# THE CHICANOS

*As We See Ourselves*

# THE CHICANOS

## *As We See Ourselves*

Arnulfo D. Trejo, editor

Fausto Avendaño

Roberto R. Bacalski-Martínez

David Ballesteros

José Antonio Burciaga

Rudolph O. de la Garza

Ester Gallegos y Chávez

Sylvia Alicia Gonzales

Manuel H. Guerra

Guillermo Lux

Martha A. Ramos

Reyes Ramos

Carlos G. Velez-I.

Maurilio E. Vigil

THE UNIVERSITY OF ARIZONA PRESS
Tucson, Arizona

*About the Editor...*

E
184
M5
C47

ARNULFO D. TREJO, professor of library science at the University of Arizona, is author of *Diccionario etimológico latinoamericano del léxico de la delincuencia* and *Bibliografía Chicana: A Guide to Information Sources*. He also edited the first *Quién es Quién: A Who's Who of Spanish Heritage Librarians in the United States*. He received an M.A. in Spanish language and literature from the Universidad de las Américas, Mexico; an M.A. in Library Science from Kent State University, and a Ph.D. from the Universidad Nacional Autónoma de México, Mexico. He was born in Durango, Mexico, in 1922, and grew up in Tucson, Arizona. He has published articles in both English and Spanish in various professional journals.

THE UNIVERSITY OF ARIZONA PRESS
Copyright © 1979
The Arizona Board of Regents
All Rights Reserved
Manufactured in the U.S.A.

**Library of Congress Cataloging in Publication Data**
The Chicanos.
   Includes index.
   1. Mexican Americans—Ethnic identity—Addresses, essays, lectures. I. Trejo, Arnulfo D.
II. Avendaño, Fausto.
E184.M5C47          301.45'16'872073          78-23693
ISBN 0-8165-0675-2
ISBN 0-8165-0625-6 pbk.

To the Trailblazers
Who Have Greatly Contributed to the Literature of
La Raza

Carlos Eduardo Castañeda
1896–1958

Aurelio M. Espinosa, Sr.
1880–1958

George I. Sánchez
1906–1972

&

Arthur León Campa

Aurelio M. Espinosa, Jr.

Ernesto Galarza

Américo Paredes

Juan B. Rael

Renato Rosaldo

Julián Samora

# Contents

About the Contributors ix

Acknowledgments xiii

A Word From the Editor xv

Return to Aztlan: The Chicano Rediscovers His Indian Past 1
    *Guillermo Lux and Maurilio E. Vigil*

Aspects of Mexican American Cultural Heritage 19
    *Roberto R. Bacalski-Martínez*

Ourselves Through the Eyes of an Anthropologist 37
    *Carlos G. Velez-I.*

The Mexican American: Am I Who They Say I Am? 49
    *Reyes and Martha A. Ramos*

The Northern New Mexican Woman: A Changing Silhouette 67
    *Ester Gallegos y Chávez*

The Chicana Perspective: A Design for Self-Awareness 81
    *Sylvia Alicia Gonzales*

The Politics of Mexican Americans 101
    *Rudolph O. de la Garza*

Bilingualism and Biculturalism: Assets for Chicanos 121
    *Manuel H. Guerra*

The Spanish Language in the Southwest:
    Past, Present, and Future 133
    *Fausto Avendaño*

Bilingual-Bicultural Education: A Must for Chicanos 151
    *David Ballesteros*

Of Books and Libraries 167
    *Arnulfo D. Trejo*

As We See Ourselves in Chicano Literature 187
    *Arnulfo D. Trejo*

Index 213

# About the Contributors

Fausto Avendaño, a professor of Spanish and Portuguese at California State University, Sacramento, was born in Culiacán, Sinaloa, Mexico, and spent his childhood in Los Angeles and San Diego, California. He holds a B.A. in Spanish from California State University, San Diego, and an M.A. in Spanish and a Ph.D. in Spanish and Portuguese from the University of Arizona. Avendaño is the co-editor of *Explicación de cien años de soledad*.

Roberto R. Bacalski-Martínez, assistant professor of Spanish at the University of San Diego since 1978, was born in Bernalillo, New Mexico. He received his B.A., M.A. and Ph.D. in Spanish from the University of New Mexico. He was the recipient of numerous scholarships including a Woodrow Wilson Fellowship at Stanford University.

David Ballesteros became vice chancellor of economic affairs for the University of Colorado in 1977. He was born in Los Angeles, received his B.A. in Spanish from the University of Redlands, his M.A. in Spanish from Middlebury College, and a Ph.D. in Latin American Studies from the University of California. He has been the recipient of a Spanish government grant and a fellowship from the U.S. Office of Education and has lectured at numerous universities and published scholarly articles on bilingual-multicultural education.

José Antonio Burciaga, an independent Chicano artist, who did the drawings for this book, was born in El Paso, Texas. He received a B.A. in art from the University of Texas, El Paso. He has had one-man shows in various parts of the United States, including one for the benefit of the United Farm Workers' Union.

[ix]

Rudolph O. de la Garza, a member of the political science faculty and the dean's staff at Colorado College, Colorado Springs, was born in Tucson, Arizona. He holds an M.A. in Latin American Studies and a Ph.D. in government from the University of Arizona. He served with the U.S. Information Agency in Bolivia for two years and has taught at the University of Texas, El Paso. An associate editor of the *Western Political Science Quarterly*, he also co-edited *Chicanos and Native Americans: The Territorial Minorities* and *The Chicano Political Experience: Three Perspectives*.

Ester Gallegos y Chávez, a public school teacher in Santa Fe, New Mexico, was born in Tierra Amarilla, New Mexico. She received a B.A. and an M.A. in Spanish from the University of New Mexico and an M.S.W. in psychiatric social work from the Catholic University of America. She has taught at New Mexico Highlands University, the College of Santa Fe, and Arizona State University.

Sylvia Alicia Gonzales, a professor on the faculties of Mexican American graduate studies and the School of Education at San Jose State University, California, was born in Fort Huachuca, Arizona. Having received her B.A. in Latin American literature from the University of Arizona and an M.A. and a Ph.D. in educational administration at the University of Massachusetts, she has published poetry and articles in several newspapers and journals and in 1974 a book entitled *La chicana piensa*.

Manuel H. Guerra became supervisor of elementary and secondary teachers and consultant for the Bilingual-Bicultural Title Seven Program at Boise State University in 1978. For three years prior to that he was a consultant for the Migrant Education Section, State Department of Education, Sacramento, California, developing a bilingual-bicultural framework for educating the migrant. Born in San Diego, California, he received his B.A. in Latin American Studies from the University of Wisconsin, his M.A. and Ph.D. in Spanish and Latin American history from the University of Michigan. He has served as chairman of the Vicki Carr Scholarship Foundation since 1975, and in 1968 received a bronze medal from Lyndon B. Johnson for his contributions to the Bilingual Education Act.

Guillermo Lux, professor of history at New Mexico Highlands University, Las Vegas, was born into a family of migrant workers. He received a B.A. in political science and history at the University of New Mexico, an M.A. in history and Spanish at the University of Southern California, an M.A. in Latin American Studies at Stanford University, and a Ph.D. in Latin American studies at the University of Southern California. He has also published several scholarly articles on Latin America and the Caribbean.

Martha A. Ramos holds a B.A. in elementary education and psychology from the University of Iowa and an M.A. in education with a specialization in reading from San Diego State University. She was born in Drexel Hill, Pennsylvania, and spent her childhood in Los Alamos, New Mexico.

Reyes Ramos, a member of the faculty of the Institute of Urban Affairs, the University of Texas, Arlington, was born in Houston, Texas. He holds a B.A. in music education from Sam Houston State Teachers' College, Huntsville, Texas, and a Ph.D. in sociology from the University of Colorado. He was formerly assistant professor of sociology at the University of California, San Diego. He has written articles for scholarly journals including *Science* and *Social Science Quarterly*.

Carlos G. Velez-I., a professor of the faculty of the Department of Anthropology at the University of California, Los Angeles, was born in Nogales, Arizona. He holds an M.A. and a Ph.D. in anthropology from the University of California, San Diego. He formerly was head of the Chicano Studies program at San Diego State University. He has done research in urban anthropology and aging in both Mexico and the Southwest.

Maurilio E. Vigil, a political science professor at New Mexico Highlands University, was born in Las Vegas, New Mexico. He received his B.A. and M.A. in political science at New Mexico Highlands and his Ph.D. in political science at the University of New Mexico. He is the author of *Chicano Politics* and has contributed articles to *Aztlan* and the *Journal of Mexican American History*. His biography appeared in the 1975 edition of *Outstanding Educators of America* and in the 1976 edition of *Notable Americans*.

# Acknowledgments

First, I would like to acknowledge my indebtedness to the contributors of the essays included in this work, for it is their expertise together with their cultural background that gives special significance and distinction to *The Chicanos: As We See Ourselves*. This, too, is the place for me to express my sincere thanks to the various Chicano writers whose works have been cited in this book. Among them are Rodolfo "Corky" Gonzales, Ricardo Pérez, Abelardo "Lalo" Delgado, Sergio Elizondo, Alurista, José Montoya, Miguel Méndez, Rafael Jesús González, Rodolfo A. Anaya, Tomas Rivera, Floyd Salas, Richard Vásquez, Luis Valdez, Jorge A. Huerta and José Antonio Villareal. In the event that I may have inadvertently omitted a name or two, *a todos mil gracias*.

I also wish to extend my gratitude and appreciation to F. Robert Paulsen, Dean of the College of Education at the University of Arizona, and Hermann K. Bleibtreu, former Dean of the College of Liberal Arts at the University of Arizona, and subsequently director of the Museum of Northern Arizona in Flagstaff, for the funds they provided for clerical and editorial assistance to get the project started. Furthermore, I am grateful to Donald C. Dickinson, director of the Graduate Library School and Richard Hosley of the English department for providing me with typing assistance. Special recognition is given to Kathleen L. Lodwick for skilled editorial assistance and thoughtful suggestions which contributed immensely to the coherence of the manuscript. Additionally, I am indebted to her for the help she gave me in the preparation of the index. A warm note of thanks also goes to the typists, too numerous to mention by name, who worked on the preparation of the manuscript. Further, I wish to acknowledge the useful bibliographical assistance received from the Reference Staff of the University of Arizona Library at various stages of this work. A special word of thanks also goes to my wife, Annette, whose interest, encouragement, and advice are deeply appreciated. Finally, gratitude is due to the University of Arizona Press for its effective editorial and production expertise in bringing about publication.

ARNULFO D. TREJO

# A Word From the Editor

I am a Chicano, educated at the University of Arizona and a professor of Library Science at my alma mater since 1966. My work as an instructor in Mexican American literature and as Latin American bibliographer has placed me in a unique position to know what has been published about, for and by Mexican Americans. *Bibliografía Chicana*, published in 1975, brought together titles of monographic works concerned with the Chicano life experience. As I worked on this book, what I had suspected became obvious—that the majority of works were written by authors who were not of my own ethnic group. In the field of education, I identified fifty different publications, of which only fourteen were written by persons of Hispanic Mexican heritage. In the field of sociology, the results were nine out of twenty-nine. Only in the field of literature were the results more encouraging. What is interesting in this case, however, is that of the fifty-three publications cited, thirty-one had been published since 1970. The *Bibliografía* confirms that only in recent years have we started to write about our own people.

The essays presented here cover a range broad enough to give the reader a better understanding of La Raza. *The Chicanos: As We See Ourselves* is a collection of original writings that has been compiled for the purpose of giving both the Chicano and the non-Chicano reader an inside view of our people. The essays deal with anthropology, culture, education, history, language, library science, literature, political science, sociology as they relate to the Chicano. In addition, there are two essays on women—one on the traditional woman of New Mexico and the other on the Chicana. The writers have expressed their opinions as Chicanos and as subject specialists.

[xv]

The Mexican American population is a heterogeneous ethnic group. One way this can be illustrated is by the many different terms used by the people of Mexican ancestry to identify themselves. *Mexicano* is one of the most preferred terms when used in conversation among ourselves and conveys a sense of pride. *Mexican American* is generally accepted as the most common term in use. *Mexican* is a direct translation of *Mexicano,* but at times it appears to carry a negative connotation. Over the years this designation has been employed in a demeaning manner in the Spanish borderlands because it implies that we are foreigners.

*Pocho* is another demeaning term applied to Mexican Americans by citizens of Mexico. In the United States, however, it does not have a negative connotation and has become popular as a result of the novel *Pocho* (1959) which narrates the traumatic experience of a first generation Mexican American.

*Spanish* and *Spanish American* are terms which have been used less and less since World War II. This is primarily due to a growing pride in our Indian heritage. Older generation Anglos sometimes use these terms as polite forms. *Hispano(a)* is primarily used by the Spanish-speaking people of New Mexico, but its variation, *Hispanoamericano(a)* is used more generally in other parts of the country. *Hispanic, Latin, Latin American* and *Latino* are terms used mostly in large metropolitan areas such as New York, Chicago and San Francisco where there are representatives of many Spanish-speaking countries; however, these terms are not common in Los Angeles, where persons of Mexican extraction predominate. *Spanish-speaking, persons of Hispanic American heritage, Spanish surnamed,* or *Mexican ancestry* are designations widely used in writing and in speeches or formal lectures as opposed to conversational usage.

*Raza* or *La Raza* (Race or The Race) are terms popularized by the literary work entitled *La Raza Cósmica* written in 1925 by José Vasconcelos, the Mexican educator, philosopher and writer. In this work, he predicted the development of a new ''cosmic race'' in Latin America. Before World War II, these terms were used largely by the working class people who maintained close ties with Mexico. Interestingly, *Raza* has come into frequent use in recent years by all social and economic groups.

*Chicano* is the name which has been selected by those initially involved in the Chicano Movement to describe our people in the process of change. In the same way that the term Chicano is a derivative of Mexicano (which in turn originates from *mexica*, the name given to the Aztecs), we likewise are descendents of the people of Mexico. A term which has long been used informally by Mexican Americans in referring to themselves, *Chicano* is the only term that was especially selected by us, for us. It symbolically captures the historical past and signals a brighter future for the people of Aztlán. Aztlán was the homeland of the Aztecs. Its exact location has not yet been verified; nonetheless, ancient traditions have placed it somewhere in the area encompassed by northwestern Mexico and the southwestern United States. Wherever it may be, Aztlán became a promised land and provided the spiritual unity needed by the people involved in the Chicano Movement. And so, when Rudolph de la Garza poses the question in his essay, "¿De dónde vienes y para dónde vas?" (Where do you come from and where are you going?), the Chicano can now say, "This is where I come from and this is where I'm going." In other words, as de la Garza further states in his essay, the Chicano now "takes pride in his cultural heritage and vigorously denies any suggestion that he is culturally deprived or in any way inferior. Recognizing the equality of all people, the Chicano, through violent or peaceful means, seeks to have the nation at large recognize the role his people have made in shaping this country and to insure that all Mexican Americans will be treated with respect and dignity."

In spite of all these different terms which we apply to ourselves, it must be stressed that we are Americans. Prior to the Civil Rights Movement of the 1960s, becoming American meant "melting" into the mainstream of society, which has been seen as a cause of psychological discomfort for many who would identify as American when cultural background and physical characteristics did not conform to the established middle class Anglo-Saxon mold. The rebellion of these "different" Americans particularly in the years of the Civil Rights Movement in the 1960s and also in the early 1970s, however, has given Americanism a much broader meaning that is more in conformity with the ideals of a democracy. As Chicanos, we advocate a pluralistic philosophy which acknowledges that this country, made up of people from the world over, unites different peoples of different principles, but all directed toward the pursuit of those inalienable rights which the Constitution of the United States guarantees its citizenry.

Prior to World War II, Mexican American neighborhoods— barrios—functioned almost completely in isolation, much the same as they had since they were established. With World War II *La Raza*, along with the rest of American society, became more mobile and intermingled both with other Americans as well as persons abroad. On the battlefields, in the factories, and in the universities we shared experiences with people different from ourselves. After the wars some of the barrios underwent drastic changes and some of the younger generations moved out. These areas were neglected and in some cases completely demolished under various urban renewal programs. During the process we began to observe ourselves more consciously and to recognize that we had assets to contribute to America's pluralistic society. Our Spanish language was now seen as a positive element of our culture. In response to our new self-awareness we saw the need for intellectual growth so that we could function more effectively in a changing society.

Since World War II, significant progress has been made toward the revitalization of our cultural heritage, the alteration of our values and the reorientation of our attitudes both toward ourselves and toward our place in American society. No longer do we silently accept the stereotypes of the past. Today, we, as Chicanos, accept ourselves as individuals and make no apologies for who we are. Progressively, more of us are becoming aware of our potential. We are now convinced that we can help determine our own destiny through intentional effort properly guided and persistently exerted.

While this book is by and about Chicanos, it also reflects experiences with which other ethnic minorities in the United States can identify, dealing as it does with the universal human quest for justice, political freedom, and equality. Our purpose is not to talk to ourselves, but rather to open a dialogue. Neither the Chicano nor any other ethnic group can live in isolation any more than American society can continue to ignore any of its ethnic groups. Therefore, increased knowledge of Chicanos can lead to greater achievement and understanding by both Chicanos and non-Chicanos as well as respect for the dignity of all people.

A.D.T.

# RETURN TO AZTLAN:
# THE CHICANO REDISCOVERS
# HIS INDIAN PAST

*Guillermo Lux and Maurilio E. Vigil*

THE CHICANO MOVEMENT with its revitalization of the Mexican cultural origins of *La Raza* has indirectly resulted in the regeneration of interest in our Indian origins which in the past have been denied or played down. This essay will show, by outlining the historical experience of the Mexican American in the United States, how the melting pot concept has affected our people. Frequently displaced in the milieu of mainstream society, many Chicanos typically now behave as though they were Anglo-Americans, sharing with many of the latter a disdain for the Indian. Some Chicanos, obviously mestizo, struggle to divorce themselves from that heritage, while others proudly embrace it. Inasmuch as myth clouds this facet of the total cultural heritage of the Chicano people, the purpose of this essay is to explain to what extent the Indian was and is an influence on the Chicano. We will show that the traditional rejection by Mexican Americans of their Indian origins is part of a larger rejection of their entire antecedent cultural identification which is both Mexican and mestizo. We will show that the reasons for this rejection are partly the result of the Mexican American's struggle to accommodate himself to a very hostile environment in the United States. That environment first of all has stressed assimilation into the Anglo society, with its use of the English language and Anglo values and normative systems. For Mexican Americans in this environment, becoming American has clearly meant rejecting one's own cultural background.

In addition to this has been the Mexican American's struggle to overcome pernicious, cruel and misleading stereotypes which have been created by Anglo society through motion pictures and other mass media. The Mexican has been portrayed as the dirty Mexican, the greaser, the pot-bellied "bandido," or the complacent, placid, fun

[1]

loving quaint personality. The Indian, on the other hand, has been cast as savage, mean, and treacherous. As such, not only was the Mexican American impelled to shed his Mexicanness because of the stereotyped picture he was exposed to, but he has not been able even to begin to consider his Indian origins. In Mexico of the 1930s during the presidency of Lázaro Cárdenas the Indian origins of the Mexican people were accepted with pride. Yet the Mexican American, because his picture of the Indian was the same highly distorted one held by the Anglo, could not accept his Indianness. The socializing institutions in American society—the schools and the mass media—and even some organizations like the accommodationist-oriented League of United Latin American Citizens (LULAC) all stressed to the Mexican American that the way to succeed in America was to enter the mainstream of American life, by emulating Anglos. In American life the "melting pot," actually an amalgam, a blending of different racial and cultural groups and creation of a new one, was a majority ideology substituted for the more conspicuous term "assimilation," even though the social processes dictated an assimilationist mold to which non-Anglo-Saxon groups were expected to conform.

The Chicano Movement with its emphasis on pride in being *La Raza* is, at least, partially a reaction to the pressure toward assimilation that stems from dissatisfaction with the social order of mainstream American society and results in a refusal to be absorbed. The concept of *La Raza* can be traced to the ideas and writings of José Vasconcelos, the Mexican theorist who developed the theory of *la raza cósmica* (the cosmic or super race) at least partially as a minority reaction to the Nordic notions of racial superiority. Vasconcelos developed a systematic theory which argued that climatic and geographic conditions and mixture of Spanish and Indian races created a superior race. The concept of *La Raza* connotes that the mestizo is a distinct race and not Caucasian, as is technically the case. *La Raza* is the term most universally accepted by Mexican Americans when referring to themselves.

Another quite opposite Chicano reaction to the pressure toward assimilation was to affiliate, or at least to accommodate, as stated before, to the extent necessary to maintain their status, or to establish rapport, in some cases, with the conqueror. This was accomplished more easily in some instances than others. For example, there existed commonalities in attitudes between the conquered and the conqueror such as those toward the *indios barbaros* (savage Indians), the nomadic Utes, Navajos, Apaches, and Comanches, the enemies of *La Raza* for the past three hundred years. Both the Mexican and Anglo settlers shared that hatred, and the frontier policy of violence of both Spain and the United States coincided. Spain adopted this policy once it was determined that the previous Christianizing program of the mission was ineffectual with the *indios barbaros*, the nomads. The newly arrived American settlers held that the "only good Indian was a dead Indian," as the frontier slogan demonstrated. That same feeling had been held in the outermost reaches of the colonial frontier by Mexican colonists who had for over a century suffered from the savage raids of Navajos, Apaches, and Utes, and who had carried out considerable, though largely ineffectual, campaigns against *los indios barbaros* before the Americans came. In fact, part of the reason for the bloodless conquest of New Mexico was that many Mexicans welcomed the military might and technology which the Americans could contribute against the rampaging Indians. The Anglo conquerors were quickly emulated by *La Raza* who gained status by association. It became a matter of good form for mestizos to become as Spanish as possible, thus disassociating themselves from their Mexican origins which necessarily implied Indian origins. Unfortunately, the universal designation given erroneously by Columbus to all Native Americans—Indians—did not allow for distinctions to be made between the sedentary Indians such as the Aztecs (from whom Mexicans derived) and the Pueblos (with whom they later intermarried), and the nomads such as Apaches, and Utes, the arch enemies of Mexican colonists. To the Americans, an Indian was an Indian, and the popular stereotype soon became one in which the Indian was viewed as an uncivilized savage, as popularly depicted in dime novels and later motion pictures. Another factor in the Mexican American's rejection of his Indianness pertained to attitudes relative to feelings of racial and social inequality among Anglos, Mexican American mestizos, and Indians.

Though it is not widely acknowledged by contemporary American social thought, the 1776 American Revolution was not for the establishment of democracy in the New World—that came later on. One could not imagine the Virginia aristocratic, patrician families of the Tidewater accepting the small farmer of the Piedmont as their equal. Neither did the *patrón* class of New Mexico, nor the wealthy landed families of California accept the Indian or the mestizo as an equal (Valdes 1971, pp. 1, 30.) Under the patina of mythological colonial grandeur, there subsisted, in a state of vile servitude, the masses. The wealthy families designated themselves with pride as *castizos*, of pure blood lines, meaning no miscegenation, often claiming a genealogy dating back to the conquistadores. The colonial tradition of being pro-White (Spanish or other European) and anti-Indian was deeply ingrained. Once the Anglos arrived, the *patrón* class which dominated the lower classes quickly formed an alliance and collaborated in many instances with the recently arrived oppressor. This was manifested in land frauds, such as the various intrigues of the Santa Fe Ring in New Mexico, the origins of the Maxwell Land Grant and so on. The miscegenated, colonial masses were again the object of racial discrimination.

Anglo-Americans shared this disdain for the half-breed—for miscegenation. Faced by such hostile attitudes the Mexican Americans embraced Anglo-American values. Like their counterparts, the black Americans, Hispanos considered *güeros* (fair-skinned mestizos) especially lucky since they would generally be more readily accepted by the dominant society.

The growth of democracy in the nineteenth and twentieth centuries and its social leveling tendency has had its impact on *La Raza* too. As Anglo America learned about equality, so did brown America. The Chicano Movement is the most recent stage of this democratizing evolution. It embraces all *Raza*. It frequently assumes a common enemy—the gringo. In its extremes it is a counter-racist surge. Those who do not comply are harshly labeled as *vendidos* or *agringados*,* sell-outs or those politically naive or unaware. The colonial hierarchy based on color, pedigree, and wealth, is summarily dismissed.

The descendants of the prestigious colonial families still frequently have difficulty in accepting democratic ideas and so they find it difficult to embrace concepts of ethnic community which would be to embrace the Indian as a brother. This would be a hard step to take inasmuch as the Indian was an enemy long before the Anglo arrived in the Southwest. Liaison with the controlling Anglo class has been more attractive.

---

*Agringado* is an anglicized term used to mean a Mexican American who has assumed the characteristics of the "gringo"; the term carries a negative connotation.

There is substantial evidence of acculturation among our people today due to pressure from the dominant society. The Mexican American can become a different person by immersing himself "in the mirror image reflected by others," by acting as a person accepted by the mainstream society. This self-rejection focuses on color and nationality and hence community. For the person who may not physiologically appear distinctive or different, it is relatively easy to pass for white. For the distinctive person, the mestizo, the recourse must be "my family descended from the conquistadores; we are Hispanos, Spanish" (Weiss 1962, p. 471). The mestizo demonstrates his obvious shame of his Indian heritage by introducing himself as Spanish. How often have Spanish-surnamed people been told "but you don't look Spanish!" The reference is, of course, to the mestizo and Indian characteristics and to the brown skin pigmentation. Little does the Anglo realize the heterogeneity of *La Raza,* whose physical characteristics are a mosaic.

More significant is the image these persons strive to project. It is through community relationships with others that one has being, context, and self-realization in the social milieu. Individuals and groups constantly react and adjust to society. To quote the social psychologist George H. Mead:

> We cannot realize ourselves except insofar as we can recognize the other in his relationship to us. It is as he takes the attitude of the other that the individual is able to realize himself as a self. (Mead 1934, p. 194.)

An example of this would be expression of nationalism and patriotism voiced with a sense of superiority or domination over others who may therefore be deemed inferior. This may be an unconscious adjustment, but basically it is a reaction. Individuals perform as they are seen by others and as they are expected to perform, and as they see themselves. This is the "looking-glass self," a "self-image."

Consequently, until the 1960s, when the great awakening of *La Raza* occurred, the people of various shades of brown who spoke Spanish and lived primarily in the Southwest were called, by outsiders, Mexicans, Mexican Americans, and even Latin Americans (Twitchell 1911–12, p. 259). Yet many of them introduced themselves as Spanish and Hispanos. One could detect very definite attitudes concerning the implied and misunderstood Indianness of these people of Mexican ancestry. They introduced themselves as Spanish because that was synonymous with white (Casavantes 1969, p. 1). Anglos called them Spanish because it was considered polite to do so. Mexican was a name used in a pejorative sense.

In the 1960s the term "Chicano" took on a new meaning and gained acceptance. It connotes people who believe in self-determination. Chicano is still a controversial term worn by some as a badge of honor and rejected by others because of the activism and militancy with which it is associated. Even among the Chicano activists some make an unconscious adjustment vis-à-vis their Indian heritage and cling tenaciously to their Spanish past; yet the term Chicano itself has Indian origins. Chicano derives from a tribe of the Aztecs known as *Mexicas*. In time references to the tribe in the Nahua language as *Mexicanos* led through contraction and pronunciation to the present spelling and pronunciation—*Mexicas, Mexicano, Xicano,* Chicano (Meier and Rivera 1972, pp. xiv, 8).

*La Raza's* journey towards recognition of *Chicanismo* has been one of struggle. In the year 1846 the Mexican army, much more numerous and powerful than that of the Americans, should have easily vanquished its enemy which arrived to revel in the Halls of Moctezuma, but the ancient Aztec cycle of history had completed its revolution again. As before, Huitzilopochtli, the Aztec god of war, and the other Aztec gods had abandoned the Mexican people. According to the ancient legend of the white god Quetzalcoatl, it was futile to resist the white gods who were more powerful than the brown gods of Aztlan.

In New Mexico, General Stephen Watts Kearny greeted the Mexican people saying that the army had come as their friends, to better the conditions of the people. It was reminiscent of the words of Hernán Cortés three and a quarter centuries earlier, in 1519, on the occasion of his first meeting with the Aztec monarch Moctezuma: "Tell Moctezuma that we are his friends. There is nothing to fear....We have come to your house in Mexico as friends." Before the conquest of Tenochtitlán was over, more than 240,000 Aztecs would be sacrificed to propitiate the white gods from Spain (Valdez and Steiner 1972, pp. 28–29, 30).

The Corteses and the Kearnys were carriers of new technologies, the representatives of different civilizations which profoundly changed the worlds of Mexico and Aztlan—modifying but not annihilating them. The Indian and mestizo world of Aztlan, now the Southwest of the United States, has metamorphosed into a different civilization. Arthur Campa has described very well the influence of Mexican culture, already tinged by Indian influence, on the Southwest and on the Anglo American immigrant to Aztlan:

> ...These newcomers [Anglo Americans], learned from the inhabitants to use water for irrigation, to break the wild *mesteño* into a serviceable mount, to work the longhorn cattle of the *ranchos*, to eat *frijoles, chile,* and *charqui* and to build with *adobe* in a land where timber was nonexistent. In California, they learned to shout *chispa* not gold.... they learned to pan the streams with a *batea,* to process quartz with an *arrastra* after bringing it up from the mine over *escaleras* [ladders].... Many Anglo Americans whether trappers, prospectors, or traders, built upon a Mexican base, much of the culture that we call today southwestern. Take the *ranchos* and the cattle industry of a century ago from the Texan, remove his *chaparreras* [chaps] and *tapaderas* (leather stirrup cover), relieve him of his *lazo* (lasso), his *reata* (lariat), his *remuda* (relay of horses), his *sombrero,* his *mostranco* (mustang)...and his *rodeo,* and he is reduced to the midwestern farmer he was before he came into contact with the civilization that made him different from the rest of the *Americanos* ...and incidentally, the American folk hero, the cowboy, vanishes (Campa 1973, p. 20).

In the Southwest the Spanish language remains as the spoken, if not official language of the people of Aztlan. Chicanos speak Spanish, the language of the conquering European, and consider it part of the Chicano cultural heritage, even though Spanish had earlier replaced Nahuatl, the language of the sixteenth century Mexican Indian. Much of the earlier Indianness of pre-Spanish culture also remains as a part of our heritage. Indian Mexico is an integral part of the Chicano culture on the north side of the arbitrary cactus curtain that separates Chicanos from their Mexican mestizo and Indian brothers. Buffer worlds such as Indian Aztlan are destined by history to surface once again.

Most Chicanos are likely more Indian than European, because relatively few Spaniards came to the New World. Initially, the Spaniards married Indian women creating the mestizo, who in turn married Indians or other mestizos. The Spanish villa of Santa Cruz de la Cañada, surrounded by three pueblos—San Juan, Santa Clara, and San Ildefonso—in what is today New Mexico, offers an interesting study of this intermarriage. The 1790 census of the town reveals that nearly the entire population listed itself as either *castizo* or mestizo; and almost none declared themselves to be *indios*. It is likely that many who called themselves mestizos were *indios,* but because they spoke Spanish and lived apart from the nearby pueblos they no longer referred to themselves as *indios.* This is a logical conclusion, given the Spanish social scale, which encouraged Hispanicization. If they were indeed mestizos, they offer evidence of considerable miscegenation. In any case, the high percentage of mestizos demonstrates the strong Indian influence on this Spanish colonial town. At the time of independence from Spain, in 1821, the population of New Mexico was approximately half mestizo. Yet one hundred and fifty years later, most of the Mexican Americans of northern New Mexico prefer to be called Hispano or Spanish American.

Evidence of the Indian culture of Aztlan is abundant. The Indian name "Aztlan" has a universal meaning that connotes a spiritual union, the beginning of Chicano cultural nationalism. Aztlan was the mythological homeland of the Aztecs, the Nahua-speaking people before their migration southward to Yucatan. The gods of Aztlan then must be Indian. Today, the *huelgas* (labor strikes), the processions, and other solemn occasions of the Chicanos are conducted under the sacred banner of the brown Virgen de Guadalupe, the patron saint of the Mexican campesino, who is the Christian counterpart of the gentle Indian goddess Tonantzin. Tonantzin was worshipped at the place where the Basilica of the Virgen de Guadalupe now stands in the Valley of Mexico. The brown Virgen protected the Indian and mestizo masses in 1810 when they struggled to throw off the cruel yoke of the Spanish gachupin oppressors who worshipped the white Virgen de los Remedios.

In Mexico, during the Conquest, the Spanish gained domination over the country and maintained their control for 300 years. Control meant maintaining a world of privilege for the gachupín and Creole overlords of colonial society. In 1810 the masses spoke and the outcry was deafening. Mexico saw blood run as it had during the reign of terror in the French Revolution. The old order was threatened even more with the rise to political power of the Indian and mestizo in the 1850s with the emergence of the *Reforma* of Benito Juárez and other Indians who ended, temporarily, the unequal position of the masses in Mexico. Later, in 1910 this struggle for real freedom was continued. Again the Virgen de Guadalupe symbolized this second struggle for independence. She is an Indian symbol.

When the Revolutionary movement was institutionalized in the Partido Revolucionario Institucional (PRI), presidents such as Lázaro Cárdenas officially declared the mestizo as the main component of the Mexican population. The Indian origins were rediscovered and reemphasized. This rediscovery undoubtedly touched the Mexicans who lived "north from Mexico."

Today many Indian symbols in Mexican and Mexican American culture are interpreted as Chicano. Some are the Aztec figures on Chicano magazine covers; the Aztec eagle on the *Huelga* banners of César Chávez and the United Farm Workers; Emiliano Zapata, an Indian, is one of the historical figures most commemorated by Chicanos in the movement. These and other unconscious symbols affirm a new trend among Mexican Americans to accept the Indianness in their heritage.

To illustrate the prevalence of the Indian influence on Mexican and Mexican American culture it is appropriate to single out highlights in the language, traditions, beliefs, and customs traceable primarily to Aztec origins and to a lesser degree to the Maya, Toltec, Olmec, Zapotec and Tarasco Indians who also lived in pre-Columbian Mexico.

More subtle, but pervasive are the many foods, words, place names, beliefs, and legends that are still replete in Mexican American culture. It is important to note that current pronunciations of the Hispanicized Aztec words usually drop the "1" or "i" endings from the original Aztec spelling, due to the phonetic differentiation in pronunciation between the two languages. Aztec words ending in "tl" usually end in Spanish "te" (*caxitl*=*cajete*) and Aztec words ending in "li" end in Spanish "le" (*tamalli*=*tamale*).

The most familiar to most Americans are the Mexican foods and drinks which are largely Aztec. Primary among these are the maize derivative foods such as corn tortillas, pinole, *gordas* (thick corn tortillas), tamales, *nixtamal* (cooked corn), *chicos* and *pozole*. *Atole*, a porridge made from corn meal; *pozole*, usually prepared with pigs' feet or shanks; *menudo*, prepared out of hominy and beef tripe; and *chicos*, made of dried corn, constitute the Chicano equivalent of Black soul food. Chili, probably the best known Mexican dish, is traceable to the Aztecs as are dishes such as enchiladas, tamales, and tacos. Other common foods, fruits, drinks, vegetables or dishes are: *cacahuates* (peanuts), chicle (gum), chocolate, *ejotes* (green beans), *camotes* (sweet potatoes), guacamole (avocado salad), *mezcal* (corn liquor), tequila (a strong liquor derived from the agave plant), *tomates* (tomatoes), and *quelites* (spinach) (Thomas 1974, pp. 49–54).

The Aztec influence is manifest in many words thought to be Spanish, but which are actually of Aztec origin. Examples are *nopal* (cactus), *elote* (ear of corn), *chapulin* (grasshopper), *aguacate* (tropical fruit tree), *guajolote* (salamander), mesquite, *mitote* (gossip), *papalote* (kite), *zoquete* (mud), *metate* (grinding stone), *cajete* (water drum), *mecate* (rope or string), *milpa* (sown field), and *chiche* (breast).

Interestingly, the slang used by the young zoot-suit Mexican separatist subgroup *pachuco* in the 1940s and 1950s in the barrios included Aztec origin words such as *calco* (shoe), *cuate* (friend), *chante* (home), and *ruco* (old man) (Thomas 1974, pp. 49–54).

Also common are Aztec or other Indian origin words which appear as place names. In New Mexico (the name of the state itself is of Aztec origin) alone there are towns named Montezuma, Tecolote, Capulin, Aztec, Analco, Chilili, Coyote, Cuates, Mesquite, Petaca, and Toltec (Thomas 1974, p. 55).

That the Indian influence goes beyond language and words is manifested in the many and varied beliefs and legends still current in New Mexico which are traceable to Aztec origins. They were transmitted, like much Mexican culture, in stories handed down through generations. Two examples are the legend of *La Llorona* and the legend of *La Malinche*.

The legend of *La Llorona* exists in several variations but all tell of a woman who roams the streets and fields at night wailing and pursuing wayward children. The story, frequently told and implanted in the minds of young children, is used to scare them and keep them at home after dark. One popular version of the story concerns Luisa, a beautiful but poor young maiden, who falls in love with Nuño de Móntez, a handsome and wealthy bachelor. Luisa bears him children out of wedlock but is kept from marrying Nuño because of class barriers. When Nuño marries another woman, Luisa goes mad, and in a rage kills her children. As a result she is tried, convicted and scourged. By strange coincidence her lover dies the same day she is scourged. As the story goes Luisa's soul is *La Llorona* searching for children to replace those whom she killed. As the cry of the *lobo* or wind is similar to the cry of a wailing woman, the story is clearly fixed in the mind of the young Chicanito who would dare wander out at night.

The story of *La Malinche* bears some resemblance and has on occasion been confused with that of *La Llorona*. *La Malinche* was the Indian mistress of Hernán Cortés and bore him sons. When Cortés abandoned her, she killed the two sons in her misery. Tradition has it that she spent the remaining years roaming the streets of Tenochtitlan in the dark of night, dressed in white, wailing over the loss of her sons (Thomas 1974, pp. 58–61).

Other aspects of Mexican Indian folklore and beliefs manifest themselves in contemporary Mexican American behavior. Manuel Gamio, in describing some folklore from Michoacan and Jalisco from whence many Mexican immigrants came, describes the Indian belief systems. The strong tradition of veneration of elders by the young Mexican American could be linked to certain Indian customs. For example, in the village of Cheran the natives bury in their fields idols called *tares* which are the symbolic remains of old men. They believe that the idols will help ensure a good harvest.

The virtue of chastity is still comparatively strong among Mexican American women in spite of the more liberal sexual mores of the contemporary period. Undoubtedly, this was influenced by Mexican customs, many of which in turn can be traced to our Indian origins. For example, one custom in Angagua and other pueblos in Mexico traceable to Aztec origins was the placing of a clean white sheet on the marriage bed by an old woman of the village on the day of the wedding. The following morning the woman discreetly enters the bedroom and removes the bed sheet. If the sheet contains the virginal blood, the happy announcement is proclaimed to the village whereupon the wedding feast continues. If the sheet is spotless, however, this indicates that the bride was not a virgin. The celebration would cease immediately. The guests in reproach of the bride would break the pottery (the perennial wedding gift) thus making it unserviceable (Gamio 1930, pp. 217–19).

Many beliefs relative to pregnancy and newborn children with roots in Indian culture are also strong among Mexican Americans. One belief is that if a pregnant woman looks at an eclipse of the moon, she will give birth to a lame child. Another belief, perhaps less current, is that a pregnant woman does not carry salt, chili or lime for fear that her child will be born deaf or blind. New mothers do not like strangers to fondle their children for fear that they will give the child "el ojó" (the evil eye), which could lead to violent illness in the child. To avoid the evil eye, a mother may tie a ribbon on the child's blouse, put a coral necklace around its neck, or otherwise distract the "eye of la bruja." Mothers still practice the custom known in Jilotlan of pulling the noses of children during the first two months of life to prevent the child from being pug-nosed (Gamio 1930, pp. 217–223).

Another practice common in some homes of Mexican Americans is that of having a religious area, usually a small niche or altar, for a special patron saint such as Saint Jude. Votive candles burn constantly and incense may burn to commemorate the saint on special religious holidays (Gamio 1930, p. 220).

Indian influence is also present in mystical beliefs surprisingly strong among some Mexican Americans today. In addition to the preceding examples, belief in *brujeria* (witchcraft) and *curanderas* (folk healers) is common among Mexican Americans in the Southwest. Rodolfo Anaya's work *Bless Me, Ultima,* one of the most popular recent Mexican American novels, reflects these aspects of our culture. Indian influence is pervasive in folk medicine, particularly in the use of herbs and other remedies. Our people use herbs to cure ailments ranging from ulcers and headache, to stomach irregularities and colic in newborn babies. Medicinal herbs are often stocked along with modern drugs in drugstores serving Mexican American clientele.

The significance of such beliefs, legends, and language to Mexican American values, attitudes, and socialization patterns is well described by Jorge Thomas who observes that "superstitions and legends, whether based on fact or fiction continue to be a very important element in the life of the Mexican American . . . A belief does not have to be fact to influence the thinking of the young. . . . These legends and language indicate the survival of Indian and Mexican culture among Mexican Americans in New Mexico today" (Thomas 1974, p. 62).

Other influences of our Indian past on Mexican and Mexican American culture may have been more covert or gone unnoticed because they were generally consistent with Hispanic cultural traits. Among these are the patriarchal tradition in which the father is the unchallenged head of the family. In Indian cultures the woman walks behind the man and generally performs most of the chores including such tasks as plastering the adobe hut. In the Spanish tradition the male is also dominant as manifested by the patronymical origin of some Spanish names such as Martínez [*los hijos de* (sons of) Martín].

In their political culture the Indian societies were characterized by a hierarchical structure where the leadership was inherited and usually the province of an elite group (such as the supremacy of Moctezuma over the Aztecs); this, likewise, reinforced the Hispanic monarchical tradition. Spain in the sixteenth century was one of the most absolutist of the European monarchies. These traditions continued and manifested themselves in the patron-peon system of nineteenth century New Mexico territorial politics and are even visible in the strong-man rule of jefes políticos in the twentieth century. In social interaction the Indians of New Mexico, like the Spaniards, had a definite caste or class structure. Together these contributed to the near feudal social structure which was instituted in the Southwest by the Spaniards.

In religion, the Christian piety of the Spanish Catholic is still evident in the strong adherence of the Mexican American to the Roman Catholic Church. There is, however, evidence of Indian influence. Although the religious rites of the Mexican American Penitentes have been traced to Spanish and Franciscan Third Order origins, there is evidence that flagellation was a common religious rite among some tribes of Indians (Weigle 1976, pp. 26–29). Although Ross Calvin lacks an understanding of the Penitentes, he, too, substantiates an Indian influence in their rites. "... Popular ignorance left without the guidance of the Church relapsed naturally into fanaticism, and the Mexican zealot, inheriting from the Spaniard a tragic interpretation of Christianity, and from his Indian forebears a recent and thinly covered savagery, evolved presently a cruel and schematic cult of scourge" (Calvin 1965, p. 217).

In familial ties, the Spanish *compadrazgo* system of the extended family was likewise consonant with the Indian tribal structure. Both contributed to close familial and tribal relationships but militated against formation of larger group associations.

In summary, we have described the more obvious as well as the subtle manifestations of the Chicanos' Indian past. Yet, what cannot be discerned are the influences of them on Chicano psychology—our thoughts, our reasoning, our logic, our choice between values. In spite of all of the aforementioned manifestations, the Indianness of the Chicano is denied by many of *La Raza*, as is its very essence of *Chicanismo*.

One is reminded of the most apropos excerpt in José Antonio Villarreal's *Pocho* which reflects so accurately the attitudes of two generations about the brown-white syndrome and Indian status, and the extent of denial of Indianness by mestizos born in the United States. Richard, the pocho, states to his Mexican-born father, Juan Rubio,

> "Do you think, Papa," he said, "that when we go to Mexico I could have a horse?"
> "That is understood."
> "A white one, and very big?"
> "If you want," said Juan Rubio. "But why do you want a white one?"
> "Because I want the best."
> "Who told you that? White horses are usually little more than useless."
> "You are playing with me," said Richard. "Everyone knows that a white horse is the best horse there is."
> Juan Rubio laughed. "Hoo, that shows how much you know. That is only in the motion pictures, but if you knew anything about horses you would know that a good horse is not chosen for his color. . . . What is this obsession about the brown?" asked Juan Rubio.
> "It is only—" Richard began.
> "Enough! A horse is a horse!"
>
> Richard asked, "Mama, was your great-grandfather a rich one?"
> "No, but he was independent and worked for different people, because he was not a peon."
> "He was Indian, was he not?"
> "Yes, he was an Indian from the South country, but do not feel superior—you are Indian, too, as well as Spanish and probably even French."
> "But my father told me I was not Spanish." . . . Richard had never understood that side of his father (Villarreal 1959, pp. 96–99).

Reading Chicano literature today, one sees obvious pride in the emerging Chicano cultural heritage—which is not yet clearly defined. The inconsistency is that the search to reestablish or recapture the Chicano cultural heritage is frequently an attempt by Chicanos to return to their European or Spanish heritage. The emphasis is on the Spanish rather than the mestizo or the Indian aspects, yet Mexico's society is very definitely an Indian one.

It is not difficult to comprehend why *La Raza* consciously or unconsciously coveted a white image when one considers first the Mexican experience. It was the white Spanish European who violated the brown Indian woman of Mexico, producing from that union the mestizo. The mestizo carried within his heart the seeds of conflict, being a bastard and part of neither of the two worlds around him. With time and numbers, however, he created his own world which he today dominates in the place of the colonial world of the white European. Yet, there is a frustration—after throwing off the white world of the Spaniard, and the Anglo, who continued the Spaniard's domination, some Mexican Americans yearn to be white. They are heard to say, "I have to wear a hat in the sun, because if I don't I'll get too dark"; other Mexican Americans romanticize both Chicanas with green eyes and fair complexions as well as white women. The reasons for this lie in the deep recesses of the Mexican American psyche, a psyche influenced by decades of relegation to an inferior racial and social status, and years of suffering from prejudice and discrimination which perpetrated probably irreparable harm in the hearts and minds of Mexican Americans.

As pointed out before, one of the most important consequences of the Chicano Movement may be an alteration of this view. But we have, as yet, not reached that point. Some Mexican Americans, still caught up in the assimilation process, remain unmoved by the Chicano Movement and its call for cultural awareness, for we are a people caught in a paradox: Is assimilation into Anglo society to be resisted to the point of complete separation? To answer "yes" is being unrealistic. However, what has been started by the *Movimiento* is not about to die. There are signs that portend a change. The Indianness in our heritage will no longer be a source of embarrassment or something to ignore, but rather a source of pride and enrichment.

Bibliography

Alport, Gordon. 1958. *The Nature of Prejudice*. Boston: Beacon Press.

Barrera, Mario; Muñoz C.; and Ornelas, C. 1972. "The Barrio as an Internal Colony." *Urban Affairs Annual Review* 6:465–98.

Calvin, Ross. 1965. *Sky Determines: An Interpretation of the Southwest*. Albuquerque: University of New Mexico Press.

Campa, Arthur. 1973. "The Mexican American in Historical Perspective." *Chicano: The Evolution of a People*. Edited by Renato Rosaldo. Minneapolis: Winston Press.

Casavantes, Edward J. 1969. *A New Look at the Attributes of the Mexican American*. Albuquerque: Southwestern Cooperative Educational Laboratory.

Cue Canovas, Agustín. 1970. *Los Estados Unidos y el México olvidado*. Mexico, D.F.: B. Costa-Amic.

*450 años del pueblo chicano: 450 Years of Chicano History in Pictures*. 1976. Albuquerque, N.M.: Chicano Communications Center.

Gamio, Manuel. 1930. *Mexican Immigration to the United States: A Study of Human Migration and Adjustment*. Chicago: University of Chicago Press.

López y Rivas, Gilberto. 1969. *Chicano; o, la explotación de "la raza."* México, D.F.: Editorial Imprenta Casa.

Mead, George H. 1934. *Mind, Self, and Society*. Chicago: University of Chicago Press.

Meier, Matt, and Rivera, Feliciano. 1972. *The Chicanos: A History of Mexican Americans*. New York: Hill and Wang.

Memmi, Albert. 1965. *The Colonizer and the Colonized*. Translated by Howard Greenfeld. New York: Orion Press.

Moore, Joan. 1970. "Colonialism: The Case of the Mexican American." *Social Problems* 17 (Spring issue): 463–72.

Pitt, Leonard. 1966. *The Decline of the Californios: A Social History of the Spanish-Speaking Californians, 1846–1890*. Berkeley: University of California Press.

Samora, Julian, and Simon, Patricia V. 1976. *A History of the Mexican-American People*. South Bend, Indiana: University of Notre Dame Press.

Thomas, Jorge. 1974. "Influencia Azteca en la cultura y lenguage de Nuevo Méjico," Unpublished M.A. thesis. Las Vegas, New Mexico: New Mexico Highlands University.

Toch, Hans. 1965. *The Social Psychology of Social Movements*. New York: Bobbs-Merrill, Co.

Twitchell, Ralph Emerson. 1911–12. *The Leading Facts of New Mexican History*, vol. 2. Cedar Rapids, Iowa: Torch Press.

Valdes, Daniel T. 1971. *Political History of New Mexico*, vol. 1. Unpublished manuscript.

Valdez, Luis and Steiner, Stan, eds. 1972. *Aztlan: An Anthology of Mexican American Literature*. New York: A. A. Knopf.

Villarreal, José Antonio. 1959. *Pocho*. Garden City, N.Y.: Doubleday and Co.

Weigle, Marta. 1976. *Brothers of Light, Brothers of Blood: The Penitentes of the Southwest*. Albuquerque: University of New Mexico Press.

Weiss, Frederick A. 1962. ''Self-Alienation: Dynamics and Therapy,'' *Man Alone: Alienation in Modern Society*. Edited by Eric and Mary Josephson. New York: Dell Publishing Co.

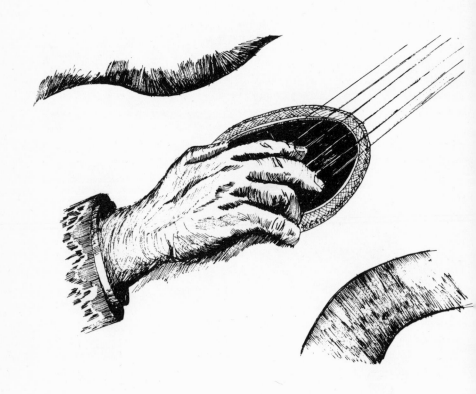

# ASPECTS OF MEXICAN AMERICAN CULTURAL HERITAGE

*Roberto R. Bacalski-Martínez*

A CHARACTERISTIC OF CHICANO CULTURE in the American Southwest is that it is incredibly ancient on the one hand, and surprisingly new on the other. Indian, Spanish, Mexican, and Anglo elements have gone into its formation, and they continue to affect it. In each case, the introduction of new elements began as a clash between two peoples which eventually resulted in a newer, richer culture. The Spanish and Mexican colonists attempted to completely transplant the society from which they came, quite unlike the Anglo-American settlers who brought little with them except the idea of creating a new society. Thus, colonial San Antonio and Santa Fe were miniature versions of Sevilla and Mexico City with respect to buildings, costumes, and social customs. The culture did not attempt to adapt itself to the new environment, rather, the new environment was molded to conform to the people and their culture.

Traditionally, the greatest single cultural force in Mexican American society has been the Roman Catholic Church. Coming to the Americas, together with the armies of Spain, Hispanic Catholicism has provided its adherents a spiritual fortitude enabling them to withstand the harshness of the Southwestern landscape as well as the utter loneliness of separation from loved ones in the Old World. In addition to the sacramental aspects of its services to the people, the church has always provided a very real cultural unity for Mexican Americans. Although today traditional cultural patterns are in a state of transformation, and many Chicanos are attempting new solutions to social, cultural, and spiritual problems, the majority of Mexican Americans are still devoutly Roman Catholic.

[19]

The annual church festivals which are celebrated date back to the arrival of the early Spaniards in the Southwest. In Bernalillo, New Mexico, the *Fiesta de San Lorenzo* is still celebrated annually as has been the tradition with many past generations. This festivity starts on the tenth of August, the feast day of the saint. Rehearsals are held every afternoon for about two weeks before the fiesta itself; then on the morning of the tenth the dancers lead a large procession of towns-people from a chapel located in one part of the village to the church, located in another part of town. The image of the saint is carried first on a portable platform by a small group of devotees. Others, on either side of the platform, sing hymns in Spanish. Still others support a canopy or an arch which seems to float above the saint's head. Afterward come the dancers, known as *danzantes* or *matachines*, dressed in fluttering ribbons and bandanas, led by the little girl called *La Malinche* in memory of Cortés's Indian paramour in Old Mexico. Finally comes the throng of villagers, singing more Spanish hymns to the glory and honor of God and their patron saint. The procession wends its way down the paved main street of the village, pausing every few minutes to allow the dancers to perform for San Lorenzo.

Upon reaching the church a mass in commemoration of the saint is celebrated by the parish priest after which the procession goes on to a public chapel made for the occasion outside the private home that has been the saint's chapel for the previous year. During that day, San Lorenzo is enthroned in his shrine waiting to receive the homage and veneration of his devotees. People who have prayed for and received his help in the past come to express their gratitude. An old woman, wearing a built-up shoe on one foot, approaches the shrine and, bor-rowing a *palma* and a rattle from one of the *danzantes*, she proceeds to express her gratitude to San Lorenzo by means of the dance. Others approach and leave their exvotos on the saint's wooden altar before his image.

The men who participate in the fiesta are not professional per-formers. They are residents of Bernalillo who might be ranchers, farm-ers, small businessmen, or who might commute on a daily basis to jobs in Albuquerque or Santa Fe. They are not rich people; life for them is a constant struggle to provide the basic necessities of life for them-selves and their families with the threat of a strike or some other economic disaster always tormenting them with the grim possibility of sudden unemployment. And yet, once a year, these men don their colorful costumes and lead the celebration in honor of their village's patron saint.

Historically speaking, the Bernalillo matachines typify one aspect of Hispanic culture which the Chicano has preserved intact from an earlier era. Elements of matachín veneration or saints go back for many centuries. They are seen in Cervantes' exemplary novel, *La gitanilla*, published in 1613. The early Spanish explorers and settlers, following leaders like Francisco Vásquez de Coronado and Juan de Oñate, brought this custom with them to the New World. Evidence of this custom is to be found in some of the villages of modern Spain and Mexico as well as New Mexico.

Until 1680 Indian and Spaniard coexisted in a precarious peace that was finally broken by the Pueblo Indian revolt, instigated by the mysterious Po-he-ye-mu of the yellow eyes and led by Popé, the courageous warrior from San Juan Pueblo. The Spaniards, determined to hang onto their northernmost colony in the New World, returned twelve years later under the leadership of Diego de Vargas. The *reconquista* was mostly peaceful, and since that time there have been no open hostilities between the Pueblo Indians and the descendents of those Spaniards who so stubbornly refused to be driven from their new homes.

Leading the return of the Spaniards in a symbolic, spiritual sense was another sacred image, *La Conquistadora*, a statuette of the Virgin Mary whose origins are lost in the past. According to legend, *La Conquistadora* predated the Moorish invasion of Spain. Hidden for almost eight hundred years near her native city of Granada, she was brought out by the victorious Christians when Granada was retaken from the Moors under Fernando and Isabel, the Catholic monarchs, in 1492. Brought to Mexico in the early years of the conquest, she remained there until the close of the seventeenth century when Vargas and his valiant band of soldiers and families adopted her as their patroness and protector for the reconquest of New Mexico from the Indians. Promising her a yearly fiesta in return for a peaceful reconquest, the Spaniards brought her north to Santa Fe, where she is still enshrined in a special chapel of the Cathedral of Santa Fe. The annual *Fiesta de Santa Fe* in honor of *La Conquistadora* has been celebrated every year in September for almost three hundred years.

The century following the *reconquista* (1692–1800) saw a great deal of colonizing activity in California, Arizona, and Texas, as well as in New Mexico. The celebrated Father Junípero Serra established his chain of missions which served as the nuclei of new Spanish-Mexican colonies in California. In northern Sonora, Mexico, and southern Arizona the Jesuit Father Eusebio Francisco Kino performed a similar job. Where the padres went, the soldiers and soldiers' families went too. The soldiers who had brought no wives with them found spouses were available from among the baptized Indian women, and the children of these unions, half Spanish and half Indian, in their turn found spouses either among their mothers' people or else among the children of other mixed marriages. Some of the problems faced by the settlers in this area which the Mexican government had been unable to solve, such as the growing conflict with certain elements of the Apache nation, were left to be dealt with in the last and largest invasion and occupation of these lands.

Initially, relations between Mexicans and Americans had not been hostile in much of the area. In 1821, the year in which Mexico won her independence from Spain, William Becknell of Missouri opened the Santa Fe Trail by bringing a wagon train filled with goods for trade with the newly independent republic. Hundreds of such trains were to follow in succeeding years, leaving their mark on the old capital, Santa Fe.

Other Americans, engaged in the lucrative fur trade, also began to penetrate the river valleys and mountain ranges of New Mexico, Arizona, and California in pursuit of beaver and other fur-bearing animals. These mountain men must have made quite a strong impression on the natives with their rough talk, uncouth manners, and barbaric costume, if the record left by one of them, James Ohio Pattie, is to be believed. At that time, the Mexican towns and villages possessed a higher degree of cultural refinement than did the majority of Americans who followed the Santa Fe Trail or the mountain passes and rivers into the Southwest in search of profit. Writing in his journal, *The Personal Narrative of James Ohio Pattie* (first published in Cincinnati, 1831), Pattie describes two *bailes* (dances), one in Santa Fe in 1824 and one farther south in the village of Perdido in 1827. These illustrate aspects of American-Mexican cultural relations in the third decade of the nineteenth century:

> At eight the governor and my father came to our quarters,
> and invited us all to dine with him at two in the afternoon.
> Accordingly we all dressed in our best, and went at the

appointed time. A band of musicians played during dinner. After it was finished, and the table removed, a fandango was begun. The ladies flocked in, in great numbers. The instruments, to which the dancers moved, were a guitar and violin. Six men and six women also added their voices. Their mode of dancing was a curiosity to me. The women stood erect, moving their feet slowly...I admired another (dance) so much, that I attempted to go through it. It was a waltz, danced to a slow and charming air. It produces a fine effect, when twenty or thirty perform it together. The dancing continued, until near morning, when we retired to rest (Pattie 1962, p. 46).

Three years later Pattie attended a party in Perdido:

On New Year's eve...the Spaniards of the place gave a fandango, or Spanish ball. All our company were invited to it, and went. We appeared before the Alcade, clad not unlike our Indian friends...we were dressed in deer skin, with leggins [sic], moccasins and hunting shirts, all of this article, with the addition of the customary Indian article of dress around the loins...not an article of which had been washed since we left the Copper Mines. It may be imagined that we did not cut a particular dandy-like figure, among people, many of whom were rich, and would be considered well dressed anywhere. Notwithstanding this, it is a strong proof of their politeness, that we were civilly treated by the ladies, and had the pleasure of dancing with the handsomest and richest of them (Pattie 1962, pp. 109–10).

Throughout Pattie's descriptions of these events a tone of self-consciousness is evident. The spectacle of a party of rough mountain men dressed *a lo salvaje* (savagely) in the midst of a refined elite performing the latest dances of continental Europe certainly struck him with its absurdity, and the fact that the Spaniards were polite about receiving him and his party in their outlandish clothing speaks well not only for his own sensitivity to the situation, but also, and more particularly, for the humanity of these early-day Spanish American colonists.

In New Mexico, prior to the American conquest of the Southwest, the Franciscan missionaries had to rely on local artisans to paint and carve representations of Christ, the Virgin, and the saints to adorn the interiors of the adobe missions. Apparently depending, in the beginning, on memories of images seen in Spanish and Mexican churches, and on illustrations in religious books brought by them, the early missionaries directed the production of *santos* by native craftsmen.

The Mexican American has a very personal relationship with God, and he has often put his esthetic sensibilities in the arts and crafts to work in order to express that relationship. Today the names of the carvers and painters of the colonial period have been lost, and the traditional *santero* art form has declined due to the ease with which mass-produced pictures and plaster statuettes are acquired. Other factors, such as the secularization of the clergy and the conflicts between civil and ecclesiastical authorities have undermined the devotional impetus that formerly inspired the village *santeros*.

The continuance of the art of the *santero* is to be found not only in its original home in New Mexico, but also in other parts of the Southwest. Esteban Villa, the painter, has among his works a picture entitled *Un hombre* which is a twentieth-century manifestation of the same religious spirit expressed in the super-realistic images of the suffering or dead Christ found in the early New Mexican missions. Villa's painting is modern in the sense that the crucified man has an aura of power and dignity, for it symbolizes man's tenacious resistance against the cosmic powers that subject him to fear, pain, suffering and death. Stronger than mankind, these powers have done virtually everything to destroy man, but man still makes one final gesture of defiance that eloquently expresses his refusal to capitulate, utterly doomed though he may be.

Villa's religious feelings may or may not be those of an orthodox Roman Catholic, and in this case it does not really matter. Nevertheless his picture and his statement, "I still believe in *el dia de los santos, el bautismo, la boda y la llorona*" (All Saints' Day, Baptism, Matrimony, and the wailing woman) (Villa 1969) reflect his religious feelings. The omission of God from his credo is significant, as is his inclusion of *La Llorona*, a legendary wailing spirit, with the traditionally Catholic feasts and sacraments of Baptism and Matrimony. These latter two are probably included because of the festive nature with which the Chicano has always regarded certain functions of the church. In Villa's case, however, the religious feeling is definitely there; what is missing is the commitment of that feeling to a particular institution, and in this Villa shows himself to be a true child of the twentieth century.

Manuel Hernández Trujillo, another of the contemporary Chicano artists, also represents the continuation of the craft of the *santero*. His work entitled *La cruz* is more traditional and less universal than Villa's *Un hombre*. Where Villa's work is readily seen as an interpretation of the human condition before the imponderable factors of man's ultimate destiny, Hernández Trujillo's work is more concerned with the blending of Spanish and Mexican folk elements and the result is a genuinely Chicano work of art, reflecting the main elements that have gone into the molding of the Chicano character. *La cruz* portrays a thick rugged, squared-off wooden cross set on a chiseled wooden block. Taking advantage of the natural grain of the wood, the artist has highlighted certain parts to produce a weird, goblinlike figure on the vertical arm of the cross. The horizontal arms have been stained a darker color, and a very Indian-looking series of motifs has been added in a lighter shade. Geometric figures, four skulls, and two abstract hands at both ends seem to flow across this transverse piece. The dark stain in the background gives a feeling of depth to this part of the cross, while the contrast it provides with the two-dimensional vertical piece is quite effective. *La cruz*, like most of the anonymous work that preceded it in New Mexico, gives an impression of primitive naiveté with its stocky bulkiness, its abruptly squared-off sides and ends, its rough grain, and its lack of true symmetry, which is so characteristic of the Latin cross. A closer look, however, reveals its modernity. The artist has employed such realism in the execution of this painting that on seeing it one would almost swear one were looking at a cross carved from living wood. The painting as a fact becomes apparent only when the viewer suddenly realizes that the artist has manipulated his perspective barely enough to intrigue the viewer, but not so much as to shock his sense of balance or make what he is doing seem obvious.

The importance of this painting, however, goes beyond its technical virtuosity. The appearance of the cross itself and the figures painted on its horizontal and vertical arms show clearly the artist's debt to his Mexican Indian heritage. As part of his artistic manifesto, Hernández Trujillo has said, *"Es aquí en este despertar que nos encontramos y es aquí en este momento que busco por medio de la expresión artística los símbolos que más bien expresan lo que soy. Así fue el arte para el antiguo azteca, después para el mexicano, y ahora aquí para el chicano''* (Hernández Trujillo 1969). These are truly significant words, and they can be applied with much validity to the whole range of modern Chicano endeavor in the arts.

Music, song, and dance have always been a salient characteristic of Mexican culture, and the Mexican American has certainly continued and added to this aspect of his heritage. Mention has already been made of some of the rich folkloric elements that continue to thrive in villages such as Bernalillo, in which the ritual dance of the matachines expresses the religious devotion of the people to their patron saint. A vast storehouse of traditional religious ballads, such as the *alabados* sung by Penitente brotherhoods, still exists and can be heard occasionally in the mountain villages of northern New Mexico.

A great deal of nonsense has been said in the past about the Penitentes, so much in fact, that some of the more negative commentaries on this aspect of popular religious expression have made them look like a weird collection of sadomasochistic freaks operating beyond the pale of official Catholic sanction. The truth is that the Penitente of northern New Mexico and southern Colorado is not a reincarnation of a flinty, cruel inquisitor from the past, nor is he a modern day sadist looking for unwary tourists to crucify on Good Friday. While it is true that an archbishop of Santa Fe did attempt to restrict Penitente activity in New Mexico several years ago on the basis of ecclesiastical policies, the action taken by the archbishop has fired the imaginations of some so that in their minds the archbishop moved to halt lurid scenes of torture and violence that supposedly culminated in some strange, occult form of religious ecstasy.

The *confradías* or *hermandades* (brotherhoods) of New Mexican penitentes have been seriously maligned, and it has been this lack of comprehension and indiscreet curiosity concerning them that has forced them into secrecy. Because of this need for privacy from the curious, sometimes mocking gaze of outsiders, the penitentes have been forced to build their *moradas* (chapels) in almost inaccessible sites adjacent to small, out of the way villages in the hinterlands of northern New Mexico.

---

*It is here in this awakening that we find ourselves, and it is here in this moment that I search, through the medium of artistic expression, for the symbols that best express what I am. This is what art was for the ancient Aztec, afterward for the Mexican, and now, here for the Chicano.

Historically, the penitentes are related to the Third Order of St. Francis of Assisi, that confraternity of lay persons dedicated to emulating the Franciscan way of life but without withdrawing from the world. The word "penitente" itself may have derived from another name by which the Third Order was known: the Brothers and Sisters of Penance.

In the past the penitentes helped to preserve and maintain the spirit and practice of the Catholic faith over the generations when no priest or friar was available to the more outlying districts of the colony. Marriage ceremonies and burial still had to be performed, even if only in the most rudimentary fashion, during the absence of the padres, and it was the penitentes who carried on these activities for the people, reminding them constantly that they were Christians even though their churches were inoperative as far as the administration of the Roman Catholic Church was concerned.

Another function of the hermandades during colonial times and subsisting even to the present time, was the purely secular one of providing financial security to its members and their families through a system of insurance. Each hermandad collected from its members dues which went into a common fund and were payable at regular intervals of time. Then, upon the disability or death of a particular member, monies taken from the fund were given to the wife, or widow, and her children so that they might support themselves without relying on public charity. Thus the dignity of a family was preserved, together with its sense of economic security.

Returning again to the more religious functions of the penitentes, it was they who utilized hymns (*alabados*). The word "alabado" is a derivative of *alabar* which means "to praise," originally used to commemorate the lives and miracles of the saints. Later, in New Mexico, their use was extended and employed in connection with the feasts of Easter, Corpus Christi, Christmas, and various other holy days. These hymns have been traced to the Iberian Peninsula from where they spread throughout Latin America. In Brazil, the alabados are known as *ladaínhas*, but the style is unmistakably the same even though they are sung in Portuguese instead of Spanish. In Mexico they are also known as alabados, and they are used on virtually the same occasions (Mendoza 1956, p. 39).

The style in which the alabado is sung is a unique one characterized by a high-pitched monotone in which an almost Moorish or Andalusian microtonality persists. Resemblances between this style and that of the more primitive areas of northern Spain, Asturias, for example, have also been noted. One of the New Mexican versions of *"Por la orilla de un arroyo"* (Along the Edge of a Stream) is known and sung in the Salamanca area of Spain. For the penitentes, the alabados provided an adequate means for expressing their own religious sentiments and kept the mysteries of Christ's birth, passion, death, and resurrection ever before the people in simple, yet lovely, imagery. Furthermore, the people themselves used these hymns at different times of the day as a part of their own devotions. Thus the head of a household might greet the dawn of a new day by intoning the lovely *"En este nuevo dia"* (On This New Day), a hymn of thanksgiving to God for having preserved the family through the uncertainties of the preceding night as well as a prayer for His continued help throughout the day. The alabado on rare occasions is also used at the funeral of a *cofrade* (brother) when the entire hermandad congregation sings prayers for the repose of the soul of the dead man. This custom may still be observed by the interested student of Mexican American folkways, though less frequently today, in some of the villages in northern New Mexico.

In a secular, contemporary context, Mexican folk and pop music continue to thrive among Mexican Americans. As an example of the former there is the mariachi style. Mariachi groups made up of local musicians and singers are constantly being formed in the Southwest. Many of these bands are made up of young people, which would seem to indicate that instead of turning away from the tastes of their parents in favor of more typically American styles in music, these young adults feel a solidarity with the culture of their parents and are actively keeping it alive.

The origins of the mariachi are obscure, although its roots can be traced to numerous orchestral groupings of colonial Mexico, and ultimately to both Spanish and pre-Columbian Indian musicians. When the Spaniards arrived in Mexico, they found, among some of the Indians there, a highly organized system of musical guilds whose social functions were the composition and teaching of hymns, songs, dances, and the manufacture and maintenance of musical instruments. According to the records left by early-day witnesses of the Aztec musical world, such as Fray Bernardino de Sahagún, music was an indispensable part of their martial and religious life, so much so that the direction of the music guilds was seen as a priestly function (Mendoza 1956, pp. 18–19).

The Spaniards, on their part, brought their own heritage of Latin and Castilian songs, together with European instruments. Spanish Renaissance music represents a glorious high point of European culture, and together with the older medieval heritage, which in Spain remained intact throughout the Renaissance, it was brought to the New World. Indians and mestizos were promptly taught to play European instruments and to sing in church choirs in the important cities of Spanish America. From the churches the singers would go to the halls of great men, such as the viceroys and the grandees of Spain who were in the colonies, and sing the popular secular airs of the times. Outlying ranchos and haciendas would eagerly listen to any wandering troubadours who put up there for the night, and soon local vaqueros were learning to play and sing the songs brought to them from the distant capitals. The Indian influence was always very close, as even today there are many Indian tribes in Mexico that have preserved their language and customs, so that from the beginning, Mexican popular music was a *mestizaje* (a mixture) of Iberian and Indian influences. The formation of local bands on the ranchos and in the villages was a natural consequence of this musical activity, and soon the mariachi band was born.

The size of the mariachi band varies according to the financial resources of the group. In 1932, for example, the Mariachi Vargas de Tecalitlán arrived in Mexico City to seek its fortune, but had to leave, temporarily at least, because, according to its leader, Silvestre Vargas, the band was too small and therefore hardly interesting. At that time the group, which had been founded in 1898, consisted of two violins, a harp, and a guitar. In 1934 the group returned to Mexico City, this time with four violins, a harp, and a guitarrón. Dressed in the costume of the Mexican *charro* (cowboy), the band did meet popular approval this time, and sometime later was able to add a six-string *vihuela*, a guitar, and a trumpet. In the latter seventies, this group was still one of the finest and the most famous and, of course, had grown quite a bit larger (Garrido 1974, p. 72). One American counterpart, *Los Changuitos Feos*, of Tucson, started in the mid-sixties with four guitars, one trumpet, one violin, one vihuela, and a guitarrón. Later the band grew to include three trumpets, four violins, and two more guitars.

The mariachi costume represents a stylized version of what the nineteenth-century Mexican vaquero of Jalisco wore most of the time: a wide-brimmed sombrero, white shirt, colorfully embroidered short-waisted jacket, and tight-fitting trousers embroidered to match the jacket. A colorful large bow tie and high-heeled Spanish boots complete the costume.

The word "mariachi" itself seems to be of unknown derivation. A popular legend states that in the mid-nineteenth century, during the French occupation of Mexico, their Royal Highnesses Maximiliano and Carlota needed some musicians to play for a court wedding. French courtiers were sent out to scour the countryside for musicians, but because they could not speak Spanish very well, the Frenchmen could only pantomime their request to the Mexicans while repeating the French word "mariage." The Mexicans apparently understood the pantomime, for they found some musicians for the court, but those who could not speak French and who obviously did not recognize "mariage" as a cognate of the Spanish "maridaje" must have thought that "mariage" meant "musician" instead of "wedding." Thus it is that, at least according to the legend, the Gallicism "mariachi" came into the Spanish language in Mexico. Be that as it may, it is a unique word in that it denotes a form of music so unmistakably Mexican that it can never be confused with any of the many other forms of Hispanic music, and it is this unique quality which the Mexican American brings onto the American cultural scene. And what is this unique quality? Part of it is derived from the nature of the musical instruments used. The trumpets lend a stirring martial air to whatever piece is played by the mariachis. The stringed instruments, harps, guitars, vihuelas, and even the large guitarrón, lend a soft lyricism which appeals to the emotions. There are no percussion instruments as such, and yet many percussive effects can be simulated on the guitar, especially in the quasi-military pieces that date from the revolutionary period (1910–1920). Another part of the mariachi's uniqueness derives from its versatility. I quote here from Randy Carrillo, alumnus of *Los Changuitos Feos,* founder and director of the *Mariachi Cobre,* and, as of the late 1970s, recording star:

> I think that the Mariachi is one of the most diverse musical forms ever to come along. We can play from classical to hoe-down music, from huapangos to corridos and rancheras, cumbias, and sones jalicienses. There is just so much, it's hard to mention everything that the Mariachi can do.

As can be seen from this statement, the mariachi is international in scope. The *huapangos* are characteristically from Mexico's eastern region (Vera Cruz north along the coast through Tamaulipas); *corridos* are the octosyllabic ballads, derived from Medieval Spanish *romances*, which narrate current events of political and social interest. They can be sung to any tune, and they are continually being composed by village bands and professional song writers so that they are both ancient (form) and modern (content) at the same time. The *rancheras* are the songs and dances popular on Mexico's northern frontier and consequently heard throughout the American Southwest, too. The *cumbia* originated in Colombia, where it remains the popular folk form, although it has achieved an enormous popularity throughout Latin America, and the *son jaliciense* refers to the folk music of the Mexican state of Jalisco. The latter especially has become the hallmark of mariachi music, with individual pieces such as the "Jarabe tapatío" becoming well-known in the United States as the "Mexican Hat Dance."

Another aspect of the Hispanic musical heritage which the Mexican American actively and creatively promotes is flamenco. Flamenco music and dance today are associated primarily with southern Spain, with the ancient province of Andalucía. Its history is complex and, in some cases, controversial. Arab, Hebraic, Latin, and Oriental influences are clearly visible in flamenco, and to some the music is overly intellectual while to others it is too crude and popular to merit serious consideration! Flamenco song is said to derive from a blending of the techniques of the Jewish cantor in the synagogues of Islamic Spain; the Arab muezzin calling the Moslem faithful to prayer several times a day from his minaret alongside one of the many mosques of southern Spain; the *a capella* singing of the Andalusian peasant as he went about his daily chores; the chanting of Latin hymns by the choirs in the Christian cathedrals and churches; the sung description of merchants' and vendors' wares in the streets and markets; and the profane songs of students in the university towns. Contemporary flamenco is divided into two main parts: *cante jondo* ("deep song") and *cante chico* ("little song"). The former incorporates the ancient, imponderable themes of unrequited love, death, and intense personal suffering into its songs; the latter is gay in spirit, often satirical in content, and more appropriately suited to the tourist trade. Each of the two *cantes* includes a large repertoire of different types of song; so large is each, in fact, that there is not space enough in this essay to allow a listing of those types. The same can be said for the many different kinds of flamenco dance; however, in spite of the bewildering variety to be found among flamenco dances, certain characteristics are common to almost all. The rapid stamping of the feet and heels (*zapateao* and *taconeo*) in definite rhythmic patterns, the snapping of the fingers (*castañeteo* or *pito),* the clapping of the hands (*palmas*), and the graceful movement of the arms, hands and fingers (*braceo*) are typical of flamenco dancing. Purists decry the use of castanets in flamenco, but certainly their contribution to the overall rhythmic effect cannot be denied.

Native New Mexicans, Arizonans, Californians, and Texans, as well as Hispanic (and even some non-Hispanic) Americans from other states have studied flamenco here and in Spain and subsequently brought their art to American audiences. Vicente Romero, María Benítez, Anita Ramos, Carla Durán, Maya Fernández, and Lydia Torea are outstanding exponents of flamenco in the United States. They are native Americans who have joined the Spanish flamenco artists who immigrated here or to Mexico, such as Mario Escudero, Pepe Segundo, Sabicas, David Moreno, and others, in keeping alive for the Mexican American a rich part of his total cultural heritage.

Mexican dance is also pursued creatively throughout the Southwest. Numerous *folklórico* groups have been created in Los Angeles, San Diego, Tucson, Santa Fe, Albuquerque, El Paso and San Antonio, to list but a few of the important places. Judging by the talent, energy, and dedication displayed by these dance companies (and many of them are made up primarily of children), Mexican folk dance here is a rich contribution to the total cultural scene in America.

Song, too, is an important feature of the Mexican American's cultural heritage. Chicano society has preserved a rich store of ancient folk songs while at the same time new songs reflecting the Chicano experience here, today, are being written. This fact illustrates the vitality and renewed vigor of a culture that continues to develop musically. The Mexican American singers are individuals who work to maintain the old traditions while striving to personalize and expand their art by experimentation with new forms. Many have made great contributions of their time and talent in public performance as well as on recordings. Some of the more outstanding singers have been Alex Chávez, Marilina Bustos, and Geneva Chávez of New Mexico. These three sing Spanish, Mexican, and New Mexican folk songs in Spanish as well as ranchera style songs in the mariachi tradition. Others, such as Freddy Fender and Johnny Rodríguez of Texas have made solid contributions to American country-western music while still pre-serving songs in Spanish in their repertoires. In the field of popular music Mexican American band leaders have found their proper medium. Trini López and the revolutionary Carlos Santana are but two examples.

Rubén Cobos, professor emeritus of the University of New Mexico, is a great musicologist who is both scholar and interpreter of the Spanish folk ballad of the Southwest. Cobos has studied the genesis and evolution of the Spanish *copla* and other musical and poetic forms throughout Spanish America, and his vast collection, the fruit of many years of labor, resides at the Colorado College in Colorado Springs.

The cultural revolution of the 1960s and 1970s among the Mexican Americans has found another medium for expressing itself: the theater. Talented young Chicano writers are addressing themselves more and more often to this art form that has the capacity for reaching a wide audience directly. In addition, when one considers the fact that the theater in the Southwest has always had a dual function, entertainment plus instruction, the appropriateness of the play for serving as the vehicle of cultural awareness and expansion becomes readily apparent.

The colonial theater in New Mexico had a few secular pieces in its repertoire. For example, *Los comanches* is a dramatized version of the conflicts between the Comanche Indians and the Spanish settlers at a remote outpost of His Catholic Majesty's empire. The play combines peculiarly local allusions as well as a series of topics that were commonplace in European art, but strangely out of place in a New Mexican context. Such, for instance, are the references to castles and the presence of the monarch himself.

The majority of plays that have survived from early colonial days are religious in subject matter and spirit. The Spanish *auto sacramental* (a one-act theological play which glorifies the Eucharist) had a great influence on the form of these plays, as did the more pastoral *coloquios* (religious plays) centered on the birth of Christ. No one knows with any certainty who wrote the colonial plays, nor even when they were written. The only definite fact about them is that their representation before an audience on religious feast days has been an unbroken tradition since the earliest days. Thus, the Mexican American residents of places as distant from each other as Los Angeles, Santa Fe, and San Antonio will present works like the *Coloquios de los pastores* (a pastoral representation of the birth of Jesus) around Christmas time, *Los reyes magos* on the Feast of the Epiphany, or any of the other plays on their respective holy days.

Aside from this traditional repertoire of colonial drama in Spanish, the Chicano, until the 1960s, had no theater of his own making. All that he had was an inheritance from the past, a rich inheritance, to be sure, but still something already completed long before his time. Since the rise of *Chicanismo* in the mid-1960s a growing number of contemporary plays have been written and performed on topics as diverse as the Delano laborers' difficulties and the reactions of barrio residents to the Vietnam war. Some of these plays will undoubtedly represent real contributions to the entire heritage of the Mexican American in the drama.

Needless to say, Chicano theater of the 1970s is no longer religiously oriented but still used for instruction in social change. Its purpose is to reach the minds of the people through the stark portrayal of the conflicts and tragedies suffered by *la raza*. In this context it is interesting to note that a character in *The Dark Root of a Scream*, by Luis Valdez, says,

> Our people have loved your God very much. We've brought little things to him—candles, *oraciones* (prayers), devotions—all that we have, even our blood in penance. Or in war. We've loved him because we saw him nailed to a cross, suffering and bleeding like us. Every time we've been cheated, worked like animals, had our lands stolen—we've cried out and prayed to him to help us. *¡Jesucristo!* Nothing has happened. But we still go on believing in him like faithful *indios* (Valdez 1973, p. 91).

In other words, the underlying reality of Chicano theater has not changed, even though its outward forms and language have. What is this underlying reality that has always been the moving force of this theater? Ostensibly, it has been the dramatization of the Mexican American's sorrows, thereby offering him a degree of hope that things will get better for him or for his children. The older plays offered the hope of redemption and salvation in the hereafter, after the soul had undergone the torments of this "valley of tears." The new drama, sociopolitically oriented as it is, offers the hope that through political and social action living conditions for the Mexican American within American society may improve.

During the 1950s and 1960s an emergence of Chicano culture became evident throughout the Southwest. The reflowering has assumed the proportions of a true burgeoning of Mexican American culture. It represents, in part, a reaffirmation of Mexican cultural values as a result of the efforts of young Chicano militants who helped in making the Mexican American more aware of himself, his identity as a Mexican American, and of the aspirations we share with the many other ethnic groups that, together, make up an important part of the American people.

## Bibliography

Barrio, Raymond. 1975. *Mexico's Art and Chicano Artists*. Sunnyvale, Calif.: Ventura Press.

Campa, Arthur L. 1934. *Spanish Religious Folktheatre in the Spanish Southwest*. Albuquerque, N.M.: University of New Mexico Press.

Chávez, Fray Angélico. 1974. *My Penitente Land: Reflections on Spanish New Mexico*. Albuquerque: University of New Mexico Press.

Comité Chicanarte. 1975. *Chicanarte*. Los Angeles: Comité Chicanarte.

Garrido, Juan S. 1974. *Historia de la música popular en Mexico, 1896–1973*. México, D.F.: Editorial Extemporaneous.

Hernández Trujillo, Manuel. 1969. "Portfolio 3." *El Grito* 2 (Spring issue).

Mendoza, Vicente T. 1956. "Panorama de la música tradicional de México." Vol. 7 of *Estudios y fuentes del arte en México*. México, D.F.: Instituto de Investigaciones Estéticas, Universidad Nacional Autónoma de México.

Pattie, James Ohio. 1962. *The Personal Narrative of James O. Pattie*. Philadelphia: Lippincott.

Quirarte, Jacinto. 1973. *Mexican American Artists*. Austin: University of Texas Press.

Valdez, Luis. 1973. "The Dark Root of a Scream." *From the Barrio: A Chicano Anthology*. Edited by Luis Omar Salinas and Lillian Faderman. San Francisco: Canfield Press.

Villa, Esteban. "Portfolio 2." *El Grito* 2 (Spring issue).

Weigle, Marta. 1976. *Brothers of Light, Brothers of Blood: The Penitentes of the Southwest*. Albuquerque: University of New Mexico Press.

Weisman, John. 1973. *Guerrilla Theater: Scenarios for Revolution*. Garden City, New York: Anchor Books.

Wilder, Mitchell A. 1968. *New Mexican Santos*. Colorado Springs: Taylor Museum of the Colorado Springs Fine Arts Center.

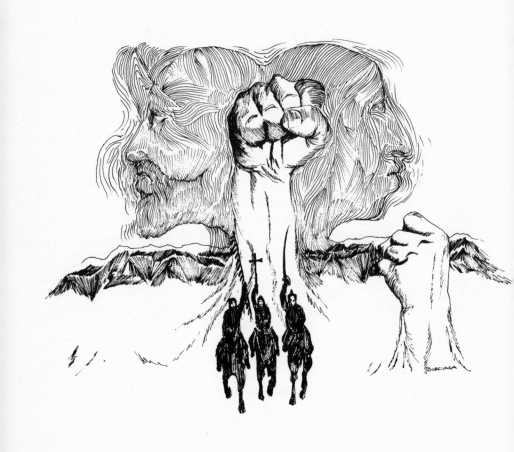

# OURSELVES THROUGH THE EYES
# OF AN ANTHROPOLOGIST

*Carlos G. Velez-I.*

WHEN I WAS ASKED TO WRITE AN ESSAY of the way in which a Chicano anthropologist looks at the group of persons with whom he identifies himself, I came to the conclusion that I could not take this look without, of course, taking a look at myself. I could not take this look without introducing my own subjective feelings, my own aspirations, failures, successes, my own inadequacies, strengths, and those things that rather than being specifically identified as "ethnic" should be considered pan-human.

Regardless of the analytical or theoretical stance one assumes in order to understand human behavior, one must always include the filtration process of experience which inevitably changes, colors, and shifts the model of explanation itself. And what should also be considered is that the model of explanation itself is the result of a filtration process which consists of many experiences which do not always coincide with the reality of the experience being perceived. What this suggests is that the models of analysis are themselves the result of historical-cultural processes that have been filtered by the individuals who have explained them, utilized them, and written about them. It seems, then, that little can be gained by claiming that any model of analysis organizes the world into its objectivę reality. That reality which we perceive in terms of enculturation and socialization is as real as we as individuals make it. We as anthropologists perceive reality also as a result of these processes with the addition of a body of knowledge which describes and has attempted to analyze those processes of which all human beings are a part. Anthropologists have attempted to explore other peoples' perceptions of their realities and the imperfect expression of this reality in social processes. In so doing, anthropologists find themselves understanding their own reality and the expression of that reality in their own social processes.

[37]

If we can utilize that body of knowledge gleaned from parts of the world, while at the same time keeping in mind that such knowledge is filtered, we can attempt to understand our own individual reality and the reality of the people with whom we as individuals identify.

What then from this filtered analytical and personal point of view can I say about the way we as Chicanos see ourselves? I can truly make no claims to truth; I can truly make no claims that my perceptions are any more or any less real than someone else's. Yet I do think that I can perhaps offer a few ideas, a few perceptions, as filtered as they are as to what I understand as a Chicano and as an anthropologist.

Let us first consider a term which may be helpful for our mutual understanding. That term is the amorphous catch-all word referred to as culture. The word culture is a result of historical processes and subject to a variety of interpretations resulting from historical filtration. It is a handy tool by which we can arrange the world outside of our minds but which ironically concerns the "stuff" in our minds. It is a scheme which organizes sets of abstractions within people's heads called values, beliefs, and procedures and also assumes that these abstractions are crucial to the development of the emotional, intellectual, and biological growth of the individual. To put it another way, this scheme states that in people's heads there are understandings which tell us what is good or bad, how to go about things in the world, and how the world is put together. These "understandings," or "stuff," are shared, transmitted, and sanctioned. In order for people to live together they have to have these values, beliefs, and procedures carried to and fro between them and passed on to future generations. These "understandings" have some kind of moral force attached to them so that if we deviate from them we might get punished and if we follow them we might get rewarded. Yet these "understandings" are not as simple as they seem. Each individual filters, transforms, restructures and reinterprets them according to his own psychodynamic processes so that our parents' culture was transformed after their parents' transmission and in turn during our socialization and enculturation process, we transformed their version's culture.

Further, not all persons even within a family unit share the same "stuff" in the same way due to the transformation process within each personality as well as the transformation process of shared understandings accumulated, transmitted, and prescribed by significant others on the job, in the school, on the streets, and wherever human beings meet in social interaction. Thus, from the point of view of the individual who is undergoing these processes, he or she may find that these understandings are incongruent with the ones accumulated in the home resulting in some type of alienation from either source of enculturation. Yet in order for human beings to participate in social interaction there has to be enough predictability of others' behavior so that group life may continue. This predictability is so important that it sometimes defines the parameters of allowable physical distance between human beings. Thus, the physical proximity of one human being to another will be greatly influenced by the sorts of shared, transmitted, and sanctioned understandings people carry around in their heads about how far and how close they should be from one another and even how much and what kind of smell will be accepted or tolerated in each others' company.

Culture partially consists of this elemental "stuff" and in reality this has little to do with great ideologies or social movements, although the quality of this "stuff" can be utilized as support for political movements of all sorts including our own. I do not deny the importance of ideology nor do I deny that culture consists of only this elemental sort of shared understandings. However, we cannot understand the peculiarity of the translation and transformation of ideologies by different cultures unless we understand the peculiarity of the "stuff" that different cultures adhere to and discard. Thus for an Anglo-American to understand the *Huelga\** he would have to understand its symbols—the eagle, black and pyramidal, on white manta surrounded by the red color of blood and of the sun. The meaning would be lost if he did not know what pyramids meant to many of us and the emotions connected with them or what white manta worn in the fields of old and for weddings meant. Of such "stuff" he would have to know in order to understand the ideology contained in the struggle.

The knowledge of other people's elemental "stuff" is crucial to the understanding of ourselves, for it is from such knowledge that we can understand the processes involved in making us "us" and perhaps determine where we might be going. In the discussion of the kind of shared understandings we as Chicanos hold, and here I use the word

---

*The cry ¡Huelga! was first heard in the grape fields of Delano, California, in 1965. It was then that César Chávez was joined by men, women, and children in a bitter strike that eventually would lead to the improvement of working conditions for farm laborers.

"we" rather guardedly since these are my perceptions of "we," I would suggest that in some ways we are no better off and no worse off than any other people. In some ways we are better off and in some ways worse off. What is important to note is the manner in which we are either better or worse off. This manner involves the totality of "stuff" which is different from or the same as other people and the historical circumstances which produced such similarities and differences. In this way it is possible to judge what is to be done for ourselves and others. This knowledge, however, from my point of view, should be based on the understanding that all culture is inherently repressive but that the expression of that repression and the nature of that repression is different in different cultures. The rationale for this assumption is that we become social animals only when we are part of social sets and to be included within social sets we usually have to adhere to shared understandings that others have set up for us. We, in turn, insist that others hold to our perceptions of what these shared understandings are, even though many times these shared understandings seem to be vague and very difficult to comprehend in their totality. The result may very well be that we miss the signals which point out which sets of understandings we are to use. In this sense we are also no better or worse off than other human beings; however, we may very well be in a period of history in which missing signals because of rapid social and cultural change becomes too frequent for our own mental health, and in this case we might be worse off.

Regardless of whether we are better or worse off, all persons are participants in these vague, repressive outlines whose totality we can refer to as their traditional culture. But traditional culture as used here is not the static concept with which some of us may have become familiar. Traditional culture here refers to the totality of shared, transmitted, and sanctioned understandings of a group at a particular historical period in time. This is further qualified by stating that as soon as a child is born the process of his translation of his parent's traditional culture begins so that the sum total of his parents' experience may be described as his traditional culture but not his culture. Instead he will have transformed and filtered that traditional culture through his own psychodynamic processes and created his own version of his culture which becomes traditional when he attempts to transmit this version to his children. To put it another way, enculturation for all human beings consists of internalizing, transforming, and discarding his or her parent's traditional culture.

As Chicanos we have also been part of these processes—processes of addition, multiplication, subtraction, and division. We have accumulated and discarded "stuff" according to the structure of our own individual personalities and have transformed our traditional culture into our own culture and, in turn, have transmitted "stuff" to our children and to those with whom we interact. Of these processes we have always been a part and the multiplicity of experiences in our barrios and with others has formed our perception of reality and the understandings which we share with others. Such processes contain our experiences, and in my case, the fact that my parents came from Mexico, one from an upper-class military family and the other from a defeated bourgeois family, provided me with a version of traditionality which, in turn, was transformed by the structure of my personality. In addition, the experiencing in my barrio of the Garcia family, descendants of original settlers in the Southwest during Spanish colonial days whose contemporary offspring have a penchant for criminal activities, became part of the making of my "stuff." The experiencing of an Anglo family in the neighborhood whose father never worked but played the banjo daily on the steps of his peeling house, also became part of the making of my "stuff" as did the Lopez family whose father, a reformed alcoholic, built with his wife and children a number of small businesses and went on to send his children through the local university. The experiencing of the Vargas clan became part of the making of my "stuff." All *machotes* (he-men), all *cabrones* (no-good bastards), the Vargas were all great fighters but not for justice rather for their own distorted kicks—beating old men and women and sometimes children in the streets, releasing their own aggressions and expressing their own futility.

Of such "stuff" my reality came to be partially formed along with my experiences across the border. During my visits to Magdalena, Sonora, I used to see a long-bearded man walking on the balls of his feet because he had been caught by the Yaquis who had sliced the tendons of his arches. Listening to the sounds of heavy breathing outside in the yard at night, covered by clean white sheets, we children whispered stories of *La Llorona** and of the brujas. It is of such and other "stuff" from across the border that I came to gain another dimension of my own "stuff." Other "stuff" across the border also showed me that I was not really one of them for their understandings

---

*See Lux and Vigil essay for a discussion of *La Llorona*.

were not shared in the ways which counted. For example, we children could be seen but not heard at rituals or fiestas where all ages attended, whereas at home this was not the case at all. I thought it was curious that female children had to hide their legs with bland-colored stockings and that they were made to pray to the Virgin to keep their legs and their "selfs" covered lest they were discovered and inadvertently discovered themselves, while we male children could roam the streets, seeking new and wonderful experiences, new colors, new smells, new sounds, and most importantly new thoughts. Upon return to our barrios, female children were still less free but their expectations of others and of themselves were different. Here, they would pray with uncovered legs and covered heads not only to the Virgin but also to Christ. This prayer they learned not only from their parents but also from Irish missionaries who repeated their own versions of celestial truth as well as strange and exotic tales of spearing lions in the African bush and of little people of the Kalahari who had been pushed off their lands by both white and black strangers. These missionaries would intersperse their tales with curses and jokes, and with each exhalation the odor of Irish whiskey serpentined in the air—just enough—not with the abandonment of their fathers nor of ours—just enough, with the expertise of athletes—not too much, just enough—enough to get the whiff that these were men unlike the Spanish inquisitors who piously sniffed but never smelled.

The differences between what was Mexican and what was mine came to be, and these differences were accentuated by my Mexican cousins, who would call us gringos *patas saladas** even though our Spanish was as good as theirs, yet they would receive no insults in kind when they came to our homes. I have often asked myself, why the differences in "stuff"? Surely a boundary cannot be the reason. In the beginning there was none and the earliest one had little effect. But, when I went across the border I was made to feel and did in fact feel differently. Then I was vividly aware of the differences between myself and them. I was told not to go a block west of my cousins' home—for here lived children of the *industria* who were not to be associated with because somehow they were contaminated. I would see the differences they created among themselves when I noticed that the *criada* (servant) sat down to eat by herself in the kitchen. She ate of

---

*This is a derogatory term applied to Anglos; literally, it means gringos of salty feet.

leftovers like a leper who somehow was capable of spreading a disease my relatives and others like them had infected her with. She sat there in the corner of the kitchen, with her brown face, downcast eyes and drooped head, tortilla in hand scooping out the generosity of my relatives and others like them. I wondered even then, why it was that she was made to eat by herself even though they called her by her first name and why they yelled at her like a disobedient child. I soon found out that, unlike us, it did not matter whether she did everything she was supposed to do, for she was not of their *clase* (class), nor according to them, of mine.

I would return to my barrio where there was no *clase* except between those of the pious and the non-pious, the strong and the weak, the employed and the unemployed, the *mujeriegos* (women chasers) and the *hombres de hogar* (homebodies, as applied to men), the *borrachos* (drunkards) and the non-*borrachos*, the good ball-players and the mediocre ones, those who went to Catholic schools and those who did not, the smart ones and the dumb ones, those who could sing and those who could not, the nice girls and the not so nice, those of el Hollywood where it was said that one received a twenty-one chain salute and those of us in the Southside, and between *las buenas familias* (the socially elite) and those that were not—as well as everything in between those different orders of things. But we all lived together in spite of these differences. We shared, as imperfectly as it was, understandings—a multiplicity of understandings that had little to do with *clase* but instead had to do with the way in which our world was ordered according to differences and similarities intrinsically tied to moral questions and not to class differences. We were also linked to each other in spite of the differences by the same dusty air, and so we met in the rocky lot behind my house to play pelota (baseball) and sit on the boulders and tell each other tales of sex and ghosts.

We did differentiate, however, even though we had a multiplicity of imperfectly shared understandings, for within those understandings were the definitions of differentiation. In our minds we categorized the world, therefore, forming moral orders within which were formed rules as to who was what, who did what, and what was good and bad. The arrangement of all of this formed a hierarchy—as temporary as it was. There came to be formed categorizations of those within us who were like "us" and those who were not like "us," until within our families there was mother or father, or uncle or aunt, or *padrino* (godfather) or *madrina* (godmother) who were like "us" or not like "us." This moral order we carried about with us as do all human beings, differentiating according to the "stuff" that made us different or the same, which included everything in between. But we all lived together though many times in opposition to the different "us's." Sometimes in competition, sometimes in cooperation, sometimes in conflict, but we all lived together. I think that the opposition may have held us together as long as the rules of the moral order and their shared understandings were believed to be implicit and as long as our expectations were at least partially met.

We carried these categorizations into wider circles of experience as do all human beings, and differentiated into another moral order those human beings called gringas and gringos. I can remember how differently we looked at the gringas from the Chicanas. We looked at the Chicanas as if they were not to be touched but coveted, but we looked at the gringas as if they were to be coveted and touched. These differentiations in expectations we carried into young adulthood and as young men we shared fantastic adventures and concluded that with Chicanas *no había nada* (there was nothing) but with the gringas, *había todo* (everything was available). And so the ground rules for the expectations of relations with females who were differentiated either as Chicanas or gringas came to be set, but not to remain.

As time progressed, we further differentiated into moral orders our perception of the male gringos. In so doing they became our enemies and not our friends although inexplicably at times they became friends too. We thought they were to be fought and beaten because they were different and not like us. They made us feel different as we made them feel different. We expected them to be different and they expected us to be different. Their "stuff" was different or so we thought, and to them our "stuff" was different or so they thought, even though we were all in the same boat. We fought them with sticks and stones, with feet and fists, and sometimes we lost and sometimes we won. And it seemed that the war never ceased. From this war of youth, we carried with us the expectations of opposition into our schools, into the swimming pools and later into our jobs. Our expectations were reciprocated, for they, too, had learned to place human beings into moral categories. They carried their oppositions into our circles of opposition—even though we were basically in the same boat. As a result of having internalized certain expectations, we were regulated and in turn we regulated them into categories called the statuses and the expectations. The result was that they, like us, became slaves to prejudices conjured up through the process of multiplication, addition, subtraction, and division. Sometimes we let loose as they did, the rage resulting in American wars, killing and being killed all in the name of predetermined categories, expectations and prejudices that were not basically of ourselves but some of us believed them to be true. When we examined them much closer we found that they were our own categories, and came to know ourselves during the process.

There were times that we let loose with these expectations among ourselves—at times of ritual, at times of dancing and drinking, at times of gaiety and happiness. There were always notable events at every dance on those great Saturday nights. Times when we would strut and show that we were worthy, that we were human, but inevitably someone would disagree with our own assessment and that was enough to let loose our own anger. Bottles would fly, chairs would project, tables would overturn, and the beautiful girlfriends and older uncles and brothers would intervene. In turn they would let loose their anger by taking sides, accusing, and claiming past deeds as causative agents. Sometimes in the resulting process, networks of families would split into feuding parties, so that years afterward cousins would not speak to cousins, and sisters-in-law would plot among themselves even though when asked no one could remember why they were doing what they were doing.

Somehow during these times we came to know ourselves and others and the content of our "stuff." Some of us knew that the knowledge of ourselves was not clear, that the processes of how we came to be were cloudy, and that the expectations of others were contradictory to the kinds of expectations we had experienced. Some of us then decided to experiment with higher institutions which might provide us with some tools by which we could figure such things out, but unfortunately these institutions provided us with little other than tools to pay for our daily bread. Oh, now we could discuss and utilize polysyllabic ideas and words, but when we went to the barbershop and Chico, the barber, asked what we had learned, we would have to admit that after two hours of argument we knew little more than he did and perhaps he had a clearer understanding of the "stuff" than we did. There came to be a space between the expectations that we hoped would be met by learning and the realization of those expectations. For some of us that space became part of the "stuff" within us so that we traveled high and wide seeking answers to some basic questions as to what made us "us." Some of us found different paths and different obstacles on our journey to self-discovery and so we joined with others in political activities, in Chicano Studies departments, in literature and in writing, while others dropped out of the journey to return to that which made them most comfortable. Some sought comfort in daily work in the mines, in the fields, in supermarkets, and in universities. It was within this searching process that some of us found that all those expectations and dragons of experience had little to do with ourselves as human beings although we were "ground" by categories to believe them as ourselves. Those shared understandings contained within them were imperfect, indeterminate, and not of ourselves as human beings. We also found that among the "stuff"within ourselves there were understandings that had little to do with being Mexican, gringo, or Chicano, but rather with being human. From that point some of us searched for models by which we could understand the quality of experience and pan-human understandings. Those models assisted us in finding ways in which to ask fruitful questions not only of ourselves but of others; the answer to those questions, in turn, provided us with a clearer picture of what others perceive and the way in which we perceive ourselves and how we came to be at this point in historical time.

For some of us, in one sense, we are no longer Chicanos and yet in another, we are very much Chicanos. In the first sense, some of us are because we have found ourselves to be in a process of "becoming": of adding, of multiplying, of subtracting, of dividing ourselves and others into moral categories—part of the process of constant creation, part of the dialectic of oppositions, and part of the process of synthesis which all human beings undergo. Gustavo Segade has suggested in "Toward a Dialectic of Chicano Literature" which appeared in 1973 in *Meester* (November issue, pages 4–5) that "the Chicano mythic dialectic...is ...based upon the historical dialectic of the Chicano people and their relationship with Mexican and North American realities [but the process itself]...is general and universal." In this sense then some of us are not Chicano, for the recognition of such processes provides us with links to other peoples of which ethnocentrism cannot be a part. In a second sense, we are very much Chicanos, for the process of experience which many of us underwent and continue to undergo is based on the continued evolving expectations of Mexicans and Anglo-Americans and the reciprocal evolving expectations of Chicanos—a historical reality from which there is no escape. As we add, multiply, subtract, and divide, so do they, and as they add, multiply, subtract, and divide, so do we. Within these processes of historical relations our "stuff" shifts, changes, and becomes something else even though we may not recognize those shifts and changes at the time in which they occur. Within those processes of historical relations the "stuff" of other peoples shifts, changes and becomes something else even though they may not recognize those shifts and changes at the time in which they occur.

The recognition of these two senses of ourselves and their processes is from my point of view an act of reconciliation with ourselves which provides us with the opportunity to celebrate ourselves as participants in the grand ritual of human experience and of the "stuff," so very human and so very rich, which we have accumulated and discarded and will continue to accumulate and discard. We will find in this reconciliation that the process of acquiring and discarding "stuff" transcends tightly-bound ethnicity and instead shows us that we have always been part of the order of things, that we have always contributed to those processes, that we have been a crucial aspect of those creative processes, and that we have always been part of the flux and flow of change even though some social scientists have refuted that participation, and unfortunately, because of their own limitations, have refuted the processes themselves.

This recognition, however, leads to reconciliation with ourselves as Chicanos for it provides us the opportunity to recognize the scope and nature of the "stuff" within ourselves, and that "stuff," whether we like it or not, partially consists of the Anglo-American and of the Mexican. That "stuff" contains historical patterns of synthesized beliefs, values, and procedures, of unique versions of what the world is about, about what is good and bad, and how to go about things. What I suggest in this second aspect of reconciliation is that we can see that we are not bicultural but instead, uniquely cultural—as participants of history and as history-makers. We are a synthesis of myriad experiences—pan-human, multicultural, and multisocial. During the course of history, such experiences and continuing experiences are added as layers of meaning, layers of orders, layers of different and similar shared understandings, and, as a result of such experiences and the discarding of layers, we constantly "become." This is another way of saying that culturally we are neither Mexican nor Anglo-American, but we are of the American continent in a technologically complex society, with a complexity of experiences of moral orders. Some of these moral orders are uniquely Mexican, some are uniquely

Anglo, and some pertain to other minorities, but in their totality and together with our own participation in the creative process of living and experiencing, may be considered uniquely Chicano.

We are not synthetic, but a synthesis of ourselves and of others as are all human beings. Within this synthesis we can utilize aspects of ourselves for strategic purposes—at one time speaking English when it suits us, speaking Spanish when it suits us, or combining both when it suits us. We can utilize aspects of ourselves when it suits us, to shut others off from us if our strategies of the moment call for us to do so, as long as we recognize that these are only strategies and not the synthesis itself. We can also do just the opposite when it suits us. We can, in fact, be the bridge—the linkage of understanding on the American continent if our strategies call upon us to do so. It seems to me that the most important aspect of this synthesis is that we serve as indicators of the social and cultural change, not only in this country but in the Americas because of our uniquely historical background. I would suggest that if we want to predict changes in the American continent, we should look at the Chicano; we must look at ourselves—for we reflect the western hemisphere in a state of cultural and social change.

# THE MEXICAN AMERICAN:
# AM I WHO THEY SAY I AM?

*Reyes Ramos*
*With the assistance of Martha Ramos*

EVERY PERSON HAS A SELF IMAGE. In this the Mexican American is no different from anyone else. He knows the qualities in himself which distinguish him from other people. His name, his family relationships, and his physical appearance make him a person different from others. Less observable qualities such as his attitudes, likes, dislikes and abilities also make him a unique individual. A person's knowledge about his own qualities is his self-image.

Sociological literature has much to say about what a Mexican American is. Most of the accounts in the literature describe my people negatively in terms of group specific culture: I label these traditional accounts. Celia S. Heller, William Madsen, Arthur J. Rubel, Florence Kluckhohn, Lyle Saunders, and Julian Samora have all written about the Mexican American. Following are examples of the characteristics these researchers have developed in describing what they consider to be the cultural values of our people:

1. Present-time oriented and desires immediate gratification
2. Non-intellectual; that is, formal education is not valued
3. Non-goal, non-success oriented
4. Fatalistic and superstitious
5. Prefers living within the extended family group
6. Believes in machismo and a male dominated society

The purpose of this essay is to challenge these long-held concepts which I do not believe accurately describe *La Raza*. In this essay I propose to enlighten the reader with different points of view. As a professional sociologist of Mexican ancestry, I have read most of the literature written about Mexican Americans. The more I read and do research, the more I realize that there is a contradiction between my own self-image and what others have written about how I am supposed to be. The above list of characteristics does not describe me, nor does it describe many other Mexican Americans I know.

The formation of self-image is a lifelong process through which a person interacts with others and acquires a sense of who he is by what he sees reflected in the responses of others. Everyone has experienced this: for example, a sincere complimentary remark may make a person feel worthwhile, but a disparaging remark may make a person feel worthless. C.H. Cooley calls this the "looking-glass self" (Cooley 1964, p. 184).

The infant and the small child interact most with parents and the immediate family. These primary relationships in the early years have a profound effect on the child's developing self-image. If a child is constantly told that he is naughty, he begins to feel naughty and to act accordingly. If, however, the majority of the interactions with his parents are positive, he begins to feel that he is a person of worth. As a child grows older, he begins to interact more and more with people outside the home. Primary relationships with friends increase. Secondary relationships, which tend to be more formal and not on a one-to-one basis, are formed with teachers and business people. The school-age child can be greatly influenced by his teacher's opinion of him, as well as by the opinions of his school friends. As he ventures beyond the home, the child begins to receive feedback about himself from a multitude of sources. He finds that the responses from some people contradict the responses from others. Perhaps the child's friends celebrate his boisterous behavior, while his teacher disapproves. A teacher might approve when a child spends much time reading while his parents feel he should put down his books and help around the house. Despite the fact that a child receives both negative and positive responses toward his behavior, he nevertheless develops a general attitude or feeling about who he is. The image a youth has of himself is not fixed. It changes as he goes through life and encounters many people—each of whom responds to him in a different way.

The Chicanito, like all others, develops in this way. From the reactions of people he encounters, he learns that he is similar to other children. Perhaps he shares with his friends a liking for ice cream or a dislike for doing homework. He also learns that he is different. In going about his daily activities, he may discover that he is taller or shorter, darker or lighter than his friends. More important, he may begin to feel different in terms of his ancestry. Within the school setting, he may find himself to be different because he is not as proficient in English as his Anglo classmates. Furthermore, his teacher may consider him to be a less capable learner if he is not highly skilled in English. Even if a child lives in a predominantly Mexican American community, differences can still be found. His family may be one of few which speaks no English, or one of the few which receives public assistance. Factors such as these tend to influence how Mexican Americans view one another as well as how institutional representatives, such as school teachers and welfare workers, view Mexican Americans.

The teenage years are characterized by ambiguity, for the young adult is treated as a child in some instances and as an adult in others. Consequently, the teenager's self-image may be in a state of constant change. The problem of not being sure who he is may often be compounded for the Chicano youth, who may have more difficulty obtaining a job because of a lack of English language skills, or who may find that parents disapprove of dating persons of other ethnic groups.

The adult self-image is still dependent on the reactions of others. Whether a person qualifies for a job influences his feeling of well-being. The Chicano adult may wonder if references are made about his ancestry before they are made about his abilities. For adults, reading can serve as another source of feedback about the groups to which he belongs. The books and articles about Mexican Americans have not gone unread. Teachers, sociologists, and other professionals as well as some laymen have read these accounts and hence some of them expect each individual Mexican American to conform to the characteristics attributed to the group as a whole. Because I am oriented toward education and success, I have been asked why I am ''different'' from other Mexican Americans. Although I do not conform to what has been written, I am influenced by other people's responses to me: I can be made to feel different.

Since the literature on the Mexican American does not adequately describe me, it is important to ask whether it describes others of *La Raza*. I argue that it does not. Therefore, it is necessary to consider how we have been characterized by traits, many of which carry negative connotations. What factors, other than culture, can account for a Mexican American's behavior? I assert that the manifestations of our behavior cannot be explained solely in terms of the cultural characteristics attributed to the group as a whole. I strongly emphasize that it is best to try to understand the Mexican American in terms of the practical circumstances of his daily life and how he copes with those circumstances. That is, it is better to learn how we use our common sense to manage our routine affairs, than to assume that we handle our practical affairs solely in terms of cultural characteristics which social scientists attribute to us.

To understand how we have been differentiated by a set of negative cultural values, one must know the methods used by social scientists to study us. A review of the literature reveals that two methods of data collection are generally used: participant observation and depth interviews. These methods are used either alone or together.

In participant observation, the researcher collects his data from the vantage point of a participant. This means the researcher lives in or near the community to be studied; he tries to interact with the people whom he is studying; and he attempts to become a member of the group. In actuality, most researchers who use this method end up concentrating more on the observation than on the participation. Furthermore, it is often difficult and time-consuming for the researcher to become accepted by the group he is studying. One way of making the research less time-consuming is to use an informant to help collect data. The informant is a member of the community being studied and volunteers or is hired by the researcher to tell him about the people involved in the study. Some problems arise from the use of informants. The informant may tell the researcher what he thinks the researcher expects to hear, rather than what actually occurs. Another problem is created if the informant gives his own interpretation of events. It is difficult for the informant to be objective about his own community's affairs.

Although the researcher usually goes into a community with some knowledge of a few people who can introduce him to others, the fact that he is a stranger still creates barriers. People in the Mexican American communities, like people in all communities, notice and are curious about any stranger within their midst. They can and do observe, listen, and evaluate a researcher as much as he observes, listens, and evaluates them. Community members may not tell the social scientist what is "really" happening in their lives in much the same way that the social scientist does not tell them everything about himself.

The depth interview method, like participant observation, has its advantages and disadvantages. The depth interview is used to get detailed information on a specific subject. It usually starts with general questions. As the interview progresses, the interviewer gets more specific in his questioning until he has been provided with a detailed account of whatever is of interest. Its major advantage is that the researcher is not bound to fixed questions, as he would be in administering a survey, and he can follow certain points of interest which are brought up by the person being interviewed.

There are also disadvantages to the depth interview. Since it is time-consuming, the researcher may not be able to conduct as many interviews as he would like. Another possible problem is one of language. If the researcher must use a translator, then he must account for the possibility of the responses being altered in translation.

After the study is completed, the researcher compiles, analyzes, and interprets his data. In studying the Mexican American, researchers usually use the comparative method to interpret the data: the researcher looks for resemblance and differences between the people he has studied and another group with which he is familiar. Inherent in this procedure is what Robert A. Nisbet calls the "ethnocentric foundation of the comparative method." According to Nisbet, researchers studying a different culture tend to describe that culture in terms of, or in comparison to, their own culture. Nisbet argues that inevitably most researchers define their own culture as a "modern" one, and the culture under study as the "traditional," "non-progressive," or "backward" one (Nisbet 1966, pp. 202–4).

Studies on the Mexican American show evidence of the ethnocentric foundation of the comparative method. A review of the literature reveals that most researchers have indeed identified their culture as "modern" and that of the Mexican Americans as "traditional." The following is an example of the types of comparisons that are made between what is said to be Mexican American and what is said to be Anglo (Vaca 1970, p. 45).

| *Mexican American Value System* | *Anglo Value System* |
|---|---|
| Present time oriented | Future oriented |
| Non-intellectual | Intellectual |
| Non-goal oriented | Goal oriented |
| Non-success oriented | Success oriented |
| Fatalistic | Non-fatalistic |
| Traditional | Progressive |

In these comparisons the Mexican American generally is described as the opposite of the Anglo. *La Raza* is presented as if we lived in a vacuum and had no control over our affairs.

A final problem which exists is that the researcher may see and record an event which was preceded by other events which he did not witness. If he does not investigate the preceding events, he may misinterpret the witnessed event. Furthermore, a researcher may accurately describe an event or behavior, and then ascribe an inaccurate cause to that event or behavior.

To get a sense of what this means, consider that a researcher might spend a short period of time in your home. Then, because you are of Irish or Japanese ancestry, the researcher writes a book of cultural characteristics of the Irish Americans or the Japanese Americans based on what he observed during that particular time. Could these conclusions be accurate? Obviously, no researcher can come into a home and learn in a few hours the many meanings that family members attribute to their interaction.

This study is based upon both participant observation and depth interviews in a town in Colorado (Ramos, 1973). The community, at the time of the research, had a total population of 21,000, twenty percent of which was Mexican American. Being aware of the weaknesses as well as the strong points of the research methods, I took steps to overcome them. I was a community member before I began my research and thus had already been accepted as a participant in community affairs. My interviews with community members came within the context of my job in a public school. I was not known to be a researcher. After observing the behavior of a family, I did back-up research on the institutions and people who had dealt with the family prior to that time. I paid special attention to what the Mexican American said about himself and his daily life as well as what others said about him. Furthermore, I was able to converse with people in English or Spanish.

Given the fact that much research has been faulty, it is still necessary to consider the possibility that many Mexican Americans do exhibit the characteristics ascribed to our culture. Are these characteristics a result of Mexican ancestry, or are there other contributing factors? Oscar Lewis, in his study of poor people, argues that some people belong to a culture of poverty. Interestingly, many of the characteristics which he attributes to the culture of poverty are the same as those attributed to Mexican Americans. Is poverty more of a determining factor than ancestry? It can be shown that being poor drastically affects a person's way of life; however, it should also be noted that the term "culture" may imply a way of life that is consciously perpetuated and defended. Surely, the culture of poverty is not willingly passed on from parent to child.

In the search for the causes of human behavior, specifically the behavior of Mexican Americans, the researcher should focus on individual people with real life histories. I will present some of the characteristics which have been said to be Mexican American traits and examine them in terms of case histories. Special attention will be given to the practical circumstances of life which underlie the actions of people studied.

Our people are said to live in the present with no thought or plan for the future. Furthermore, this present-time orientation is said to cause people to seek immediate gratification for their desires. Most American taxpayers frown upon the individual who receives public assistance but who is still able to make a down payment on a new automobile. If the individual happens to be Mexican American, this seemingly irresponsible behavior is attributed to his present-time orientation. Research may show, however, that, in truth, other factors are behind the individual's behavior.

Consider the Ortiz family,* who followed the crops from Texas to Michigan. Every fall they arrived in Colorado to pick sugar beets. Although they lived there only for the picking season, the children enrolled in school and were signed up for the government-subsidized hot lunch program. The Ortiz family felt that there was some reluctance on the part of the school personnel to give the children free lunches. After all, the school personnel observed, the parents drove the children to school in a new car and had probably bought it with no thought for the children's future.

Why does the Ortiz family own, or at least have a down payment on, a new car when they cannot buy lunches? It is simply because it is impossible to be a migrant worker without dependable transportation, and when one car breaks down another must replace it. Actually, the car represents the future rather than the present. If the Ortiz family can forego some essentials today, the chances are that with the aid of a new

*All names used are fictitious.*

car, they can travel faster and pick more crops to get ahead in the future. As Mr. Ortiz once told me, his hope is that the car will get his family to the jobs before the other pickers arrive and thus enable him to get the better jobs. On the surface the Ortiz family's actions appear to confirm the present-time orientation, but upon considering the circumstances we find the opposite to be true.

Sociological literature has also described *Raza* people as being non-intellectual with little regard for formal education. A common complaint heard from public school teachers is that Mexican American children do not attend school regularly. Documentation verifies that Spanish-surnamed persons in the Southwest average fewer years of school completed than any other group (Grebler 1970, p. 151).

Teachers who actually talk with parents concerning their children's absences, however, often find that the reasons given to explain the absences may have nothing to do with a disregard for education. In fact, many parents express the hope that their children might attain a better education than they themselves have, and thus be eligible for better jobs. This statement would certainly conflict with the traditional literature. Of chronically absent students, the following reasons given by parents and their attitudes toward education allow for a better understanding of the reality of daily life.

> We try to send them to school, especially the older ones, but it seems that for one reason or another things happen and they are unable to go. For example, Jimmy has missed since Monday. Today is Wednesday so that is three days he has been out. On Monday we kept him home to take care of the younger kids because my husband was to go and see about another job and I was also going away to see about a job too. We just cannot make it on what my husband makes. Well, I didn't get the job and on the way to see about this other job my husband was stopped by the police. He was thrown in jail. He doesn't have a driver's license. He can't take the test because he can't read or write.

> On Tuesday, Jimmy had to stay home again because I had to go and see about my husband and then I had to go out and try to borrow money to pay the fine to get him out. That is why I wasn't here yesterday when you people came by. I was out trying to find the money for the fine. Today he had

to stay home again because I was still looking for money. It was not until this afternoon that I was able to get some more money to make the $35.00 for the fine.

They go to school as much as they can but it is impossible for them to go everyday. Right now they are all sick. When they are not sick, it's too cold for them to go all the time. They don't have winter coats, and I can't send them out in the cold without coats. I am not an animal. I want them to go, but I can't send them out when it's cold. My wish is for them to go and finish (high school) because I didn't, but the way things are I doubt if they ever will. We just don't have that kind of money.

Although what these two women have to say is straightforward, it is important to point out a few things about their accounts. Both women tell about the circumstances in their respective families which keep their children from attending school regularly. Mrs. Alvarez tells about their efforts to get ahead by getting better employment, and about how these efforts turn into problems that prevent their children from attending school regularly. An important aspect of Mrs. Alvarez' family condition is that their problems are created when they interact with other people. Consequently, their problems can be solved not by dealing solely with the family, but by also working with the others who interact with the family members.

Mrs. Barajas's problem is mainly financial. She does not have the money to clothe her children adequately for school. Consequently, she keeps them home, not because she does not value formal education, as specified in the literature about the Mexican American, but because they are sick or she fears they will become sick without adequate winter clothing.

It might be argued that Mrs. Barajas' financial problem could be solved if the family applied for welfare, but for families such as the Barajas, it is not simply a matter of declaring their need and getting assistance. The family, for example, had applied for welfare and was rejected when Mr. Barajas was declared to be an able-bodied person, even though he was underemployed. The caseworker with the department of welfare felt sorry for the family and regretted that Mr. Barajas did not earn enough money to support his family. Nonetheless, it was felt that if the welfare department helped the family they would violate the law. It was clearly explained that able-bodied heads of households were not to be given assistance. An unfortunate aspect of this situation was that Mr. Barajas lost a whole day's work when he went to apply for welfare. After this experience they were reluctant to follow any suggestion to apply for help. It was hard for them to forget that all they got from applying for welfare was a day's less pay. Now they take such things into account when deciding how they are going to manage certain aspects of their lives.

A third trait often ascribed to the Mexican American is that he is non-goal oriented. More realistic is the fact that our people have rarely had the chance to be successful. Although he may have a goal, the circumstances of poverty often keep him from attaining that goal. This is not to say that any given individual does not want success, but both discrimination and lack of training make success difficult to attain. For the Mexican American, success often means a state of independence, achieved by a stable job which provides enough money for the worker and his family to live above a subsistence level.

For example, Mrs. Morales is a widow who was considered by her local welfare department to be unable to follow up on her goals. Since her house was inadequate for her ten children and herself, the welfare department approved her request to rent a larger house. The welfare department would raise her rent allocation when she found a house. On the surface, this would seem to be a fair arrangement. In actuality, the odds were against her ever having success in reaching this goal. Since she did not own a car, it was necessary to find someone to drive her around to look at houses. This was troublesome because she not only had to ask friends to help her find a house, but she also had to search when it was convenient for her friends. Furthermore, when she did look at prospective rentals, the landlords turned her down when they discovered she had ten children. After looking at more than a dozen houses in two different towns, she decided that it was unrealistic to look further. The caseworker from the welfare department labeled her as irresponsible and unable to follow through on a goal.

Another seemingly non-success-oriented person was Mr. Jiménez, a forty-five-year-old, seasonal farm worker. During the winter months he was unemployed. When asked by community workers if he would like to receive job training, he agreed. When the time came to report to the job training site, however, he never arrived. This happened several times until the community workers (both Anglos and Chicanos) stopped asking him, calling him lazy, non-motivated, and unwilling to help himself. After getting to know him, I discovered that he was unable to read or write and was afraid that the job training would put him in the embarrassing position of being unable to understand. Pride had kept him from attending. He said, "They want me to go and I want to go, but if I find myself with a piece of paper in my hand, what do I do?" He also told me that he would have gone if he and the community workers could have gotten to know each other better. But, as he said, "They are so busy trying to get people on jobs that they never have time to know me and my problem. So we've never been able to communicate with one another and I've never learned what goes on at these job training places. They tell me nothing, except go to this place or that place. That doesn't help."

Both Mrs. Morales and Mr. Jiménez exhibit behavior which appears to be non-goal and non-success oriented. It is clear that their lives have been unsuccessful simply because the obstacles were too great, and not because they did not want to be successful. Furthermore, they were not helped by community workers because the helpers were unable to learn the particular circumstances surrounding their lives. Had the workers done so, they would have been able to deal more effectively with both of them.

When listening to Mexican Americans speak, one would find it easy to believe that two qualities, fatalism and superstition, do characterize *Raza* people. The phrase *Si Dios quiere* (God willing) is heard frequently, and it would seem that the people who say this feel they have little or no control over the outcome of future events. What is the cause of this pessimistic outlook toward life? Simply stated, it is past experience which has created this attitude.

Any person who does not make enough money to be independent of others is in some way controlled by those who help him. Mr. and Mrs. Maestas are a case in point. Mr. Maestas earned a living by doing agricultural work and unskilled labor until he was disabled in a work-related accident. At that time he was not aware of welfare, and so the family subsisted for a while on practically nothing. During this time he saw a doctor who declared him totally disabled. Later, when Mr. Maestas learned about welfare and applied for it, the welfare department did not approve of the doctor he had seen. The Maestas family could not receive welfare until he was re-examined by an approved doctor, and he could not see a doctor until he received money. Simply, he had lost control over the affairs of his life. After quite some time the welfare department re-evaluated his case and awarded him $250 a month to provide for himself, his wife and seven children. During this time, Mrs. Maestas became severely ill with a gall bladder ailment. The welfare department would pay for twelve visits to a doctor during the year, but did not pay for the medicine required which was purchased from the $250 monthly allocation. With so many outside forces controlling their lives, the Maestas family naturally responded to the future with the attitude of *con el favor de Dios* (with God's favor). Quite realistically, because of past experiences, they had little hope that circumstances would change. There were other factors which contributed to the Maestas's problems. Although the parents spoke both Spanish and English, neither of them could read or write. Both Mr. and Mrs. Maestas had attended only elementary school, but quit school to go to work at an early age. Many of their health problems as adults resulted from the lack of medical care during their earlier years. Although the Maestas family had many friends and neighbors who wished to help them, they, too, had limited financial resources, and thus were unable to help.

It is a known fact that most Mexican Americans live with or near their extended families. This means that parents and children often live in the same town, neighborhood, or house with grandparents, aunts, uncles, cousins and other relatives. Not only do they live near each other, but they share the responsibilities of child care, help with expenses during a crisis, and get together for many social events. Although people do remain within the extended family, it is not always by choice. Unskilled laborers who have a secure job are not likely to move because they know the difficulties they would have to face in finding another job. Another economic factor which influences this life-style is the inability to buy any type of insurance. Thus, when a calamity such as illness or fire arises, the uninsured must rely on relatives for help. For example, Mr. Méndez is an unskilled laborer who lives in a three-room house with his wife, five children, mother-in-law, sister-in-law, and her two children. They cannot afford a bigger house. As Mr. Méndez said:

> It's very difficult to live like this. It would be easier for all
> of us if we didn't live like sardines. We all work hard,
> but we never seem to make enough to get a bigger house,
> not to mention our own individual houses. It seems

something always happens just when we start to think
about a bigger house. If one of the kids doesn't get sick
something else happens. One day we'll get a bigger house.
I know.

Thus, it is not always by choice that a person remains near his relatives. Even when a person reaches an economic level which would
allow him to move away, he may feel an obligation to remain near and
help the relatives who helped him in the past.

Machismo is a trait which has been romanticized beyond reality. A
man is said to show machismo if he is super-manly and domineering in
his relationships with women. He is expected to be honorable, physi-
cally superior, and self-sufficient. Few men, of any ethnic group,
would be able to fulfill the exaggerated concept. Despite the miscon-
ception of machismo, women do play a critical role in managing the
affairs of *Raza* families, even though this is not acknowledged publicly. Mr. Armijo is a man who publicly downgrades his wife and
upgrades his own abilities and accomplishments. In actuality, he finds
it difficult to hold down a job, and he drinks heavily. Still, he talks
constantly of his machismo. Mrs. Armijo carries the whole burden of
managing the family. In explaining her husband's unrealistic view of
himself, she literally says, "He is full of hot air. He says what he says
because it makes him feel good." Mrs. Armijo says that her husband's
boisterous and crude behavior, which he calls machismo, is really a
result of alcoholism. For other men, machismo may be a way of
feeling capable in a world which makes it difficult for Chicanos to
demonstrate their capabilities.

Obviously, not all Mexican Americans are like those who have
been presented in these case histories, but it is important to realize that
there are many reasons for behavior and they are not always cultural
reasons. Many aspects of the life-style of Mexican Americans are
shaped by the circumstances of life rather than by Mexican ancestry.
We must also look back to the concept of self-image. So many articles
have been written describing the Mexican American in terms of cultural traits that it is now commonly believed that our people "are that
way." We have so frequently heard negative things said about us that
we may have begun to believe them.

The people in the case studies presented are poor. We have focused
specifically on them because the majority of Mexican Americans are at
the poverty level and it is they who are described in the literature as

being traditional in culture. Why have such a vast number of Mexican Americans remained in poverty? Historically, many have moved from an agricultural society into a highly complex industrial one. In some instances, new immigrants have come from Mexico, where a large percentage of the population is engaged in non-mechanized agriculture. Oxen and donkeys still pull plows more often than tractors. In other instances, Mexican Americans have moved from predominantly agricultural areas of the Southwest to large cities as a result of mechanization which has taken over their farming jobs.

The social skills necessary to manage everyday life in a complex urban area are different from those needed in rural areas. For example, Mr. Montoya lived in a rural area and generally heard about jobs by word of mouth (Ramos 1968). His cousin or his friends would tell him of someone who needed workers. Upon arriving in the city, however, Mr. Montoya no longer had an adequate network of relationships to help him. He was not aware of employment bureaus, and since he could not read, the newspaper want ads were no help. He could not find a job in the city and he found the situation so baffling that he eventually went back to the rural area. Upon his return he said, "I couldn't make it. I was out looking for something that I didn't know where it was or how to get to it if I knew where it was." Just learning how to take the right bus was difficult for him.

Discrimination against *La Raza* is another factor which has kept many people in poverty. Acts of discrimination need not always be overt. Subtle discrimination occurs when a person, having read about the Mexican Americans as a group, reacts to an individual in terms of what he has read. For example, many teachers have read or heard that we do not value education. Believing this, the teacher may not expect as much effort from Chicanitos who in turn sense that not much is expected of them. It becomes a vicious cycle, with the students' low performance confirming the teacher's beliefs.

Another reason the poor often remain poor is that a person who lives at the subsistence level rarely has the energy left to better himself. Generally, the diet which the poor can afford consists of carbohydrates with little protein. Women especially may appear to be fat and well-fed when they are actually fat and poorly nourished. Illnesses are more frequent and are allowed to continue before the expense of a doctor is warranted. Simply making it through the day is more time-consuming for the poor, who may not have transportation or household appliances such as washing machines to ease their tasks. The man's work is generally physical and, therefore, exhausting. It would be difficult for an illiterate man doing eight or ten hours a day of unskilled heavy labor to return to school at night to help him gain skills to get a better paying job.

Another obstacle for the Mexican American is language. Recent arrivals speak only Spanish, and this obviously limits the possibilities of finding a job, getting a driver's license, or of doing a multitude of things in the United States. Second and third generation children are often in the peculiar position of not learning either Spanish or English adequately. Because their language development is split between two languages, a limited vocabulary in both may result and, in turn, school problems arise from limited language skills.

Over the years various institutions have been established to aid the poor: welfare departments, charitable organizations, on-the-job training, and a variety of programs under the direction of the U.S. Department of Health, Education and Welfare. With all of these groups attempting to solve the problem of poverty, why is it that so few people are able to upgrade themselves? Why have the helping institutions not had more of an impact on the Mexican American poor? Governmental welfare departments form the largest single group of service agencies and are probably the most controversial ever set up to aid the poor. The primary function of welfare departments has been to give money to people who do not make enough to live on. However, the money given is only sufficient to maintain them at the most meager level. When a person receiving welfare takes a job, the money he earns is usually subtracted from the welfare allocation. Thus, his total income remains at the same subsistence level. All too often welfare itself creates a cycle which is difficult to break. Caseworkers are often burdened by the official details of filling out request forms and writing reports. Thus, they have little time for counseling clients about educational and job opportunities. Case loads are often so high that the caseworker must spend his time with only the most essential duties. The poor person's problems are much more complex than just monetary ones, but the aid he receives is almost strictly monetary. Agencies, other than welfare, are often beset by many problems and find it difficult to help even a small percentage of the poverty-stricken population.

There are solutions to the large-scale poverty of the Mexican American. Welfare reform, with changes in case loads so the caseworkers might know their clients as individuals, might be attempted. Some form of subsidized day care for children would help women obtain jobs. Men on welfare could receive larger grants to cover family expenses while going through job training programs. As long as welfare grants are only enough to cover the bare minimum, few people will have the energy or ability to better their position.

People who coordinate job training and employment opportunities must consider the total complexity of a person's life rather than just the working aspect. In the past, job-training programs for Mexican Americans have had a high dropout rate due to the difficulties of illiteracy, lack of transportation, misunderstanding of expectancies, illness, and fatigue. Too often a number of people have been trained in areas which have only a few available jobs.

Schools, too, must make some radical changes to help the poor. They might have smaller classes, so that each child could have more individual attention. Teachers might be given release time to visit families, so they can work with the total child. Bilingual programs could certainly help, but they are not the cure-all for our children. If the total environment in which the child lives is not altered, he will have many obstacles to overcome before being able to benefit from bilingual programs.

Obviously, such changes would require placing new priorities on the spending of tax monies. Altering the opportunity structure for the poor would be expensive, but in the long run, money would be saved if the poor became self-sufficient. Other less grandiose schemes involve person-to-person relationships. Mexican Americans, like all people, are individuals with individual characteristics. It is most important to know people as individuals rather than to stereotype them. One should not expect a person to behave in a certain way simply because he is of Mexican ancestry, for his environment and the circumstances of his daily life are more influential in shaping his behavior.

Person-to-person relationships are especially important when it is realized that a person forms his self-image from the way other people react to him. If most of his relationships with people are negative and he senses that little is expected of him, the Mexican American may come to feel negative about himself.

This essay has focused on the socio-economic conditions of daily life which are frequently more important than cultural traits in shaping the life-styles of the Mexican American. The poverty-stricken Mexican American can enjoy more aspects of his own culture if provided a better standard of living. He may be limited to eating beans and tortillas simply because he cannot afford more. He may never have the chance to travel out of his neighborhood or city, but with improved income the Mexican American might partake of a more varied cuisine, or actually travel. In closing, it is necessary to determine what aspects of the life of *La Raza* are a result of his poverty-stricken conditions and what aspects are a result of his ancestral roots in Mexico.

Bibliography

Cicourel, Aaron V. 1964. *Method and Measurement in Sociology.* New York: The Free Press.

Cooley, Charles H. 1964. *Human Nature and the Social Order.* New York: Schocken.

Grebler, Leo, et al. 1970. *The Mexican American People: The Nation's Second Largest Minority.* New York: The Free Press.

Hawkes, G.R., and Taylor, Minna. 1975. "Power Structure in Mexican and Mexican-American Farm Labor Families." *Journal of Marriage and Family* 37. (November): 807–11.

Hernández, Deluvina. 1970. *Mexican Americans: Challenge to a Sacred Cow.* Chicano Studies Center, Monograph No. 1. Los Angeles: Aztlan Publications.

Nisbet, Robert A. 1966. *Social Change and History: Aspects of the Theory of Western Development.* New York: Oxford University Press.

Ramos, Reyes. 1973. "A Case in Point: an Ethnomethodological Study of a Poor Mexican American Family." *Social Science Quarterly* 53 (March issue): 905–19.

———. 1974. "Beyond the Bilingual-Crosscultural Classroom: The Effects of the Social Environment on the Classroom." Unpublished paper.

———. 1968. "Urbanization of the Migrant: Processes and Outcomes." Unpublished paper.

Romano-V., Octavio I. 1968. "The Anthropology and Sociology of the Mexican Americans." *El Grito* 2 (Fall issue): 13–16.

Shibutani, Tamotsu, and Kwan, K. 1965. *Ethnic Stratification.* New York: MacMillan Co.

Vaca, Nick C. 1970. "The Mexican American in the Social Sciences: 1912–1970." *El Grito* 4 (Fall issue): 17–51.

Zinn, Maxine Baca. 1975. "Political Familism: Toward Sex Role Equality in Chicano Families." *Aztlan* 6: 13–26.

# THE NORTHERN NEW MEXICAN WOMAN:
# A CHANGING SILHOUETTE

*Ester Gallegos y Chávez*

THE CONCERN OF THIS ESSAY is to give a few observations on my personal interpretation of the Spanish-speaking woman of New Mexico. One must define the confines of a commentary when attempting to describe women since the New Mexican woman may have many commonalities and similarities with all women and certainly more with other Latin women in Spain and Latin America, but she has many differences as well, and her character is unique by virtue of a mosaic of influences of history, culture, language, geography, economics, politics, and status as a minority within the United States. One can discern tones, attitudes, particular qualities of life that are similar among women of many groups, but to try to lump them together would be a grave mistake. This is the reason that I have chosen to limit my essay to a personal view of the New Mexican woman as her own image has changed through the generations and through my eyes and reflection. I cannot neglect her heritage, but I must not forget her circumstances in the past as well as the present.

The young or the weathered face of the New Mexican woman has been etched by the artist of nature, carved by the sculptor of circumstances and tempered by her own nature and destiny as a woman. She sees herself differently from the way anyone else will see her. The painter, the social scientist, the sculptor, the husband may find her in different stages of evolution or revolution, whichever is befitting at the time.

No one can ascertain the original or the definitive portrait of any woman, least of all, of the woman of the late 1900s. We must accept, however, that woman herself has perhaps the only valid and accepted portrait, for it is she who has lived her life. Some of the chapters of that life are the concepts of other generations. They are the voices and the echoes of the past that may tell us a little about the melodies of childhood. There are memories of joy and the pains of adolescence. Together these thoughts of yesteryears represent the total experience of our conscious adulthood. This is how the picture unfolds to me. This is how the silhouette assumes form, color, and style. It is really never a finished and fixed creation. Woman is a dynamic, moving, changing subject, of a history, a time, an age, a generation, a type, an ambient, a mood, a feeling, and countless other influences and facets.

I do not pretend to speak for all women, not even for all New Mexican women, for I am well aware that my interpretation has the hues that have colored my own life, my own time and space, my own environment, my own abilities and limitations, my preference, and my own reality. To reflect on the past while trying to analyze the now is no small task. Yet, with all the boundaries of the topic itself, all its sensitivities that cannot be securely tied down, including my own foibles and shortcomings, I believe it is possible to give an outline of the northern New Mexican woman in her special setting. This is the story that I wish to share with the reader.

The Spanish-speaking woman of New Mexico has basically identified herself with her Spanish ancestry. The core of her being, the basis of her thinking is usually expressed in the special maternal tongue—Spanish. The Spanish that she uses has survived many changes common to all living languages, but it has maintained and sustained a flavor of the past because of the isolation of New Mexico and her people who long ago became separated from Spain and from the political and social connections with Mexico and became part and parcel of the barren land that they now inhabit. The technology that the Anglo brought and the sounds of the Native American are reflected in the Spanish of New Mexico, but structurally and philosophically it reflects the heritage of Spain.

The strength and the rugged individualism of the peoples of New Mexico created a fusion of race, culture, language, and atmosphere that are all a part of the synthesis of a rich way of life that has created a singular type of woman. The European heritage from Spain and the Indian culture of the New World left their indelible marks on the New Mexicans. Generally, it could be said that there is a sense of comfort and pride in a social identity with European Spain and Indian New Mexico, as well as with the political identity with the United States because we are Americans by birth or by adoption. Visible are the deep roots in the New Mexican character that manifest the fundamental aspects of needs and fulfillments of all those that preceded us. First, the New Mexican woman has managed to develop an appropriately healthy concept and esteem of herself and her history. She has been nurtured by simple, strong, and courageous people who bequeathed to their children the stamina needed to withstand the overwhelming odds of a severe and austere land.

The Spanish woman has been described as a woman of grace, charm, discretion, and integrity. She has also been viewed as arrogant and demanding. Others see her as stern, self-disciplined, and honest. Perhaps these are all part of a more profound truth that is but a fragment of the essence of the New Mexican woman. In her weakest moments she can be frightened, bewildered, and even unresponsive, but she can also muster all attributes which have been hewn by the demands of a country that was hard and filled with contradiction and strife. Her most salient feature, as I recall my grandmother, my mother, and countless other women, is her stoic demeanor and her sense of austerity. Her sense of humor had to be borne out of the sense of tragedy, the weaknesses of the individual, and the compassion necessary to accept all that human beings offer. Her courage and vigor were strengthened out of necessity, not only for survival and existence, but because of her love and respect for life.

If one were to ask one of the women of our past what the ideal woman should be, undoubtedly she would ascribe to her many qualities among which would be an unfaltering faith in God, honesty, loyalty, and affection to husband and family and parents. These qualities would all be unconditional. In a region where life was hard, and where poverty was accepted as part of the destiny of a people, the possibilities for compliance with such an ideal were often unrealistic because health, need, disillusionment and the certain betrayal by the elements of nature were sufficient to break even the strongest character. In times of plenty there was enough to eat, but in times of drought, a severe winter, or an epidemic, all suffered. The hovering uncertainty of the present and the dim hopes of life and all its requirements were great equalizers and there was little difference between those of means and those without. Ownership of land and livestock, as well as the number of workmen one employed, were the determining socioeconomic factors between groups. Liquid assets were not readily available. Such economic conditions have existed for centuries, and only in recent decades has there been a substantial money economy. There had to be a certain equity between husband and wife, and between patron and worker since all eked out a living from the same piece of land. Although there might be class distinctions and differences as the people themselves defined them, their roots, their beginnings and their plights were similar. They worked together, and frequently died together. They had concerns about the same issues and they had equal means to express their concerns. There was a democratic spirit borne out of an equally crucial necessity. Women participated actively for they often had to solve the daily problems, including caring for their ill. The development of the *médica* (folk doctor), *partera* (mid-wife), or *curandera* (folk healer) was the result of a great need for medical care. The center of life was the family. The Church and God were the culmination of the highest aspirations among both women and men, although women seem to have been more active participants in the official Church than were men. The *Penitente* brotherhood was the religious refuge for men. It was the legacy of medieval Europe and found reputable fruition in New Mexico due to the scarcity of priests. The scourging and penance for the atonement of sin perhaps gave full meaning to a concept of man's virility or machismo.

Marriage was solid and a woman never saw her status as homemaker and wife as demeaned or devalued in itself. It was highly respected and equal to the role of the husband as provider and principal spokesman for the family. Young girls aspired to marriage as did the young men for this was how the family was forged, and it was through the concept of family that one survived. In it were the most important and fundamental realities that maintained and sustained the body, the mind, and the soul. Divorce, it has been said, was the invention of the foreigner. It had no place in the New Mexican family. It was unacceptable and though a woman might have tremendous struggles in her marriage, she did not succumb to it as a solution to the problems of marriage. The status of the single woman, whether by choice or chance, was not easy. If she entered the convent she had accomplished one of the hopes that parents had for one of their children, and her life was secure and was understood as a life on a much higher plane than that of the ordinary single woman. She seldom gave it up except for illness, because to do so was socially undesirable and an ex-nun was censured. Like marriage, the nun's bond was insoluble.

If a young woman did not go into the convent she remained with her parents and took care of them until they died. A poor woman worked out of her home as a domestic, taking care of children, sewing, and doing other work associated with the home. She occupied her leisure hours with handiworks such as embroidery. The Church was the center of her life. She did not enjoy the same status as the married woman or the nun and was often suspect. Opinions included the possibility that she might have been rejected because she would make an unsuitable wife. There was always a question as to what might be wrong with her. Her social life was restricted and became even more so as she grew older. Stories about witches or evil women always seemed to be about women living alone, without parents, husbands, or children. It appeared unthinkable for a woman to want to be alone. There were women with well-deserved bad reputations, as in all societies. They might include those who simply did not adhere closely to the prescribed traditional ways of living as well as those who chose outright immoral conduct. Discretion, of course, was part of a woman's protection in her relationships with the community.

Unsuccessful marriages were tolerated and endured by both partners. Indiscretion was far more damaging to an erring wife than to an erring husband. The woman who was alone because her husband had deserted her remained with her children and made a life for herself with them. The divorced woman was ostracized. Regardless of her conduct or behavior she had little or no place in the community. Her situation, as opposed to that of her spouse, was far more painful.

As the single woman in the community grew older her status changed. She might become a *medica* or a *partera* or even a *curandera*. A *medica* massaged, made teas and other healing medications, and diagnosed illness. A *partera* delivered babies. Sometimes the same person performed both functions. The *curandera,* on the other hand, was believed to have magical powers and her source was considered evil. Despite the attitude toward the *curandera* her vocation flourished, but even today a *medica* will be highly offended if one should refer to her as a *curandera*. The *medica* used prayer and invoked the saints. The difference between incantations and prayer was very definite. The *curandera* could tell fortunes, put hexes on people, provide magic for the lovelorn or the jilted.

As the person who spent the most time with the children and who worked with them during their formative years, the mother held the most influential position in the home. With patience she endured all the inadequacies brought by poverty. With the customary calmness of the stoic, she persevered and accepted her role. It did not even occur to her to question her status or to flee from it. When dissolution of a marriage occurred it was because extraordinary circumstances threatened the moral fiber of the family. Separation and divorce had an inherent destruction with which she could not cope.

A family was sometimes deserted by the husband, but the woman seldom, if ever, deserted her family. If a husband abandoned his family the wife managed to keep her children together. The erring husband might reappear years later when the children were grown. With the same stoicism that she had borne his desertion she accepted his return, in obedience to the marriage vows, but he was made to feel that he was no longer welcome.

A woman who deserted her family was quite different. In the first place, it was very unusual for a woman to leave her family. If she did, it would be even more unusual for her to return and even more so to be accepted into the family again. It was just not done.

When separation was the only answer to an impossible marriage, the children remained with the mother. Divorce was a legal matter only and in the people's minds did not dissolve the bond of matrimony. It carried such negative implications that it did not occur very often. The Roman Catholic Church did not recognize divorce, but under very unusual circumstances a marriage could be annulled. Often the struggle of the woman alone with her children was a mammoth task to endure, but the mother did everything to keep the family together until the children grew up and got married. I recall a woman with seven children whose husband deserted her and went to live with another woman. It was a struggle for her, but she managed to educate her children, and even got them to accept their father. The village extolled her virtues but they did not particularly censure the husband.

Within the context of the family, children were always of tremendous importance to parents who awaited the birth of a child with great exuberance and happiness. Preference for a girl or a boy was not important. Large families were very much accepted and respected. Children have often been seen as the wealth of the poor. This might be considered a characteristic of some New Mexican families. Children were considered assets and were a realistic resource to the livelihood of the family. No special consideration was given to the woman who bore a child every year. It was simply expected of her. As a matter of fact, when her childbearing days were over she anticipated with great joy the coming of her grandchildren upon whom she could bestow her affection and care.

Pregnancy out of wedlock was not accepted easily by the family of the girl. Sometimes there was a great upheaval in the family and punitive measures were taken to "right the wrong," such as forcing the couple to marry to preserve the good name of the girl and her family. *Ese bribon no va a burlarse de ti* (that rascal is not going to make a fool out of you) was the usual attitude. Many of these marriages turned out well because both partners responded to prevailing social customs.

In former years the size of the family was not a problem. Most families were large. Recently, however, when birth control has become an issue that must be realistically assessed, families have been placed in a quandary. Nonetheless, New Mexican women still see themselves as the procreators of the human race and continue to orient their children to the view that children have a right to be born. The question of when life begins never presented problems to the families since pregnancy was accepted as a very natural event. The advent of birth control devices, pills, and surgery is producing a source of conflict between the young people and the old. There are deep philosophical dimensions that must be resolved and certainly the traditions of the past are at stake.

Just as the beginning of life was heralded and considered a blessing from God, one's state in life was considered a destiny which was part of the divine plan and accepted. So it was that death was also the acceptance of the will of God exercised on His children once their mission in life had been fulfilled. The natural emotions felt at the loss of a loved one were openly expressed and the *velorio* (wake) was an important and necessary ritual, not only for the survivors, but also as a tribute to the deceased. Women, as the principal guardians of human life, interpreted this reality to the young. God was calling one of His own to a life eternal. Reward depended on how one had lived life on earth. The mercy of God was felt at this time. All knew that *uno no se va sin pagar las que debe* (one does not leave (this world) without paying one's debts). One was treated with justice tempered by mercy. One of the traditional customs when a loved one died was to observe a period of mourning for about one year. This was called *luto*. Women observed *luto* more formally than did men. They wore black for at least one month and sometimes for the entire period of the mourning.

Sometimes they simply wore dark clothing, and I recall, as a child, seeing young women wearing shawls on their heads as an expression of deep *luto*.

Certainly there were joyous occasions in the lives of the people and they celebrated with dancing, festive food, wine and music. These were informal affairs that included the whole family. Some of these occasions were engagements, weddings, and the village feast days such as the *Día de Santiago*, patron of the Spanish people, *Día de Santa Ana* which was part of the Santiago feast since they were on July 25 and 26, respectively. There was always more *negocio* (business) than *ocio* (leisure), but people knew how to celebrate and when they did they threw caution to the winds and thoroughly enjoyed themselves. It has been observed by some that religion had a kind of feminine auspices and sponsorship. Because of this, most celebrations were very much a part of a religious feast.

Education as a formal institution was slow in coming to New Mexico, but learning and teaching were never matters to be ignored. Certainly, the scarcity of schools made it necessary for the people to learn from experience, and information was passed on orally from one generation to another. Schooling was difficult to acquire because of distances and costs, yet some women did get an education as teachers, nurses, and secretaries. Men often had many more difficulties in becoming educated since they were the providers. As a consequence, education became more readily available for women, but only a few professions were considered acceptable. Until the last decade, I cannot recall New Mexican women in the fields of law, medicine, engineering, or architecture. Not only were these professions considered more in the realm of men, but also were not available to women.

Perhaps there is a relationship between the concept of woman in general and the concept of the Virgin Mary. As a mother and as an intercessor, Mary and the New Mexican woman have played a similar role in the minds of New Mexican men. This concept is indeed confirmed by the many *Virgenes* in Spain and in the New World. The bullfighter asks for the help of *La Virgen de la Macarena*. De Vargas reconquered Santa Fe through the intercession of *La Conquistadora*.* The *Macarena* and the *Guadalupe* are part of Mexico's religious tradition deeply rooted in New Mexico. This fervor and devotion to

---

*La Conquistadora* was a Virgin from Spain who gained popularity in New Mexico at the time of the reconquest (1826).

the Mother of Christ carries by extension the regard in which women are held.

As the concept of machismo exists in New Mexico in a modified form, I should like to comment on it since it has an important relationship to the identity of women. For New Mexicans, the word macho means simply donkey. The word *machismo* which now expresses the concept of certain masculine powers, rights and behavior to other Spanish-speaking people, did not enter the language of New Mexico until the militant attitude of the 1960s became widespread.The concept of machismo, however, has existed in New Mexico for as long as there have been New Mexicans, but its form is different from the commonly accepted definition of the term. It meant that by virtue of his manhood, a man had a word of honor that was more binding than a written contract, was totally responsible for his family's support, protection, discipline, and direction. It did not reduce his wife to a chattel, but as in the case of the *Virgenes* of the Hispanic world, he revered, honored and respected her mostly on special occasions. In times of need, a man consulted the Mother of God, his own mother, his wife or his sweetheart, and perhaps even a *curandera*. In times of triumph he thanked *La Conquistadora* or *La Guadalupe*, celebrated his triumphs with his wife or sweetheart, but on ordinary days, he was the all powerful man who dominated his house, his workers, his children, and his wife. In his moments of weakness, he saw his strength in becoming the great Don Juan, but this was more myth than reality. The lore of machismo is perhaps far richer than its reality as a living concept.

The part that women played in the design of machismo was far-reaching. It is the mother who has the most influence on her children in their formative years. It is she who assigns roles and gives them guidance in forming an identity. Just as she has helped her son to formulate a self-identity, she has also introduced him to the cult of the Virgin Mary and nurtured his attitudes about women. In school where the elementary teacher was usually a woman the process continued. The natural results were a certain type of machismo which made men totally responsible and which was perhaps frequently overwhelming. It removed responsibility from woman and freed her, but it also diminished her role as an equal with men. It further retained the symbiotic relationship between mothers and sons to a stage that can be viewed as unhealthy. Unconsciously it made men dependent on women, and placed an overwhelming demand on both which has sometimes become their undoing and has limited woman's role. The concept of machismo is not necessarily negative, but carried to extremes it can have dire results for both men and women. In its healthy aspect, it has spurred men to greater accomplishments and has preserved for women the role many think they should have while protecting the solidarity of the home. It is a concept that is so interwoven with the role of a man and his relationship to women that it sometimes becomes merged with the role of women as well. It is difficult to explain this idea, but perhaps citing an example will help. The name Maria is common for men, as may be witnessed in the names José Maria. Another common name is Dolores which has reference to *Nuestra Señora de los Dolores* (Our Lady of Sorrows). These names for men carry a certain strength of character and do not have feminine connotations. A man carries in his full name the name of both his father and his mother. If his mother is Martinez and his father, Gonzales, his name is Gonzales y Martinez or Martinez-Gonzales. There is recognition of both parents on an equal basis. A married woman keeps her own name. If her name is Martinez and her husband's name is Gonzales she becomes Martinez de Gonzales. In New Mexico this has not been used for many years. The influence of other cultures has limited the need for such long names, but they still exist and within the last ten years have regained prominence.

When the New Mexican woman of the 1970s compares her life to some of the traditional beliefs and practices described above, she can see radical changes in the economy, effecting changes in social orientation, and in the educational system. She has often been among those who have resisted change, holding to her beliefs and practices based on tradition, but the advance of technology and land development have ushered in a change in role and identity for her. The changes have often been jolting. Perhaps the most dramatic changes for all New Mexicans have come since 1940 and the Second World War. The men went to war leaving behind women, old men, and children. Poverty drove many to the West Coast where there were opportunities for jobs in industry. Women with few skills and only a limited knowledge of English packed up and left their homes in search of jobs. Rural people attempted to bridge the gap of culture, language, and economy in one fell swoop. They became shipbuilders, riveters, clerks, and secretaries in the work forces of Los Angeles, San Francisco, and San Diego. They worked hard and long and many lived in the little hovels of the poor, but they persevered and they prospered. They had to learn

English quickly. The opportunities for education increased. The aspirations of both men and women expanded. In the meantime, the soldier in the Pacific or in Europe could see his world changing. There was a world beyond the mountains of New Mexico. There were unlimited opportunities in the industrial cities and when the soldiers returned it was to the cities, not to New Mexico.

The isolation and the poverty of New Mexico was a protection to the people who did not leave. It made them hardy and rugged. It kept them equal and democratic, but it had not really prepared them for prejudice on the basis of nationality or origin.

As the financial circumstances improved the status of the family, it also put the role of women in a different context. Marriage was only an alternative. A family could be a choice. Work was exciting. It made financial independence possible. It provided alternatives. It, too, tended to make men and women equal, but the tradition and culture of the past were very strong and the ferment of change slow.

The Korean War continued the exodus to California. The city opened new horizons. Even young people who had been part of the pachuco culture soon became a part of the society that seized the opportunity to work, to learn, to aspire.

New Mexico remains very traditional in the late 1970s, but the tradition has taken on a different form. The people who left for California have kept their ties to *La Patria Chica* (native land) and many make a yearly pilgrimage to their former homes in Chimayo, Tierra Amarilla, or Chama. They long for the typical New Mexican foods and after a visit they return to the city with *chicos* (dried green corn), dried meat, *rueditas* (dried sliced squash), chile, and all the other foods which represent inner security. They continue their family customs in the city. They are still very much New Mexican. They still cherish *compadres* (godfathers) and *primos* (cousins).

For the ones who remained in New Mexico the changes were slower. They kept many of the old customs alive. They gathered the piñon nuts in the forest; they raised the cabrito; they ground the chile and dried the squash and when the relatives from California and other states came to visit, they all tried to retrieve the flavor of the past, the style of life they had known but could no longer live in the complexity of the city or the changing New Mexico. The scientific laboratories at Los Alamos and Albuquerque, and the proving grounds at White Sands had their impact on the people. Most affected were those from the smaller villages for whom employment opportunity had been limited. Previously, they had had to go to Colorado, Wyoming, or Texas for jobs. There was room for people with limited education to be trained and employed in these new industries. They found jobs, bought cars, and commuted daily from their villages. A new sophistication came from it. Their horizon expanded: it affected their children even more. The role of women took on still another dimension. They became providers and modified their views about the family. Grandmothers, aunts, and other relatives became baby-sitters. The extended family served a new but valuable purpose. In other cases, the employment of both parents left the children to fend for themselves. The same situation developed in the city when the mother wanted to work. The economy changed the villages and the valleys and the mountains of New Mexico. The destiny of the woman was changed. Family relationships were altered, especially between mother and child. A certain coldness and businesslike approach was born. As those children grew up and had children of their own, a different style of life and new values emerged. They became more utilitarian, more industrial, more materialistic. This is not said in a negative context, although for many it has been destructive. The silhouette of the New Mexican woman, especially the one from northern New Mexico has changed. Some would say that the demeanor, the carriage, the patience and the compassion of that woman have been irreversibly changed. Some call it the destruction of the good values while others consider it change that is progress—a change necessary for the more complete appreciation of women. The quiet, eloquent manner, once characteristic of Hispanic women of northern New Mexico like my grandmother and my mother, is now history. Those women were part of an era that began centuries ago and lasted well into the twentieth century.

The decade of the mid-1960s to mid-1970s has been a worrisome one. It has brought changes we were not prepared to understand. The New Mexican woman is trying to construct the future on the foundation of the past. Societal change is not easy to understand. Sometimes the changes have appeared far more desirable than they really are since one can only see the surface of their significance. The pressures of the technological society, the peer groups, materialistic environment, growing population, the glitter of what is chic, have all contributed to the change. Furthermore, in all this, a certain disdain for the past began to permeate the thinking, and this is unusual in a group where tradition has been so important and the wisdom of age has been so highly respected.

What will this change mean to the New Mexican woman? Since she is the culmination of all the past events and experiences she must learn to survive and adapt herself to the new rules. Undoubtedly, she will make some very fortunate changes and she will make some unwise changes. She may be giving up very important strengths that the old way provided her, but the changes of the day are necessary. There will be times when traditions and the discipline of culture will be obstacles and she will try to disregard them, but they will haunt her in a million ways. She will have to be flexible and able to appreciate what she has been and what she has become; otherwise, she will be unable to understand and fulfill her potential in the future.

The religious nature of the northern New Mexican woman is not easily changed. Her spirituality is a strong and vital part of her being. Although there have been environmental and cosmetic changes in her world, when it comes to the fundamental values that New Mexican women have felt and treasured, she feels an intimate responsibility to uphold them. The casual ways of the 1960s and 1970s are readily visible, yet the bonds and ties of strong family life are still there. The modern New Mexican woman is part of the new breed of American women who have emancipated themselves from the shackles which they saw as bondage. She may live alone, travel alone, be alone, but she will do so out of choice and a sense of independence. No doubt, she will have to make some modifications even in her new self-concept to tailor it to her own perceptions of reality, and to examine her underlying motivation for the changes she is making. The New Mexican woman, however, still represents history and traditions. The task which is hers is that of learning to integrate her cultural heritage with her present needs and her goals for tomorrow.

# THE CHICANA PERSPECTIVE:
# A DESIGN FOR SELF-AWARENESS

*Sylvia Alicia Gonzales*

The problems of the Chicana, her identity, and her aspirations for the future are the topics for discussion in this essay. I am speaking from my own experiences, and those of other Chicanas whose opinions will also be incorporated into the text, relating my own interpretations of events and history and giving my own analysis of where we Chicanas, as a minority within a minority, are in our struggle. The logical place to start is with the historical origins of the Chicana. While her heritage is many faceted and will differ with individuals, I will deal with one historical presentation which will promote understanding of the foundations of women's rights among native-born and first generation Mexican American women.

In the period following the 1910 Revolution in Mexico women emerged with a new sense of values and a higher level of consciousness in the nation that produced the precursors of the Chicana. As a result of the war, male hierarchy was seriously challenged for the first time. The static, rigid, male-oriented, pre-Revolutionary society underwent tremendous change. War dramatically altered female roles. Feminine participation in Mexican society was augmented on a massive scale. Consequently, *la mujer Mexicana* (the Mexican woman) became more vocal and militant in her struggle for emancipation (Carreon 1972, p. 3).

Mexican women began demanding the right to vote in the early days of the 1910 Revolution. Enfranchisement for women became, in fact, a formalized goal of the Revolution. Some of the more active women organized the feminist league, *Hijas de Cuauhtémoc* (Daughters of Cuauhtémoc), which advocated suffrage and emancipation for women in all areas ranging from politics to intellectual development. Occasionally, their activities were met with violence such

[81]

as a suffrage demonstration held in Santa Julia on June 5, 1911, where nine people lost their lives and many more were wounded. Because women were generally considered conservative, religious, and submissive, opponents charged that if women were given the vote the political system would regress to a reactionary, pro-clerical one (Rascón 1973, pp. ix–xiii).

The Mexican Revolution of 1910 not only created a more democratic Mexico, but unintentionally contributed to the emancipation of the *Mexicana*. Up until this time, the woman's role was a traditional one, concerned mainly with her family and the church. She was isolated from civic affairs, lacked education, and rarely was employed outside the home. With the impact of the Revolution, the *Mexicana* was forced into a new situation—a change in her environment and her role. Hunger, loneliness, and abuse, all characteristics of war, made it impossible for her to go on living in isolation. When men left to fight, women had no alternative but to fill the positions the men vacated. Women became train dispatchers, telegraphers, druggists, nurses, office clerks, reporters, newspaper editors, teachers, businesswomen, and factory workers. They also provided supportive services for the Revolution, such as delivering medicine, ammunition, clothing, food, mail, and military equipment to men at the front lines. Through her active participation in the Revolution, she developed a new insight, a third dimension, and met for the first time on an equal basis with men.

Thus began the suffrage movement of 1910 in Mexico. Both revolutionary forces and federalists appealed to the women to support their causes, and even went so far as to enact legislative measures to ensure equal rights. In May 1911, a petition was submitted to the interim president, Francisco León de la Barra, requesting the woman's right to vote. Since the Constitution made no mention of sex, after a series of conferences the state of Chiapas finally gave women the right to vote in May 1925. Sincere and dedicated revolutionary leaders attempted to carry out promises made to women during the war. In an attempt to elevate the status of women, Gen. Salvador Alvarado incorporated in his reconstruction plan for Yucatán an educational program for women; moreover, he encouraged feminist congresses in his state (Ward 1962, pp. 65–74).

Legislation favoring women was enacted during Venustiano Carranza's term in office. Divorce laws were liberalized, making it easier for women to obtain a divorce and broadening the grounds for dissolution of marriage. Statutes protecting women and unwed mothers were also passed. It was during this decade (1910–1919) that feminist literature sprang up in Mexico. *Mujer Moderna* and *Revista de Revistas* were two magazines very popular among *Mexicanas*. Novels and short stories romanticized the woman's role in the Revolution. Music and art followed the trend and depicted women as heroic, without whose aid the revolutionary cause would have been defeated. Such praise served in upgrading the woman's image. Among the most widely acclaimed heroines were *La Adelita* and Hermilia Galindo de Topete. Even though the new and more open society was becoming sensitized to the needs of Mexican women, they still encountered many obstacles in achieving greater political and social rights. Full suffrage was not granted to women in Mexico until 1953 (Novo 1964, p. 105).

While some research has been done on the *Mexicana*, the existing literature on the Chicana gives a distorted and inaccurate image. Much of the small body of knowledge which exists on the Chicana has been collected by Anglo writers who have lacked sufficient understanding and sensitivity to the culture of Mexican Americans to portray the Chicana accurately. This research has had dysfunctional consequences for the Chicana, because it perpetuates false and stereotypical images of the role and function of women within the Chicano community. In large measure, this research emerges from the activities of Anglo social institutions which, lacking counter-images of the Chicana, tend toward unquestioning acceptance of prevailing myths. For instance, educational, health, welfare and law enforcement institutions have many times utilized these distorted pictures in developing programs to respond to the needs of the Chicana. By relying on these incorrect stereotypes, these institutions and related service organizations inevitably are misguided and misinformed. This approach has contributed to both the relegation of Chicanas to a position of passivity and subservience and to effectively barring them from a full and creative role in our society.

An example of a work which has influenced attitudes and contributed to the perpetuation of inaccurate stereotypes of the Chicano is William Madsen's anthropological study *Mexican Americans of South Texas*. It portrays the Chicana as weak, submissive and overly respectful toward her husband and portrays Mexican American society as male-dominated in general. Madsen writes that "...the Mexican

American wife who irritates her husband may be beaten...Some wives assert that they are grateful for punishment at the hands of their husbands for such concern with shortcomings indicates profound love" (Madsen 1973, pp. 35–36). This study, used in many colleges and universities as an authoritative source, advances a number of erroneous conceptions about Chicanas.

While some oppression may exist within the Mexican American family structure, what writers on the subject have failed to do is the kind of in-depth research that would reveal the nature and *multiple* sources of oppression and, further, delineate accurately the Mexican American woman's reaction to oppression, and finally her true role within the family. María Adorador, a human relations specialist in Berryessa School District, San Jose, California, helps to clarify many misconceptions in a straightforward account of the interpersonal relationships within the Mexican American family including the woman as wife and mother; in her writing she reveals that the earliest sources of oppression for the woman are from within the family.

> ...The Chicana mother is the family's most influential socializing agent, if not by design, certainly by default. During the formative years mother and children establish a strong emotional bond. Mother is the center of the child's world and vice-versa. Mother teaches children eating habits and manners. She toilet trains them, nurses them, changes their diapers and sees them take their first step. She teaches them moral standards, right from wrong. Mother and child establish emotional interdependence through constant verbal and non-verbal communication. Father remains aloof and distant during this period in his children's lives and does not receive the benefits of a warm inter-personal relationship. But relations between mother and children continue to remain close through the years. While sisters and brothers might have been close when very young, socialization along rigid lines creates a chasm and brother and sister seldom interact on a personal level.
>
> Work relationships are also established along sexist lines. Boys are taught to do work outside the home. They are encouraged to experience sex at an early age. They are taught to watch over their sisters and protect them. When

son reaches the age of eight or so, father begins to deal with him and continues the process that mother started; to make "a man out of him." Son is allowed to listen to "men talk" and pursue activities that prove he is becoming a man. In the home boys learn to expect from sister much of what father expects of the wife. On the other hand, girls are taught to be feminine, ladylike, quiet, reserved, demure, delicate and womanly. She learns to sit properly and not to play rough games with boys. She is taught to become a woman by learning responsibility in the home and especially how to take care of the men in the family. Mother makes sure she remains within the confines of the home. She must not be a *callejera* [streetwalker]. Both sexes are taught to be obedient and respectful to parents and adults. Young children are taught to obey older ones. Girls are taught to serve all males in the family.

Friendship relations are also determined along sex lines. The establishment of friendship relations between a female and male as two human beings is frowned upon. Consequently, peer group friendships are confined to one's own sex. As a young lady, she will be allowed to establish a relationship with a male, but only after the family gives its approval. Approval is usually given after the young man has stated that his intentions are honorable, which means that he has marriage in mind. Above everything else, the Chicana is not encouraged to display outward affection towards her boyfriend or husband.

Thus, mother teaches the norms and values of the group. Father is not encouraged to participate in child-rearing and in fact, does not participate. This is especially true for new-born babies and children up to the ages of seven or eight. However, father-son relationships become closer as son becomes old enough to go to work with him. But girls seldom establish a close relationship with father. Nothing within their respective roles encourages either a close relationship or communication with each other.

Concerning the nature of the multiple oppressions experienced by the Mexican American woman Adorador writes:

Much of the literature written by Chicanas, Chicanos and Anglos treats the subject as a problem of oppression by males. The Chicana is not only oppressed by the Chicano but that oppression is superseded by the oppression of a white, male-dominated society. Based on these assumptions, writers conclude that the Chicana is doubly oppressed. The literature on this topic of Chicana oppression which points out male dominance highlights the following issues:

Higher wages for men

Unequal pay for equal work

Head of household

Control of government processes

Control of policy-making agencies

Focusing on the role of the Chicano we can conclude that he is dominant because:

He is the head of household

He is the wage-earner and provider for the family

He is the decision-maker and protector of the family

Based on these assumptions, father is blamed for all the problems and ills dealing with the internal functioning of the Chicano family. Father is the tyrant, the ogre, the unquestioned authority and oppressor. However, his oppressive attitude is easy to understand since he is the one who goes out and faces a hostile environment, and, therefore, deserves understanding. In his job he is treated like a peon, so logically, he treats his family likewise.

What is the Chicana woman doing all this time? Once again we turn to the literature explaining the traditional role of the women. We find her to be *abnegada y sufrida* [self-denied and long-suffering], unselfishly giving to her family day and night without expecting to be rewarded. In fact, this is what has been defined as her area of strength. Her strength lies in supporting her man, not in being a decision-maker. An often-cited example of this strength is in *las Adelitas*. Literature points to this example of women in the Mexican Revolution where they marched alongside their men. These women remained behind the front lines cooking, washing, mending and tending to the emotional and sexual needs of men. A supportive role at best! Supportive because cooking, washing, and mending are within her role. Chicana woman's strength seems to lie in the fact that she is able to withstand whatever physical or emotional abuse her macho directs at her. I remember my mother telling me that a woman once married, *se debe aguantar* [she must endure]. As long as your husband provides the basic needs for survival, you are obliged to give him support and if need be, tolerate injustices. If a Chicana is abused by her husband, too often there is no one to turn to. She does not dare complain to her father or mother because invariably the answer is, "you belong with your husband." Her mother will tell her that *la vida de la mujer es dura y así ha sido siempre,* [woman's life is hard, and that is the way it has always been]. Or she will say, *tu fuiste la que quisiste casarte* [you were the one who wanted to get married], as if to say *ahora aguántate* [now you must endure]. On the other hand, if a son treats his wife poorly, it must be because she is not "doing things right at home." This role behavior would seem to identify father as the most influential person in the socialization process of children. It would also appear that he is the one who is responsible for the internalization of values and attitudes according to group norms.

However, returning to the focus of my discussion, mother has started the process along sexist lines and it is later perpetuated by everyone in the group. The relationships are established bilaterally along a set of ascribed, strictly-defined roles that do not allow any intermeshing. Mother has created in her son an oppressive nature and a submissive one in her daughter.

One of the most pressing problems that has kept the Chicana in a subordinate position in Mexican American society is the fact that she marries early. By the time the Chicana is fourteen or fifteen, she may think of marriage as her only available role. Early marriages of Chicanas lead to social dependency and lack of education beyond the eighth grade. Because she is burdened with children and responsibility at a very early age, her economic and educational development is curtailed and continuation programs are made inaccessible to her. Therefore, the Chicana misses the opportunity to become not only a professional, but also a part of the decision-making process of Chicano society; yet, even if the Chicana does finish at least high school, she is still faced with attitudes of Chicano society which present marriage as the only vehicle by which she can improve herself as a human being. Delving still deeper into the complex relationships within the Mexican American family, María Adorador points to the respective roles assumed by Chicanos and Chicanas within the marriage relationship as being the source of the inner culture oppressiveness of male over female.

There are many different roles in our society, each with a series of implied rights and responsibilities. Every role is complimentary and interrelated. Roles can become dysfunctional when carried to extremes and/or over-emphasized and exaggerated. The strong emphasis placed on the role of mother in the Chicano family and the de-emphasis of wife, father, and husband roles has created a double neurosis in males and females. The role of father is de-emphasized, especially when the children are very young, because of his non-participation in the initial child-rearing responsibilities. The role of protector is oppressive because of its double standard application of relative freedom allowed to boys and over-protection that limits freedom for girls. She is limited in the choosing of a mate, sexual expression and oftentimes in her education.

In respect to husband-wife roles in the family, the role of head of household and authority figure can be oppressive if it is abused, rather than tempered and applied fairly and equitably. It becomes oppressive to both father and family when it requires distant and aloof behavior on the part of the father in order to maintain authority. Father is still mainly responsible for the economic support of the family. This role can become a problem if the economic situation is such that father is unable to provide adequately for his family and mother works outside the home. Father views this as his inadequacy rather than a role to be shared with his wife.

Sexual intercourse is the most intimate expression of the love relationship between spouses. It requires equal and active participation of both spouses. In this situation, the Chicana is "damned if she does and damned if she

doesn't." Mother has taught her to remain passive in this
role. In this situation, wife is bound to feel like a repository,
a thing to be used. A mistress is more inclined to feel loved
than a wife! The wife's passivity does not allow for the
development of support mechanisms necessary for establishing a close emotional and spiritual relationship with her
husband, leading to a healthy marriage and a healthy family, emotionally and psychologically. On the other hand, if
she becomes active in her role, her husband wonders
"where she learned," becomes suspicious and questions
her about her past sexual life. Heavy emphasis on her role
of mother prevents her from carrying out her role as wife in
its fullest sense and prevents him from viewing her as his
wife and lover.

Finally, María Adorador makes an evaluation of what attitudes
will have to change before the Chicana achieves equality and where
the greatest propensity for change lies.

Mother has created a situation that ultimately denies the
development of her sexuality as a wife, and her self-
actualization as a person. Consequently, she transfers her
need for significance (we all strive for significance) which
she does not receive as wife and individual into her mother
role. This transfer takes the form of an overwhelming and
conditional love. This kind of love is evidenced in her inability to "let go" of her sons, insisting on remaining *núm-
ero uno* in their lives above wife. While she professes to
want more freedom for her daughters than she had, by her
very actions she prescribes for them the same exact role she
had. Mother has indicated she would like to change in her
role without a change in her position. While she may encourage her daughter to learn a skill and attain a profession,
these are to be viewed as alternative and supportive systems, "just in case you need to work to help your husband
or your family." She continues to instill in her daughter the
importance of marriage. Marriage must take priority over
everything else.

We have been re-evaluating the position of the Chicana
since the advent of the Chicano movement. Many Chicanas

and Chicanos, especially those active in the movement for liberation, have begun the slow and painful process of attitudinal changes. However, Chicano attitudes are not changing as fast as those of the Chicana. This situation is fraught with the danger of polarization and this polarization will disrupt our family structure. Communication between Chicanos and Chicanas is sorely lacking because too many Chicanos are not seriously listening to what Chicanas are saying. I believe that mother has not prepared the Chicano with a coping mechanism that prepares him for a change in the position of the Chicana. Perhaps she has made his position seem much too comfortable for him to want to change. On the other hand, mother has unwittingly prepared her daughter with a malleable, coping mechanism stemming from her being directed towards the supportive role. The role of the long-suffering mother has, in spite of itself, inspired in the Chicana the ability to change.

The Spanish term most commonly heard which describes the relationship between men and women in the Mexican American culture is *machismo*. Although many Chicanas are testifying to the fact that the situation within their homes is changing, they and many more Chicanas are now confronting the same attitudes of oppression and inequality in colleges and universities or in their professions. For example, Mirta Vidal describes the form of *machismo* confronted by Chicanas within the Chicano Movement itself.

When a freshman male comes to MECHA (*Movimiento Estudiantil Chicano de Aztlán*—a Chicano student organization in California) he is approached and welcomed. He is taught by observation that the Chicanas are only useful in areas of clerical and sexual activities. When something must be done there is always a Chicana there to do the work. "It is her place and duty to stand behind and back up Macho!" ... Another aspect of the Macho attitude is their lack of respect for Chicanas. They use the movement and Chicanismo to take her to bed. And when she refuses, she is a *vendida* [someone who sells out] because she is not looking after the welfare of her men (Vidal 1971, pp. 5–6).

This behavior appears to be consistent with the traditional attitudes which are being perpetuated in the Movement itself. The increasing struggle against *machismo* is one factor which Chicanas feel distinguishes them within the larger Chicano Movement. They are participating in a multi-faceted struggle—fighting for equal rights as women within their own culture in addition to their support of the overall Movement. Vidal points out that when Chicano men oppose the efforts of women to move against their oppression, they are actually opposing the struggle of many women in the United States aimed at changing a society in which Chicanos themselves are oppressed. In other words, they are defeating their own purpose while also denying one-half of *La Raza* their basic rights. They are denying *Raza* women the right to struggle against their specific, real and immediate needs. "In essence, they are doing just what the white male rulers of this country have done. The white male rulers want Chicanas to accept their oppression because they understand that when Chicanas begin a movement demanding legal abortions, child care, and equal pay for equal work, this movement will pose a real threat to their ability to rule" (Vidal 1971, p. 7).

Among the many distortions about the feminist movement listed by Vidal is the argument that women are simply fighting against men. Thus, since the feminist movement is considered anti-male, Chicanas attempting to organize against their own oppression are accused of trying to divide the Chicano Movement. While it is true that unity for *La Raza* is the basic foundation of the Chicano Movement, it need not be an appeal for unity based on the continued submission of women. On the basis of the subordination of women there can be no real unity.

All arguments aside, the fact is that Chicanas are oppressed and that the battles they are now waging and will wage in the future are for things they need: the right to legal abortions, the right to adequate child care, the right to contraceptive information and devices, the right to decide how many children they do or do not want. In short, they are asking for the right to control their own bodies. Vidal concludes that the struggle for women's liberation is the Chicana's struggle. And only a strong independent Chicana Movement, as part of the general women's liberation movement and as part of the movement of *La Raza*, can ensure its success.

There is no one Chicana perspective, but instead, several different points of view which have not yet been identified and developed so that Chicanas of varying persuasions can cooperate at a faster pace. In reference to the question of *machismo*, too, there are various perspectives expressed. The following quotes solicited from various Chicanas reveal opinions of a somewhat diverse nature, but each adds in its own way to a more thorough understanding of the subject. Some offer formulas for solution to the problem of oppression within the relationship of Chicana to Chicano. Blandina Cárdenas, appointed in 1977 as commissioner, Administration for Children, Youth and Families, Department of Health, Education and Welfare writes:

> Whether Chicanos survive as a people in the United States will ultimately depend, in my opinion, on the sensitivity and vision which we bring to the formulation of a new social contract between Chicano men and women. Chicanas have long known the difference between giving and submitting and the understanding of that difference allowed our grandmothers and our mothers to emerge as strong, positive human beings carrying on the most important business of Chicano life—that of maintaining rich and satisfying relationships as human beings.
>
> Today many of us are engaged in a multiplicity of additional concerns. I would hope that the wisdom of our *abuelas* [grandmothers] would prevail and that we would continue to know the difference between giving and submitting. Chicanas, too, must approach the task with both the sensitivity and wisdom of our past and a clear vision of our future. My own professional development could never have progressed as rapidly and as positively had not the models provided by my family and community been strong, positive women, and had not many men of personal and professional excellence provided a support system filled with *respecto y cariño* [respect and love]. Clearly that support has not been extended to enough women of our culture.
>
> I believe that it is the *respecto y cariño* between Chicanos of both sexes that will make the difference in developing the climate in which Chicanas are free to realize their own professional potential as the full range of options for realizing the cultural and feminine dimension of their identity remains substantially intact.

Elizabeth Sutherland, an Anglo author, has written with a great deal of insight concerning the Chicana's position within the family. In *Sisterhood Is Powerful* she encourages other Anglo women to understand the context in which the Chicana, as part of a colonized group, must achieve her liberation. The Chicana's oppression as a woman comes after the oppression suffered by both male and female. The Chicana, according to Sutherland, feels strongly that she must side with her man who is daily fighting a hostile world. The Chicana fears she will become another oppressor of the Chicano. Besides, the author points out, the Chicana in the context of her culture, does not necessarily see herself as the oppressed one. In fact, in most cases, it is the woman who makes many of the important decisions, but to protect the man, this role is usually recognized only in private. Sutherland cites María Varela, a Chicana, who stresses the role of the woman as the center of the family and as its source of strength. The Chicana feels that this role is important for the survival of her people. Sutherland concludes with the suggestion that even though the Chicana's apparent resistance to women's liberation is understandable, she should be able to realize that the struggle for the liberation of her people is directly linked with her own liberation as a woman (Sutherland 1970, pp. 376–79).

As is true of any complex problem with deep psychological and emotional roots, not all experiences within the family have been negative for Chicanas by any means. On the contrary, many Chicanas attribute their zeal in fighting for equal rights to courageous examples set by both parents, or their mothers, or their grandmothers. Many feel that because of the oppression experienced by their ancestors over the years, they are equipped with an inner strength to resist further oppression—a strength developed out of necessity, and learned by example. Bertha Pérez, who was assistant professor of education at the University of Texas, El Paso, when she wrote this, tells of a grandmother whom she feels influenced her life considerably:

In analyzing the influences which have provided me the courage and commitment to participate in the struggle for the rights of Chicanos and Chicanas in particular, the most outstanding ought be that of my grandmother. Amá Andrea was what we called her. As a child I remember hearing stories recited by relatives about life's struggles. But the

most moving was that of the true experience of my grandmother as a young girl. The story, as told to me, was that in
her youth, a handsome, wealthy son of a prominent, Mexican landowner fell in love with her. The entire family was
thrilled at the prospect of a union between the two. However, although his family thought her attractive, they felt
she required refinement and education to be socially acceptable. An agreement was reached and my grandmother went
to live with the family of the young man. She was exposed
to social graces, wealth, and comfort. But she soon learned
that all of this was meant for her alone and her future would
not include her family. A decision was made. Amá Andrea
loved her family and decided to commit herself to them and
their struggles rather than the luxuries of life.

And a struggle it was. She worked hard at everything
from breaking horses, tilling the soil, harvesting, to taking
in washing and ironing after her marriage. The men in her
life, her husband and brothers, rather than giving her
strength looked to her for support in the aftermath of many
adventurous escapades. Yet, all of her energies produced
only the mere necessities of life. But she continued to grow
strong. She was patient and understanding, warm and en-
during. She actively sought and assisted in the development
of the lives of those around her. She was the support, con-
fidante and counselor of her family and the entire *vecindad*
[neighborhood]. She was always willing to lend her ear and
sometimes an occasional *yerba* [herb] for those who needed
more than spiritual curing. The profession of community
*curandera* [folk healer] brought her no additional income,
however, as her clientele consistently looked to the Lord for
the resources to pay for my grandmother's services. And
the Lord responded only through my grandmother's continued dedication.

In my youth, I always sought the strength and understanding of this independent woman who had diplomatically
established a matriarchal line of communication between
generations. My father respected her and always conceded
to her advice. This courageous woman laughed with spirit
and cried with tenderness. She was involved with life and

life was involved with her. Life demanded from her and she was always willing to give. She sacrificed her own comfort out of love and commitment to her family. It is my hope to follow her example and demonstrate an equal love and commitment to *mi familia de La Raza* and especially to *mis hermanas Chicanas* [my Chicana sisters].

It gradually becomes clear that what many Chicanas are striving to establish is a personal identity out of which they can relate to their husbands as equals and then communicate to their sons and daughters—this in addition and complementary to their struggle for identity and acceptance along with all Chicanos in American society. In this she is a partner with her Chicano man, for this is the struggle of all Chicanos. Longeaux y Vásquez, Chicana writer and spokeswoman says: "We want to be a Chicana *primero* [first], we want to walk hand in hand with the Chicano brothers, with our children, our *viejitos* [elderly], our familia de La Raza" (Longeaux y Vásquez 1971, p. 17).

Perhaps one of the clearest explanations of what Mexican Americans, both men and women, achieve in identifying as Chicanos comes from a student at San Jose State University, San Jose, California. Elvía Castillo wrote:

A Chicana is someone like myself. Someone who can't be called a *Mexicana* because my values are different. I am no longer accepted as a *Mexicana* just like I've never been accepted as an American because of my differences. I'm caught between two cultures and rejected by both. I can't completely fit into either group. So, I call myself a Chicana, a new breed of awareness. I feel the Chicana knows what is going on. We are no longer going to stand around and pray that things will be better for us than they were for our mothers. Now we are organizing and demanding what is rightfully ours alongside our Chicano men. We are going to school, reaching higher goals in education so that we might earn a better living. Our parents are too old and too broken to do the great task of improving our lives. But, they look upon us for this great change because they realize that we are different. We are young and have been

made strong by the many injustices incurred upon us. By
uniting *La Raza*, we will be even stronger in demanding
what we want.

The problems of oppression and discrimination for the Chicana
have been shown to be complex. She is oppressed within the family
structure. Outside the home she suffers the same discrimination as a
member of a minority as practiced against Chicano men. Since the
majority of Chicanos are workers, Chicanas are victims of the exploitation of the working class. In addition, Chicanas are relegated to an
inferior position because of their sex. Thus, outside the home, *Raza*
women suffer a triple form of oppression: as members of an oppressed
minority, as workers, and as women. But Chicanas also understand
that the struggle now unfolding against the oppression of women
throughout the United States is not only relevant to them, but is their
struggle. At the same time, in getting to know themselves, they have
realized that characteristics and experiences unique to their culture
require more specialized study and analysis than can be provided by
national women's organizations. Chicanas, here again, have various
opinions on what the extent of the Chicanas' involvement in the Anglo
women's movement should be.

Longeaux y Vásquez urges that Chicanas study the women's liberation movement in order to come up with some anwers of their own.
When examining the issues of the women's liberation movement, it is
not hard to relate to a struggle as a struggle. However, she adds, "we
understand this because the *Raza* people are not newcomers to struggles, we can sympathize with many basic struggles; however, [it] is
not our business as Chicanas to identify with the women's liberation
movement as a homebase for working with our people" (Longeaux y
Vásquez 1971, p.18). She emphasizes that *Raza* is our home ground
and family and we have basic issues and grievances as a people, as a
movement.

The very existence of Chicana organizations is an indicator of
attempts by Chicanas to attract attention to the issues that are of interest to them. Such conferences reflect their efforts to coalesce and
examine their position vis-á-vis each other, the men in their communities, and other women's groups. The National Chicana Conference held in Houston, Texas, in May 1971, attended by more than six
hundred Chicanas, indicates the vast spectrum of viewpoints held by
Chicanas. At this first national conference of *Raza* women, resolutions

called for legal abortions and birth control and twenty-four hour child-care centers so that Chicanas with children would have greater opportunities for educational, political, social, and economic advancement. While these resolutions articulated the most pressing needs of Chicanas today, the conference as a whole reflected a rising consciousness of the Chicana about her oppression by society. It also indicated a growing alignment with the goals of the women's liberation movement in this country.

In *Chicanas Speak Out*, published in 1971, Mirta Vidal clearly indicates the mutual needs and goals of both Anglo and Chicano women. Her opinions also reflect those of many Chicanas throughout the country, and she deals not only with the special needs of Chicanas, but proposes that Chicanas align themselves with the women's liberation movement because she believes the struggle of all women is the same.

> With their growing involvement in the struggle for Chicano liberation and emergence of the feminist movement, Chicanas are beginning to challenge every social institution which contributes to and is responsible for their oppression, from inequality on the job to their role in the home. They are questioning machismo, discrimination in education, the double standard, the role of the Catholic Church, and all the backward ideology designed to keep women subjugated (Vidal 1971, p. 3).

This growing awareness was illustrated by a survey taken at the Houston conference, and published in *Regeneración* in 1971. It stated that "84 percent [of the Chicanas] felt they were not encouraged to seek professional careers and that higher education is not considered important for Mexican women . . . 84 percent of the participants agreed that women do not receive equal pay for equal work" (Flores 1971, p. 3). The survey found that on one question the replies were unanimous. When asked whether married women and mothers who attend school are expected also to do the housework, be responsible for child-care, cook and do the laundry while going to school, 100 percent said yes. Eighty-eight percent agreed that a social double standard exists. The women were also asked if they felt that there was discrimination toward them within *La Raza* and 72 percent answered yes and 28 percent voiced no opinion (Flores 1971, p. 3).

Surveys help to identify social trends, but the Chicanas' achievement is better recognized by noting that in the last few years the spotlight of the feminist movement has been projected on the women of La Raza. For example, when the National Woman's Studies Association held its founding convention in San Francisco in 1977, a Chicana was designated as the executive director of the association. This is the first time that a Chicana has held a leadership position in a national feminist organization. At a pre-International Women's Year conference held in Phoenix during the summer of 1977, six Chicanas were elected as official delegates for the international IWY meeting to be held in Houston, Texas in November 1977. This was the largest number of delegates chosen from any one single ethnic group of women.

Ironically, the awakening of Chicana consciousness has been prompted, in part, by the machismo we have encountered in the Movement. Linda Peralta Aguilar stated in an article published in *Civil Rights Digest* that Chicanas are discriminated against by Anglo employers, and especially by Chicano employers. It has been her experience that Chicanos are more reluctant even than Anglo males to give an administrative position to a Chicana (Aguilar 1973, p. 33).

Chicana growth, therefore, is greatly dependent upon original, innovative and insightful research into the everyday experiences of Chicanas whether it be in the barrio, colleges and universities, or in their relations with public service agencies and institutions. If such self-understanding coupled with the interest, understanding and change in attitude of the Chicano can be achieved, then, and only then, can Mexican Americans successfully challenge and resist Anglo racial oppression wherever it exists.

Bibliography

Aguilar, Linda. 1973. "Unequal Opportunity and the Chicana." *Civil Rights Digest* 5 (Spring issue): 31–33.
Cabello-Argandoña, Roberto; Gómez-Quiñones, Juan; and Herrera Duran, Patricia, eds. 1975. *The Chicana: A Comprehensive Bibliographic Study.* Bibliographic and References Series. Los Angeles, California: Chicano Studies Center.
Carreón, Vera, ed. 1972. "La Historia." *Chicana Service Action Center Newsletter,* no. 2 (February issue): 1–4. Los Angeles: Chicana Service Action Center.

Flores, Francisca. 1971. "Houston Conference." *Regeneración* 1:1–12.

Gonzáles, Sylvia. 1974. *La chicana piensa*. 3rd ed. San Jose, California: Spartan Press, San Jose State University.

Longeaux y Vásquez, Enriqueta. 1970. "The Mexican American Woman." In *Sisterhood Is Powerful: An Anthology of Writings from the Women's Liberation Movement*. Comp. by Robin Morgan. New York: Random House.

————.1971. "Soy chicana primero," *El Cuaderno* 1:17–22.

Madsen, William. 1973. *The Mexican Americans of South Texas*. New York: Holt, Rinehart and Winston.

Novo, Salvador. 1964. *La vida en México en el período presidencial de Lázaro Cárdenas*. México: Empresas Editoriales.

Rascón, María Antonietta. 1973. "La mujer mexicana como hecho político—la precursora, la militante," *Siempre*, no. 1019 (enero 3): ix–xii.

Sutherland, Elizabeth. 1970. "Colonized Women: The Chicana." In *Sisterhood Is Powerful: An Anthology of Writings from the Women's Liberation Movement*. Comp. by Robin Morgan. New York: Random House.

Vidal, Mirta. 1971. *Chicanas Speak Out: Women, New Voice of La Raza*. New York: Pathfinder Press.

Ward, Morton M. 1962. *Suffrage in Mexico*. Gainesville, Florida: University of Florida Press.

# THE POLITICS OF
# MEXICAN AMERICANS

*Rudolph O. de la Garza*

THE POLITICS OF MEXICAN AMERICANS must be viewed from two perspectives to be understood. First, it is essential to know how Mexican Americans have been treated by American society, and to what extent they have been allowed to participate in United States politics. Second, we must examine how Mexican Americans have modified their own behavior in response to the treatment they have received, and how they have attempted to alter the way in which they have been treated. The purpose of this essay is to trace in general terms the evolution of this relationship which is the essence of the Mexican American political experience.

So as to avoid confusion I would like to define some of the terms I use in this essay. Most important is the distinction between Chicano and Mexican American. Whatever the origin of Chicano, today this term refers to Mexican Americans who are no longer willing to be treated as second-class citizens. The Chicano takes pride in his cultural heritage and vigorously denies any suggestion that he is culturally deprived or in any way inferior. Recognizing the equality of all people, the Chicano, through violent or peaceful means, seeks to have the nation at large recognize the role his people have played in shaping this country and to insure that all Mexican Americans will be treated with the respect and dignity promised to U.S. citizens by the Constitution. The Mexican American might also have a great pride in his cultural heritage, but unlike the Chicano, the Mexican American does not recognize any systematic inequalities specifically affecting him, or at least is unwilling to challenge them if he recognizes them. The difference between the two, then, is a difference in perspective, in levels of political consciousness. Because all Chicanos are Mexican

[101]

Americans, but not all Mexican Americans are Chicanos, unless specifically referring to the former I will use Mexican Americans to refer to both groups.

Another term that I will define is Anglo. When I say Anglo, I am referring to all persons of European ancestry who are of light pigmentation. This, of course, excludes groups such as Blacks, Asian Americans, American Indians, and Mexican Americans. Also, when I describe the attitudes or actions of Anglos I am not saying that every Anglo subscribes to the attitudes of the group. Rather, I mean that it has seemed to Chicanos that Anglo leaders have certain attitudes, and that, by and large, the majority of Anglos actively or passively support these attitudes.

Analyzing the Mexican American political experience reveals two basic patterns. First, Mexican Americans have been more or less irrelevant to the political process in this country. Second, from 1848 to the present, Mexican Americans have employed a variety of tactics in order to gain a voice in the political process. Overall these efforts have met with limited success. I hope to show how these patterns summarize the essence of the Mexican American political experience and explain how these patterns developed.

Mexican Americans have been politically irrelevant in the United States. By this I do not mean that they have been complacent, or apathetic, or have accepted their fate in the tradition of *lo que Dios manda* (whatever God wills). I mean, instead, that having conquered northern Mexico and established control over what is now the Southwest, Anglos organized a society in which the separation between Mexican Americans and Anglos stabilized with the Anglos remaining in control of Southwestern society. As Chicanos see it, the political process has not, in this stabilized state, responded to the needs, demands, and rights of the Mexican American community. In other words, it has seemed to us as Mexican Americans that the impact we have had on decisions concerning the political system has been minimal to the point of being irrelevant.

Many Chicanos believe that in maintaining a political system such as this a certain combination of tactics and devices has been employed, and the message to us has been: "know your place and keep it." Mexican Americans have at times been forced to remain in this posture by means ranging from expulsion from school to jailings and even murder as I will show later in this essay. It has also seemed to us that any efforts to correct these injustices through election of our own officials, or establishment of our own political parties, have been thwarted by Anglo electoral and political rules. The result has been to keep Mexican Americans politically impotent.

Another aspect of Mexican American thought is that Anglos conquered the Southwest by means of violence, and from that time on violence has played a major role in maintaining the Anglos' dominance over Mexican Americans. Indeed, the history of the Southwest offers many examples of violence suffered by Mexican Americans.

Although misleading in most respects, Hollywood and Italian westerns accurately portray how killing Mexicans was not a crime; historians tell of gunslingers who boasted of their totals "not counting Mexicans" (McWilliams 1965, p. 98). The Texas Rangers "often killed Mexicans who had nothing to do with the criminals they were after . . . perhaps the majority of innocent Mexicans who died at Ranger hands were killed much more deliberately than that." This violence was so widespread that Américo Paredes, the distinguished Mexican American scholar, argues that the Rangers killed these innocent victims to terrorize the community and make it submissive (Paredes 1958, p. 26). The Rangers have and continue to be so effective at intimidating Mexican Americans that many Chicano activists in Texas see them as little more than a western version of the Ku Klux Klan. Because of this one of the planks of the *Raza Unida* platform in the 1972 gubernatorial campaign called for the elimination of the Texas Rangers.

On several occasions California police have emulated the example set by the Rangers. A California sheriff who helped break a protest by Mexican American workers in 1932 explained his actions by saying: "We protect our farmers here in Kern County. They are our best people. They are always with us. They keep the county going. They put us here and they can put us out again so we serve them. But the Mexicans are trash. They have no standard of living. We herd them like pigs" (Grebler et al. 1970, p. 533). In 1943 Los Angeles police stood by and watched while mobs of Anglo servicemen attacked young Mexican Americans. Rather than restrain the attackers the police seemed to give them moral support (McWilliams 1965, pp. 245–46). In 1960, the Los Angeles Chief of Police argued that the Mexican Americans were a grave problem, "some of these people being not far removed from the wild tribes of the district of the inner mountains of

Mexico. I don't think you can throw the genes out of the question when you discuss behavior patterns of these people'' (Grebler et al. 1970, p. 530). Again during the 1970 Chicano Moratorium Los Angeles police fired a tear gas projectile into a tavern where numerous Chicanos had gathered. The projectile struck and killed Ruben Salazar a well-known Chicano newsman. Even the Los Angeles *Times*, which supported the police during the 1943 strikes, was highly critical of the way in which the police handled the demonstrators. No policemen were indicted (Herrera 1971, p. 238).

Other examples of violence, albeit much more subtle, which police officials direct against Mexican Americans can be found in the selective application of the law. Throughout the Southwest, Chicano activists claim that police enforce laws much more strictly in barrios than in more affluent Anglo neighborhoods. These assertions have been supported by a study of police practices in Los Angeles which shows that even though the official policy was to assign patrol cars to neighborhoods in relation to crime rates, significantly more police were assigned to Mexican American neighborhoods than to Anglo areas even though the latter had higher crime rates (Morales 1973, pp. 173–74). In Denver, Rodolfo "Corky" Gonzales, one of the more prominent Chicano activists, protested that police harassed young Chicanos who were out after curfew while across town young Anglos could be seen leaving theaters and restaurants after curfew without police interference (Personal interview, August 20, 1972).

Differences in law enforcement can even be seen in the issuance of traffic violations. In Tucson, Arizona, new recruits noted that ''a Mexican American was much more likely to be ticketed for traffic violations than an Anglo'' (U.S. Commission on Civil Rights 1971, p. 9). These are but a few examples illustrating how police authorities in some instances have become the perpetrators and supporters of violence and injustice directed against Mexican Americans.

Other institutions have been equally effective in suppressing Mexican Americans within U.S. society. Most important among these have been the schools. For decades educators have systematically ignored and degraded Mexican American culture, and they have worked diligently to cleanse Mexican American students of their values and language. As of 1972 less than 8 percent of secondary schools and fewer than 4 percent of elementary schools in the Southwest offered courses on Mexican American history. When they were offered, such courses focused on customs and eating habits rather than on significant historical and cultural issues (U.S. Commission on Civil Rights 1972, pp. 31–33). Students have been prohibited from speaking Spanish because the Spanish they speak is "of such an inferior quality that it does not warrant classification as a language" (Carter 1970, p. 52) and because it "fosters anti-Americanism" (U.S. Commission on Civil Rights 1972, p. 20). The prohibition against the use of Spanish has been so strong that as late as 1970 it was outrageous for a teacher in South Texas, an area where the great majority of residents are Mexican American, to use Spanish in ordinary school activities (U.S. Commission on Civil Rights 1972, p. 14). These and other similar practices taught Mexican American children that they would be "rewarded in school and in church when they look and act like Anglos, and punished (or ignored) if they look and act like Mexicans." Mexican American children thus often chose Anglos as role models and candidates for leadership positions (Carter 1970, p. 82). The lesson that Mexican Americans were supposed to learn is illustrated in the words of an Anglo teacher who explained why she selected an Anglo child to lead a group of students at play.

> I think Johnny needs to learn how to set a good example and how to lead others. His father owns one of the big farms in the area and Johnny has to learn how to lead the Mexicans. One day he will be helping his father and he will have to know how to handle the Mexicans. I try to help him whenever I can (Carter 1970, p. 83).

The universities of the Southwest have for the most part reinforced the lessons taught Mexican Americans in the public school system. Only recently have these institutions begun developing programs designed to serve the Mexican American people. For a brief period in the late 1960s and early 1970s, many of these universities responded to government pressures and student demands and began hiring Mexican American faculty, recruiting Mexican American students, and establishing courses and programs focusing specifically on the Mexican American experience. The value of these efforts has been seriously questioned by groups such as the Western Political Science Association Chicano Caucus and the National Chicano Social Science Association because such efforts have usually been funded on soft money, and Chicano academics charge that many of these programs were cut back or terminated as soon as it was politically feasible to do so. Supporting these indictments are the low numbers of Mexican American students in higher education. In 1970 there were 1,178 Mexican American students at the University of Texas at Austin, 944 at the University of Arizona, and 565 at UCLA (U.S. Department of HEW for Civil Rights 1970). These universities, it should be emphasized, all have well over 20,000 students and all are in areas where there is a high concentration of Mexican American residents. The conditions Mexican American students have encountered when they attend universities is suggested by the experience of students at the University of Texas at El Paso where not one Mexican American was among the "Top Ten Miners of the class of 1973." An Anglo member of the awards committee was so upset by the selection process, which, in his judgment, deliberately excluded Mexican Americans, that he informed the UTEP Chicano Faculty Association of the problem so that they might take action to prevent any repetition of such discrimination in the future (personal interview). It should be added that the administration, faculty and students at UTEP have successfully put an end to this type of exclusion.

Once out of school, whether as a dropout or as a graduate, Mexican Americans continue to be taught that they are inferior. I recall that as a young man in Tucson I was told never to bother applying for a job with the telephone company because "they don't hire Mexicans." Raul Castro, former U.S. ambassador and governor of Arizona elected in 1974, told my students at the University of Arizona that when he first applied for a teaching job in a major school district in Southern Arizona it was made clear to him that Mexican teachers were not hired (Lecture, Minority Politics class, Spring, 1972). In a similar fashion, as I was completing a graduate degree in international business, a college official offered advice on my professional future. He suggested that I not expect too much because "no matter how good you are, you will never be a company president."

Although such flagrant discrimination has ended for the most part, Mexican Americans still suffer discrimination in the labor market. As late as the 1960s want-ads such as the following clearly indicated that Mexican Americans need not apply: "Neat, dependable Anglo short order cook...."; "Maintenance, 30–45, Anglo" (Bullock 1970, p. 145). In 1970 Mexican American miners in Arizona filed suit in federal court against their employers charging that they received less pay, more difficult work assignments, and fewer promotions than fellow Anglo workers with similar training and experience. That this is not an unusual situation is evident from the fact that Mexican American workers in general earn less than Anglos doing the same work (Grebler et al. 1970, p. 235). Mexican American foremen in 1970, for example, earned only 67 percent of what their Anglo counterparts earned (Shannon and McKim 1974, p. 99).

Mexican Americans have in common many experiences such as these. Those who have resisted and refused to tolerate injustices have confronted numerous obstacles when they have attempted to alter the conditions around them. One of the greatest obstacles, as will be shown, has been the political system of the United States.

The myth of American politics is that all citizens are encouraged to vote and run for office. Mexican Americans, however, have been discouraged from voting and have had major obstacles placed in their way when seeking elective office. Several practices illustrate how Mexican Americans have been discouraged from voting. Until declared unconstitutional by the U.S. Supreme Court in 1967, Texas citizens had to pay a poll tax in order to vote. Although it applied to all citizens, this tax worked a particular hardship on Mexican Americans because most of them had relatively low incomes. Once the tax was removed, the number of Mexican American voters increased dramatically. In 1966, only 53 percent of eligible Mexican Americans registered to vote; in 1968 and 1970 this increased to 65 and 70 percent, respectively (McCleskey and Merrill 1973, p. 787). Until 1970 the only citizens who could vote in California were those who were literate in English. This disenfranchised large numbers of Mexican Americans who paid taxes, contributed to national development with their labor, and accepted all the other responsibilities of citizenship.

Politicians also employ a variety of legal but unethical tactics to discourage Mexican American voting. Many Mexican Americans report that they have been intimidated, insulted and embarrassed when attempting to vote (California State Advisory Commission on Civil Rights 1971, pp. 35–55). Sometimes they risk economic retaliation in the form of loss of employment or of welfare benefits or food stamps if they try to vote (Shockley 1973). In Texas such tactics were allegedly widespread during the 1972 election. José Angel Gutíerrez, founder of *La Raza Unida* party, vigorously protested these activities, but rather than respond to his protests, election officials had him arrested for disruptive behavior (Fry 1972). In Arizona the Republican-dominated legislature called for a total cleansing of the voter-registration rolls and a subsequent re-registration of all voters prior to the 1970 election. Since Mexican American voters would be the least likely to be informed of the need to re-register (because of language difficulties and low education), many Democratic party activists and political analysts suggest that this action was motivated by the desire to prevent Mexican American voters from turning out in large numbers and swinging the election to Raul Castro, the Democratic candidate. The actual impact of the re-registration law is difficult to measure, but Castro did lose the election by only several thousand votes (personal interview, John Crow, University of Arizona, 1972).

Even if these obstacles are overcome, Mexican Americans will find it difficult to elect their own representatives because of gerrymandering and at-large elections. The impact of gerrymandering is most clearly seen in California. In 1971, east Los Angeles—where more than 600,000 Mexican Americans live—was divided into nine state assembly districts, seven state senate districts, and six U.S. Congressional districts. None of these was more than 40 percent Mexican American, and in none did Mexican Americans make up more than 35 percent of the registered voters. No major elected official in California at this time had more than a 30 percent Mexican American constituency and thus Mexican Americans had no representative completely dependent on their support. The California State Advisory Committee to the U.S. Commission on Civil Rights concluded that: "The Mexican American in California has been gerrymandered out of any real chance to elect his own representatives to the State legislature or the United States Congress in a proportion approaching his percentage of the state population" (U.S. Commission on Civil Rights 1971, p. 8).

At-large elections, common to most cities in the Southwest, also diminish the probability of Mexican Americans winning local office (Cotrell 1974, p. 5). Originally designed to escape the corruption of machine politics, in the Southwest at-large elections have served to exclude Mexican Americans from political office. In at-large elections all voters in the city vote for all councilmen, but in ward or district elections each ward nominates and elects its own candidates. Most Southwestern cities have a Mexican section, and ward elections would allow Mexican Americans the opportunity to elect candidates responsible only to them. Such officials would probably be in the minority, but they would at least be in a position to voice the demands of the barrios. At-large elections, on the other hand, allow a simple majority of the people to control all of the positions and thus tend to exclude minority representatives. Elections throughout the five Southwestern states (Arizona, Texas, New Mexico, California, and Colorado) often reflect the racial divisions I described earlier. Because Mexican Americans are in the minority in these cities, at-large elections result in few Mexican American officials being elected. In Tucson, for example, Mexican American candidates carry the Mexican American districts with overwhelming majorities but seldom win office because Anglo candidates win large majorities in the Anglo areas. In California as of 1970 there were extremely few Mexican American locally elected officials. In Los Angeles county with a population of over seven million people, for instance, nearly five percent of which are Mexican Americans, the representation of elected officials in 1970 was negligible and in 1977 the situation did not show any significant change.

TABLE 1

Participation of Mexican Americans in Local Government

By Size of City*

| Population | Mayors | | Councilmen | | Others | |
|---|---|---|---|---|---|---|
| | Non MA | MA | Non MA | MA | Non MA | MA |
| 0–10,000 | 175 | 6 | 680 | 44 | 3,059 | 39 |
| 10–50,000 | 151 | 4 | 600 | 33 | 1,772 | 42 |
| 50–500,000 | 63 | 1 | 312 | 20 | 911 | 15 |
| over 500,000 | 3 | 0 | 32 | 1 | 66 | 0 |

*Source: U.S. Commission on Civil Rights 1971, p. 85.

Overall the tactics described here have been successful in limiting the impact of Mexican Americans on politics. This is evident not only by the relatively few Mexican Americans who are politically active, but even more so by the few Mexican Americans who have been elected to public office. As of 1972 there were four Mexican American congressmen, one Mexican American senator, no Mexican American governors, and only token numbers in state and local offices. Until 1974, California, which is considered the most progressive of the Southwestern states socially, politically, and economically for Chicanos, had no Mexican American state senators, and only five state representatives, none of whom had a constituency over 28 percent

Mexican American, and no Mexican Americans were on city councils. Appointed officials also contribute significantly to major political decisions, but few Mexican Americans hold appointive offices. As of 1971, less than 2 percent of all elected and appointed officials in California were Mexican Americans (see Table 2). Underrepresentation in the national bureaucracy is even more glaring. As of 1973 less than .3 percent of office holders as listed in the Congressional Directory for the departments of the United States government were of Mexican origin (Gómez 1977, p. 13).

## TABLE 2
### 1970 California Roster of Federal, State, and County and City Officials*

| Category of Office | Total in Office | Total Number of Mexican Americans |
|---|---|---|
| Federal Elected and Appointed | 525 | 7 |
| State Legislators and Advisors | 195 | 2 |
| Executive Offices of State | 2,291 | 13 |
| State Boards, Commissions and Advisors | 1,732 | 47 |
| City and County Government Officials | 10,907 | 241 |
| Total Government Positions At All Levels | 15,650 | 310 |

*Source: U.S. Commission on Civil Rights 1971, p. 81.

Mexican Americans did make some gains in the 1974 elections, however. New Mexico and Arizona elected Mexican American governors, and numerous Mexican Americans were elected to the state assembly in California. Less significant changes can be seen in the other Southwestern states. Despite this increase in office holders, the Mexican American people continue to be underrepresented in decision-making arenas, and political decisions continue to be made and priorities set that do not reflect the interest of the Mexican American people. Since office holders are not elected by Mexican Americans, they feel free to ignore Mexican Americans. We are, in sum, politically irrelevant. We have not, however, been politically inactive. This is an important distinction which scholars in the past have mistakenly ignored. It was argued that Mexican Americans were uneducated, poor, and politically passive because of their culture. The argument, in essence, was that we lacked the Protestant ethic and rather than actively endeavor to change our environment we accepted our situation as *lo que Dios manda*. While this may be true for a few Mexican Americans, it is patently absurd for most of us. Since 1848 our people have used a variety of means designed to end the injustices we suffer and to ensure that the rights guaranteed us by the Constitution are respected. That these efforts have been unsuccessful should not be interpreted to mean that we have not tried.

The Mexican American people have responded to their environment with at least five different strategies. These include violence (particularly guerrilla warfare), dropping out (becoming apolitical), acculturation, large scale political mobilization, and *chicanismo*, which includes a return to some violence as well as a more sophisticated approach to the problem via legal channels. Each of these strategies was developed during a different time period and thus reflects the milieu of the times. All were designed, however, to achieve common objectives. However formulated or articulated, the essence of these objectives was the desire to be treated with respect and to have the freedom and equality of opportunity promised to all citizens by the Constitution and the insistence on the right to maintain a culturally distinct and vital community.

Mexican Americans responded to the violence of the Anglo invaders with their own violence. Having defeated Mexico in war and gained much of what is today the American Southwest, the Anglos in 1848 agreed to allow those Mexicans who lived in the newly acquired territory to remain on their lands with the promise that their rights would be respected. The promise was not kept, and from Texas to California, Anglos began cheating Mexican Americans out of their land and wealth, and thought little of killing those who protested. Many Mexican Americans resorted to arms to defend themselves, and for decades men such as Juan Nepomuceno Cortina and Gregorio Cortéz and groups such as *Las Gorras Blancas* in New Mexico responded to violence with violence. By the end of the nineteenth century, what might be considered an incipient guerrilla threat had been eliminated, but the place of Mexican Americans in U.S. society had not significantly changed.

The defeat of the early militants left Mexican Americans temporarily disheartened. They had chosen to remain in the United States because this was their home and because they were guaranteed the rights of citizens. By the time they realized that they would not be treated as equals and that not even counter-violence would force the Anglo to keep his word, they had no place to go. Under Porfirio Díaz, Mexico offered neither political nor economic asylum. Thus they stayed in the United States, their homeland, uncertain of how they should go about gaining the rights that had been promised them. Convinced that Anglo society would repel them, Mexican Americans essentially dropped out of Anglo society and strengthened their own institutions so that through these they would be able to meet the needs of the community. Mutual assistance societies such as the *Alianza Hispano Americana* satisfied social as well as welfare needs that Anglo American institutions neglected.

By the 1920s Mexican Americans again changed tactics and renewed their efforts to become fully accepted members of U.S. society. Now, however, the tactic devised was acculturation. Mexican Americans attempted to convince Anglos that they, too, were Americans. No doubt they adopted this strategy because many Mexican Americans genuinely subscribed to the ideals of Anglo America. It is equally certain that others went along with this tactic because they sought to protect what small economic gains they had made. To do so, they felt they must convince the Anglos that they, the native-born Mexican Americans, were Americans and committed to the ideals and principles of this nation, and therefore should not be confused with the Mexicans who were immigrating by the thousands to this country. The League of United Latin American Citizens (LULAC), founded in 1929, epitomizes this attitude. As stated in its by-laws, LULAC had as one of its aims ''to develop within the members of our race the best, purest and most perfect types of a true and loyal citizen of the United States of America.'' In sum, during these years Mexican Americans led by groups such as LULAC saw acculturation as the means for achieving equality. If they behaved, dressed, and spoke like Americans, Mexican Americans hoped they might be treated as such. In some respects they were; in most respects they were not. In general, they were treated in a schizoid fashion during the 1930s and 1940s. On the one hand, during the Depression, government agencies rounded up Mexicans and Mexican Americans alike and shipped them to Mexico since this was a relatively inexpensive way of reducing public relief rolls (Hoffman 1974, pp. 174–75.) On the other hand, many of President Franklin D. Roosevelt's programs benefited Mexican Americans and contributed to their feelings of belonging. The Civilian Conservation Corps, for example, recruited many Mexican American youths and taught them valuable job skills. Once World War II broke out, many Mexican Americans were called into military service. There, for the first time, many were rewarded for their performance and competence. Those who did not serve in the military joined the urban labor force, and they, too, found opportunities previously denied them. By the time the war ended, it seemed that the LULAC approach was working. Mexican Americans had "Americanized," and it seemed that at last they had won their rightful place in society.

The end of the war brought a resurgence of old attitudes, however. Symbolic of the return of Mexican Americans to second class status was the refusal of a mortician in Three Rivers, Texas, in 1948, to hold services for the remains of a Mexican American soldier who died in battle in the Philippines. Outraged, Mexican Americans capitalized on what they had learned about the Anglos from having worked so closely with them during the war years. They developed political organizations designed to strike the Anglo where he might be most vulnerable—at the polls. The American G.I. Forum, the Community Service Organization and later the Mexican American Political Association (MAPA) and the Political Association of Spanish Speaking Organizations (PASSO) sought to mobilize the Mexican American people so that as voters they could have an impact on society. Although founded at different times these organizations all saw direct political participation as the means which would gain equality for Mexican Americans. But by the mid-1960s it was painfully evident that direct participation within existing political processes and parties was not achieving the desired goals. Anglo politicians had structured the political system so that mass mobilization would be extremely difficult for any group and if successful, would have a minimal impact. Influenced by black radicals, a small but significant number of Mexican Americans realized that no matter what they did, it would never be enough. This realization gave birth to the Chicano Movement.

The Chicano Movement evolves around a cultural axis. Above all else, we Chicanos take pride in our heritage, our language, and the humanistic values governing our interpersonal relationships. As Chicanos we also insist that our role in shaping American society be recognized, and that those values we cherish be treated with respect. We also insist that we be given the freedom and equality of opportunity that is our birthright.

In many important respects the Chicano Movement differs substantially from earlier strategies employed by Mexican Americans.

First, *Chicanismo* explicitly rejects any suggestion of "Americaniza-
tion." In this way it breaks with the traditions established by LULAC
and adhered to by all subsequent Mexican American political organizations. Second, *Chicanismo* recognizes violence as a legitimate political tool much as did the guerrilla fighters of the late nineteenth century. Not since then have Mexican Americans been willing to take up
arms to defend their rights. It is not clear how widespread this view is,
but what is important is that a significant number of Mexican
Americans are willing to admit that violence may be a necessary evil.
Third, unlike all earlier strategies, *Chicanismo* reflects a deep and
perhaps irreparable alienation of Mexican Americans from Anglo-
American society. The naive trust of the past has been replaced with
cynicism, frustration, and intense anger. A fourth difference is that
*Chicanismo* reaches across the Southwest and into all areas with large
Mexican American communities. In the past, the various Mexican
American movements were poorly coordinated and, in fact, tended to
be local or at best statewide in scope. The Chicano Movement, how-
ever, has been influential across the nation, and the rise of *La Raza
Unida* party and numerous associations of educators and professionals
such as the National Chicano Social Science Association suggests that
*Chicanismo* will become increasingly well organized.

Striking similarities also exist between *Chicanismo* and earlier
strategies. Most important is that *Chicanismo* is directed toward
improving the place of Mexican Americans in U.S. society much as
earlier Mexican American strategies sought to do. With very few
exceptions, no one in the Chicano Movement calls for the total segregation of Mexican Americans and Anglos, and there is no evidence of
a "back-to-Mexico" movement. *Chicanismo*, instead, reflects the
American milieu and is best understood as the most recent and most
viable effort of Mexican Americans to exercise their rights as citizens.
Another similarity is that *Chicanismo* is not monolithic. The earlier
efforts suffered from localism: *Chicanismo*, while more encompassing
than any earlier strategy, also reflects local and regional differences.
This should not be interpreted as a shortcoming of the Movement, for
after all we should recognize that the Mexican American people are
not homogeneous nor are the problems we face. It would, therefore, be
as absurd to expect *Chicanismo* to be monolithic as it would be to
expect unanimity within the Democratic party. A third similarity is
that *Chicanismo* is imbued with optimism; Chicano activists believe

they will be able to succeed where others have failed. This is the same attitude Mexican American leaders have held since the days of Tiburcio Vásquez and *Las Gorras Blancas*.

The fourth and perhaps most significant similarity is that after an impressive beginning it has become clear that *Chicanismo* has not yet attained all its objectives. Like the earlier efforts *Chicanismo* has made some inroads, but overall major changes are still forthcoming. After years of struggle, César Chávez has won the right to negotiate contracts, but he still has to battle for contracts from the major agro-businesses where he has been organizing since the mid-60s. His major efforts have been successful in California, but as of 1977 the problems that await him in Arizona and Texas will be at least as formidable as those in California. In Arizona he must confront anti-strike legislation that cripples unionization efforts, and in Texas he will encounter a powerful agro-business complex armed with vast economic and political power.

Other Chicano leaders have experienced some setbacks. Reies López Tijerina and the *Alianza Federal de Los Pueblos Libres* shocked and frightened the Anglo world. López Tijerina and his followers forced Anglo society in New Mexico and elsewhere to admit that they had cheated the Mexican Americans out of their lands. For a brief time it seemed that some of those injustices would be corrected. But López Tijerina was jailed, and even though he has since been released, the *Alianza* never again regained its initial vigor. Needless to say, the lands stolen from Mexican Americans have not been returned. In Colorado, Rodolfo "Corky" Gonzales founded the Crusade for Justice, and it too seemed pregnant with promise. For a time Colorado politicians seemed uncertain as to how to deal with Gonzales and the Crusade. By the 1970s, however, it was clear that, by and large, they would ignore the Crusade just as they had ignored Mexican Americans for generations. Leaders in Los Angeles and Arizona have suffered similar fates.

Chicano activists have been somewhat more successful in Texas, but even there their achievements are localized and do not yet affect the majority of the Mexican American population. In Crystal City, Texas, Chicanos under the leadership of José Angel Gutiérrez mobilized their community and in 1977 had total control of local political life. They ran the school board, police and city governmental agencies. The new administration had made a dramatic impact on local affairs, and Chicano activists across the Southwest have seen Crystal City as an example to be emulated. Nonetheless, *Raza Unida* organizers have failed in their efforts to effect similar takeovers in neighboring areas, and recent developments suggest that internal problems are beginning to plague Crystal City.

This, then, is where we were in 1977. Anglos control the political machinery throughout the Southwest, as well as throughout the nation, and their control of politics insures that they will also control the major social, economic and legal institutions with which Mexican Americans must deal. Despite our efforts, we have been unable in any consistent or substantive way to influence U.S. society to respond to the needs of our community. Thus, we have been and continue to be politically irrelevant. Therefore, it appears that we cannot force the political Anglo machine to deal with us in an equitable and just manner. Bobby Seale's attempt to become mayor of Oakland is perhaps the clearest example that black militants have come to the same conclusion. The problems confronting blacks, however, differ somewhat from those we face and we must, therefore, develop strategies suitable to our needs and reflective of our situation. In suggesting some strategies, I would emphasize that all Mexican Americans will have the opportunity to live the life we choose. I would be surprised if everyone agreed on the tactics I propose, but I would hope we would all agree on the goals.

My first suggestion is that those of us who are active in the movement should not promise more than we can realistically hope to achieve. Too often Chicano activists imply that if we were organized we could make the Anglo listen to us. With the few exceptions I will discuss subsequently, I see no evidence that we have such potential power. By mobilizing massive support on the basis of such rhetoric, we greatly raise the expectations of our people. If we then do not achieve what we promised, the people will lose confidence in us and it will become increasingly difficult to regain their trust. Rather than risk such a loss of confidence I suggest that we begin by admitting how difficult our struggle is. If we do not organize and work together, we will have no chance of achieving our objectives. If we do organize and use our resources wisely, we might realize our goals, but even if we are organized we must recognize that there is no guarantee we will succeed.

My second suggestion is that we be willing to use a variety of strategies to elect our own candidates and to influence other office holders. In communities that are predominantly Mexican American such as Crystal City, it makes sense for *La Raza Unida* to run complete slates of candidates and to make no deals with either Democrats or Republicans. In cities such as Denver, El Paso, and Tucson the possibility of *La Raza Unida* candidates winning is minuscule. Here it would seem more profitable to channel our efforts toward influencing the selection of candidates within the major parties in order to insure that at least one of the parties nominates candidates acceptable to our community. To do so, however, we must first organize ourselves so that Anglo politicians realize they cannot afford to disregard our views. In Tucson, for example, most local contests are close enough that Mexican Americans could determine the outcome of any given election by turning out in large numbers and voting as a bloc. Once local party leaders are convinced that Mexican Americans will give their votes to those candidates who respond to their demands, I am reasonably certain that Anglo politicians will become considerably more responsive. On the other hand, running *La Raza Unida* slates and having them receive minimal vote totals reinforces the Anglo politician's view that Chicanos are really unorganized and should be ignored. It seems to me that Chicano activists and *La Raza Unida* can be most effective if we devote our energies to organizing the community and to developing the intellectual and organizational skills necessary to support the community in dealing with government agencies and party leaders.

Because we comprise around 12 percent of the population in each of the Southwestern states except in New Mexico, where we are approximately 32 percent of the population, I would argue that we should follow the same strategy in statewide and national elections as in local elections where we are not in the majority. Unless Anglo voters are somewhat divided, we will not be in a position to influence election results. If they are divided, then we can deal with Anglo party leaders from a position of strength. Either they commit themselves to meeting our demands or we will not support them. In 1960, 1968, and 1976 for example, we were in a position of strength in dealing with the Democratic party, but we did not take advantage of it. In 1964 and 1972, on the other hand, neither the Democratic nor the Republican party needed our vote to win and thus we were in no position to make demands on them. To maximize our electoral resources therefore, I suggest that we use whatever strategy will most benefit us. If we can win by running our own candidates, we should run them. If it is clear that our own candidates will be defeated, we should organize ourselves so as to be in a position to influence the existing party structure.

We should also make extensive use of non-electoral strategies to influence Anglo decision makers. In many cities this is a more viable tactic. In San Antonio, for example, a Mexican American neighborhood organization, Citizens Organized for Public Services (COPS), has pressured city officials into changing local spending priorities so as to allocate millions of dollars to public projects in the barrio such as street lights, curbing, and park improvements (de la Garza and Cotrell 1976, p. 42). COPS has enjoyed significant success by functioning exclusively as a pressure group, and its achievements suggest the effectiveness of non-electoral strategies.

My third suggestion would be to explore all possible tactics short of violence for dealing with the problems which we are confronting in the political arena. For some Chicanos the solution has seemed to lie, at particular times and in specific circumstances, in the use of violence. I personally do not advocate "an eye for an eye" as the tactic to follow to resolve the injustices which we have suffered. Neither do I pass judgment on the action of others who have reacted in violence or with other aggressive types of responses.

Another minor issue which has been blown out of proportion and which threatens to divide us irreparably is the question of leadership. Too many Chicanos and Mexican Americans claim to speak for our people. No one—not César Chávez, not Corky Gonzales, not José Angel Gutiérrez, not Edward Roybal, not Maclovio Barraza—speaks for all our people. We have worked hard to convince Anglos that there is no such thing as a typical Mexican American. It seems strange that we would have to convince ourselves of the same fact. No one speaks for us because we are not a homogeneous people. We are, however, united in our objectives, and those who claim to be our leaders should work at combining their resources to attain our goals rather than expending their energies in fruitless activities designed to promote their views and enhance their claims to leadership.

In sum, I am suggesting that only by coming together, identifying our resources, and planning strategies suited to each specific situation will we be capable of effecting substantive changes in our environment. There is no one way to attack the problems we face because there is no one problem we all face. By pooling our resources and working together we will at least have a chance to overcome some of these injustices.

In closing I would like to make one final observation. It should be clear by now that I am convinced that American society has never dealt justly with Mexican Americans and that Anglo politicians have systematically deprived us of our political rights. Nonetheless, it is also my belief that we must accept some of the responsibility for the situation in which we find ourselves. César Chávez has shown us that we must develop strength and discipline within ourselves if we are to succeed in our struggle. Too many of us, however, have ignored the example that Chávez and the farm workers have given us and instead have resorted to rhetoric and have blamed others for all our problems. We must never allow Anglo society to deny the oppression imposed upon us, but we must also recognize that unless we admit our own weaknesses we can never correct them. We must, in sum, accept that the struggle in which we are engaged begins *entre nosotros* (among ourselves). Once we have developed a sense of commitment and discipline, we will have the foundation on which to build our political future.

## Bibliography

Acuña, Rodolfo. 1972. *Occupied America: The Chicano's Struggle Toward Liberation*. San Francisco: Canfield Press.

Barrera, Mario; Muñoz, Carlos; and Ornelas, Charles. 1972. "The Barrio As An Internal Colony." *People And Politics in Urban Society*. Edited by Harlan Hahn. Beverly Hills, Calif.: Sage Publications. pp. 465–99.

Bullock, Paul. 1970. "Employment Problems of the Mexican Americans." In *Mexican Americans in the United States*. Ed. John H. Burma. Cambridge, Mass.: Schenkman Publishing Co.

California State Advisory Commission on Civil Rights. 1971. *Political Participation of Mexican Americans in California*.

Carter, Thomas P. 1970. *Mexican Americans in School: A History of Educational Neglect*. Princeton: College Entrance Examination Board.

Castro, Tony. 1974. *Chicano Power*. New York: Saturday Review Press.

Cotrell, Charles. 1974. "The Effects of At-Large Elections on the Political Access and Voting Strength of Mexican Americans in Texas." A paper presented at the Rocky Mountain Social Science Association Meeting.

de la Garza, Rudolph O., and Cotrell, Charles L. 1976. "Chicanos and Internal Colonialism: A Reconceptualization." A paper presented at the International Studies Association Annual Meeting.

Fry, John R. 1972. "Election Night in Crystal City." *Christianity and Crisis* 32, no. 20 (November 27 issue).

Garcia, F. Chris, ed. 1974. *La causa politica*. Notre Dame: University of Notre Dame Press.

Gómez, Rudolph. 1977. "Mexican Americans in American Bureaucracy." In *Mexican Americans: Political Power? Influence, or Resource*. Edited by Frank Baird. Lubbock: Texas Tech University Press.

Grebler, Leo; Moore, Joan M.; and Guzman, Ralph C. 1970. *The Mexican American People: The Nation's Second Largest Minority*. New York: Free Press.

Herrera, Albert. 1971. "Chicano Moratorium and the Death of Ruben Salazar." In *Chicanos: Mexican American Voices*. Edited by Ed Ludwig and James Santibáñez. Baltimore: Penguin Books, pp. 235–41.

Hoffman, Abraham. 1974. *Unwanted Mexican Americans in the Great Depression: Repatriation Pressures, 1929–1939*. Tucson: University of Arizona Press.

McCleskey, Clifton, and Merrill, Bruce. 1973. "Mexican American Political Behavior in Texas." *Social Science Quarterly* 53, no. 4 (March issue).

McWilliams, Carey. 1965. *North From Mexico: The Spanish-Speaking People of the United States*. New York: Greenwood Press.

Moore, Joan W. 1970. "Colonialism: The Case of the Mexican Americans." *Social Problems* (Spring issue), pp. 463–72.

Morales, Armando. 1971. "Police Deployment Theories and the Mexican-American Community." In *Voices. Readings From El Grito: A Journal of Contemporary Mexican American Thought, 1967–1971*. Edited by Octavio I. Romano-V. Berkeley: Quinto Sol Publications, Inc., pp. 167–79.

Paredes, Américo. 1958. *With His Pistol in His Hand*. Austin: University of Texas Press.

Shannon, Lyle W., and McKim, Judith L. 1974. "Mexican American, Negro and Anglo Improvement in Labor Force Status Between 1960 & 1970 in a Midwestern Community." *Social Science Quarterly* 55, no. 1 (June issue).

Shockley, John Staples. 1973. *Chicano Revolt in a Texas Town*. Notre Dame: University of Notre Dame Press.

U.S. Commission on Civil Rights. 1971. *Political Participation of Mexican Americans in California*. A Report of the California State Advisory Committee. August 1971. Washington, D.C.: Government Printing Office.

U.S. Commission on Civil Rights. 1972. *Mexican American Education Study Report III* (May).

U.S. Department of Health, Education and Welfare, Office for Civil Rights. 1970. *Racial and Ethnic Enrollment Data from Institutions of Higher Education* (Fall).

# BILINGUALISM AND BICULTURALISM: ASSETS FOR CHICANOS

*Manuel H. Guerra*

EDUCATIONAL REFORM FOR CHICANOS in the American Southwest is the logical first step toward providing them equal opportunities for a better life. Such reform involves reappraising the Spanish language, which is part of the cultural heritage of approximately seven million Mexican Americans, looking specifically at the needs of this bilingual-bicultural society, and attempting to meet those needs. Reform, in part, could be accomplished through study programs which would emphasize that (1) Spanish was the language in which the constitution of California was written; (2) Spanish was one of the two languages officially recognized by the New Mexico State Legislature until 1942*; (3) Spanish is one of the five official languages of the United Nations spoken by over 220 million people around the world; (4) Spanish is the predominant language of the South American continent and the Organization of American States.

Many people believe that the bilingual and bicultural nature of the Mexican American is something unique among Hispanic peoples. This belief comes from the comparison of Mexican nationals who are monolingual and Mexican Americans who are bilingual. This idea is misleading, however, and many people would be surprised to learn that most Spanish-speaking people are bilingual! All of the Basques, the Catalans, the Galicians, the Valencians, and the Mallorquinos are bilingual. In the Americas, in addition to Spanish, the Paraguayans are bilingual using also Guarani; many Peruvians use Quechua, and many Bolivians use Aimara. In addition to Spanish, a number of people in

---

*Ed. note. The use of Spanish in certain government proceedings has continued in practice, but the congressional requirement providing for bilingual approaches to official proceedings in New Mexico ran out in 1931. The dates 1942 and 1953 reflect the termination of the use of Spanish in particular circumstances. (See Avendaño, 3, and U.S. Commission on Civil Rights 1970, pp. 66–67.)

Mexico also speak Indian languages. It was on this bilingual background that the Spanish-speaking people of the southwestern United States built their linguistic capacity which enabled them to adapt themselves to English, particularly in the psychological and emotional realm. The problems which Chicanos face do not stem from a lack of bilingual tradition, but from a number of arbitrary and extrinsic barriers. Mexican Americans have not been ready to cope with resulting problems of identity crises, conflicts of loyalties, and bilingual suppression. It is in problem areas such as these that educational reform can do the most good.

Actually, in spite of these facts, the language problems and talents of the Chicano people of California, Arizona, New Mexico, Colorado, Texas, and several midwestern cities such as Chicago and Kansas City have never been fully and properly researched, documented, or published. The works of such eminent scholars as Herschel T. Manuel, Robert Redfield, and George Sánchez, who have explored parts of these problems, have made us acutely aware of linguistic differences of the people of these areas. Anthropologists, like William Madsen and Oscar Lewis have stressed in their studies the importance of language in the social life of the Mexican American. Some earlier studies like those of Emory S. Bogardus, Carey McWilliams, and Manuel Gamio have emphasized linguistic barriers, adjustments and problems. In California, we have heard repeatedly from contemporary Mexican American educators such as Marcos de León, Leo López, Simón González, and Gilbert Martínez that language problems are the primary handicaps of the Mexican American people; yet intensive and conclusive scientific research in bicultural studies of the Mexican American child, adolescent, and adult had not been initiated as late as mid-1977. The Massachusetts Institute of Technology, the University of Michigan, home of the Linguistic Society of America, as well as Georgetown University School of Linguistics, possess ultramodern linguistic equipment, but such research has never been undertaken. Indeed, neolinguistic study of the Chicano has lacked the prestige and sophistication of other studies, and it has not enjoyed the serious concern of the Modern Language Association of America. Language societies have been very conservative and traditionalistic. This lack of foresight by the linguistic guilds of America has contributed to Spanish instruction's being geared to traditional academia, classical philosophies, and educational expediencies for college entrance.

In considering what the nature of educational reform ought to be, based on my own years of research, I submit that linguistic research of Mexican Americans should begin with an accurate historical analysis of (1) the region of Spain where the colonizers and discoverers originated and the language of those people; (2) the nineteenth-century migrations from Spain, Mexico, and other Spanish-speaking countries to the Southwest; and (3) the regional speech patterns of Mexico. A comprehensive study would then include twentieth-century migrations of Mexicans to the United States, mobility and ethnology of Mexican Americans, contact of Chicanos with Mexican nationals whose speech represents different regions, and analysis of both individuals and groups in the American community to trace language origins and patterns.

Such a study would reveal, among other things, that the language of Chicanos is rooted in the Castilian language which is, in turn, spoken with a variety of Mexican regionalisms. The exception, of course, may be found in the San Luis Valley of Colorado and New Mexico, as well as some other parts of New Mexico where archaic seventeenth-century Spanish expressions may still be heard. More study of Southwestern Spanish might discover other places, particularly in geographically isolated areas, where archaic Spanish is still heard. Ironically, many Spanish words and forms, brought to the Southwest by Spaniards, such as the verbs *platicar* (to converse, to chat) as a synonym for *hablar* (to speak) or the verb *amarrar* (to bind or tie up) for *atar,* are retained with consistent vigor in the Spanish-speaking Southwest, whereas they are no longer popularly heard in Spain.

Linguistically Mexican Americans fall into many heterogeneous classes, and only since World War II have we begun to understand that these linguistic categories also correspond to different social and cultural and economic classes, different origins, different geographical and climatic environments. Thus, when we speak of the Chicano community, we think in terms of ethnic and cultural unity, but linguistically, variances outnumber common denominators, and patterns are often the exception, rather than the rule. The lack of linguistic unity is a symptom, not a cause, and it is probably the best proof of the instability, insecurity, and lack of cohesion in both social and political activities—a lack more often attributed to Hispanic individualism than to bicultural incompatibilities.

In the course of my study over a period of nine years, I have categorized a number of linguistic situations found among groups of

Chicano children whom I have studied in northern and southern California. Congressman Edward R. Roybal published in the *Congressional Record* (Guerra 1968) these five categories which I hope will guide the public school systems of the Southwest in their determination of language level and instructional procedure. Categories include (1) children whose father or mother or both speak fluent Spanish and reside in a Spanish-speaking barrio; (2) children whose grandparents or other household relatives speak fluent Spanish, but whose parents do not; (3) children whose father and mother do not speak fluent Spanish; (4) children who reside in a neighborhood where Spanish is seldom or never spoken; (5) children whose father or mother or both speak Spanish and English with equal fluency.

In all categories, certain patterns have emerged. First, children with Spanish-speaking mothers, who actually speak Spanish to the children from infancy, speak Spanish without inhibition when they enter kindergarten (age 5) or Head Start Programs (age 4). Linguists have previously noted this (Levenson 1967, p. 57) and our study confirms it. Children whose mothers do not speak or prefer not to speak Spanish usually do not speak Spanish when they enter school. This is true regardless of whether the father speaks Spanish. Most children who hear Spanish at home from either parent understand spoken Spanish but do not necessarily speak it readily (Guerra 1968). The bilingual family who speaks more English than Spanish, or who permits the child to reply in English when spoken to in Spanish, a characteristic of most children observed, does not give the child the strength and reassurance to develop both languages equally.

Children who are bilingual have language assets to share with children who are monolingual, but they, in effect, do not have the opportunity of sharing their language skills because they are isolated in neighborhoods which have limited contact with the English-speaking community. Ironically, even children who attend school with the foreign language in the elementary school program are deprived of the opportunity to have the best foreign language lesson that is available—on a playground where children speak and hear Spanish. The quip "children learn from children" is especially true of bilingual Chicanitos. Children who regularly use Spanish in play, and who can transfer their games and processes to English with equal poise often come from non-English-speaking parents. Spanish-speaking children in the barrios, on the playground, and in the classroom exert a much greater influence upon their peers than had originally been believed.

The implications of this phenomenon, in the debates of de facto segregation in American public schools, are far-reaching.

Chicanitos who learn Spanish from infancy, and speak Spanish with fluency, express themselves more articulately in Spanish than in English even though English is taught to them in school. Educational experiments involved with the teaching of English after a period of Spanish instruction corroborate this fact and lead the linguist to believe that the first educational rapport should be made in the domestic language, thereafter making instruction progressively bilingual until English is mastered on an equal level with Spanish. Rather than building upon familiar experiences of the child in his native language we have viewed this natural talent as a barrier to learning English, and throughout the Southwest we have in the past many times given the Mexican American child a sense of guilt because of his use of Spanish. Here responsibility must be accepted by the federal, state, and local governments, which coupled with the apathy of Mexican Americans, has allowed the provisions of the Treaty of Guadalupe Hidalgo, insofar as Spanish and culture are concerned, to be ignored. Feliciano Rivera, an established Chicano historian, states in his commentary on the Treaty that article 9 guarantees: "Protection of culture, and protection against anything that would make them [Mexicans who chose to remain in the United States acquired territory] strangers in their own land. Hence, language, clothing, music, food or anything else that can be reasonably construed as culture" (Rivera 1970, p. 186).

An example of one observed speech difficulty for the Mexican American child is that he pronounces "ch" in English in the initial position, in a word such as "shop." We are familiar with the modification of English vowels which, unlike Spanish vowels, have a distinct phoneme and a narrow spectrum. We are familiar with the mispronunciations of labial-dentals, fricatives, and velar sounds. We know that phonemic analysis of Mexican American English shows that phonemes, alliphones, and diaphones sound confusing, like the phoneme "pero" and "perro," with or without the trilled Spanish "r." Transference from English sounds to Spanish sounds often results in the substitution of phonemic timbre and structure of one language for the other. The result is often English structure with definite Spanish phonetics. Sound patterns are substituted; intonation and inflection are often carried over from one system to the other; sometimes syntactical structure is reversed, and the normal positions of modifiers like adjectives and adverbs, or of verbs, suffer dislocation. Spanish genders are frequently transferred to English. Also, Spanish accentuation (many times on the next to the last or last syllable) is often carried over into the English, and the intonation of sound patterns peculiar to southern and central Mexico may be heard in English giving the sound an effect of changing the declarative sentence to an interrogative.

The Mexican American child with many such speech difficulties frequently reveals emotional, psychological, or psychoesthetic conflicts which are expressed in his language (Córdova 1970, pp. 161–62). Language is not the primary source of the conflict, but largely an outward manifestation of inward maladjustments. The emotional fabric of the Mexican American child is often overextended. The child is disturbed, confused, and disoriented as the result of being pulled between two worlds, neither of which gives him a sense of security necessary for learning experiences nor a feeling of belonging. The child comes from the love and warmth of his home into the school situation in which he is made aware that he is different; sometimes this is traumatic. Perhaps the child's mother and father images are crushed when he learns at school that foreigners are people who do not speak English at home. Up until this time, the child had felt a sense of security, a sense of belonging, a sense of pride in his home and family. Now a conflict of loyalties arises when the obvious cultural differences between school and home, home and society, himself and his classmates, appear irreconcilable, and at times, unbearable. In extreme cases the child may sublimate his feelings and withdraw altogether from playmates, teachers, and parents, or the child may retreat to the compensatory behavior of gang activity in which a subgroup of his peers finds security and identity in one language and culture while suppressing the other.

The realization of the difference between school and home can be understood by the child, if guided by an understanding teacher, or a sympathetic parent. Yet the difference can be aggravated if schools, teachers, and textbooks do not teach the child that differences are a basic part of American life and that different people, customs, and languages enrich our nation. If the schools contribute to the myth of a homogeneous America, they shortchange the child by depriving him of good mental health, American identity and personal dignity.

My documented research has shown that, with only one exception, all of the juvenile delinquents, psychologically maladjusted, and violent militants among the youth studied have a characteristic language handicap in either English or Spanish, and often in both. Pochismo (mixture of Spanish and English) is very common, and often reflects a low class dialectical Mexican Spanish. The underlying causes, however, reside just as much in the lack of empathy of teachers, indifference of society, alienation of parents and inability to cope with the social and cultural adjustments of two ways of life as in a language handicap.

There is also a correlation between school dropouts and bilingual studies. My research in Los Angeles County shows that schools with the highest dropout rate also have the poorest rapport with children, the poorest rapport with parents, and inadequate means of communicating in Spanish. The negative attitudes of teachers and principals toward Spanish-English bilingualism, and the customs and traditions of Mexican American children, have created an invisible wall between pupils and teachers.

In many schools personnel have difficulties communicating with the Mexican American child. To illustrate, some schools with a predominant number of Spanish-speaking children have never had an assembly program using Spanish, or featuring community leaders of Mexican American descent, or Mexican American Congressional Medal of Honor recipients, despite the fact that there are many residing in the Southwest (Morin 1962, pp. 10,12,16). Some schools have never played Mexican music, never organized an orchestra or band for Mexican American youth and never taught Mexican dances. Few schools have encouraged children of Spanish-speaking backgrounds to organize Chicano clubs.

In looking toward a solution to the Chicanos' language problems, it is worth noting that among the more educated, affluent, and successful Mexican Americans in professional and vocational occupations, bilingual and bicultural attributes, capacities and talents are commonly found and utilized. Based on my research, I have concluded that there is a definite correlation between the talented, successful Chicanos and bilingual-bicultural abilities. And conversely, there is a correlation between the insecure, unstable, and frustrated Mexican American and his lack of bilingual development. Of course, there are exceptions, but they are few, and these difficulties have far-reaching implications concerning the acculturation concepts and goals of our American public schools.

Examples of successful bilingual-bicultural Mexican Americans throughout the Southwest are as numerous as are the professions they represent. Of the more than one hundred Mexican American attorneys of Los Angeles, most are bilingual-bicultural and conduct inquiries, discussions, and conversations in both Spanish and English. Judges Leopoldo Sanchéz, Phillip Newman, and Benjamin Vega are but a few of the outstanding Mexican American lawyers in the Los Angeles Municipal and Superior Courts.

In the field of government Edward R. Roybal, U.S. Congressman reelected in 1976 from California's 30th District located in Los Angeles, was author of the Bilingual Education Act of 1967. And anyone who understands the politics of the Southwest would not minimize the importance of the Spanish language in the life of the people of New Mexico. It would be impossible to visualize a politician seeking election to office in New Mexico who could not speak Spanish.

Many other Mexican Americans, successful partly because of their bilingual-bicultural abilities, could be named from the medical and education professions. In the field of entertainment Vicki Carr, Eddie Cano, and Trini López are representative of how the Spanish language and Mexican customs enrich the arts. Vicki Carr also established a scholarship foundation in 1970 which has provided scholarships for more than one hundred outstanding Mexican American students, and Eddie Cano, a graduate of the Los Angeles Conservatory of Music, is considered by many critics to be the outstanding stylist of Afro-Hispano jazz.

There is nothing about the bilingual problems of the Chicano child which money, electronic laboratory equipment, and appropriately trained, understanding teachers cannot solve. On the last point, it is not essential that only Mexican Americans teach our children. Non-Mexican American teachers who have a sincere and sympathetic regard for their Spanish-speaking youngsters often help them make the necessary adjustments while indifferent Chicano teachers can compound the child's problems. As far as adequate facilities are concerned, I would recommend the establishment of at least two regional bilingual centers, perhaps one in the Los Angeles area and one in San Antonio, Texas, equipped to study Mexican American speech patterns and make the phonemic analysis which is needed. Such scientific findings would provide guidelines and material for textbooks, tests and measurements, evaluations, manuals, tapes and records. Moreover, I would recommend that the U.S. Office of Education hold annual conferences on bilingual teaching and research. The participants from all over the United States would have an opportunity to see and hear the latest findings in bilingual phenomena. They would presumably return to their schools and communities with a better understanding of the problems.

With regard to ESL (English as a Second Language) programs which make use of community resources, I would like to make a few suggestions as both an evaluator of ESL textbooks for the California State Curriculum Commission as well as a consultant for the Los Angeles Public Schools.

ESL is a valuable component of bilingual-bicultural education. In the Migrant Education Program, for example, it has proven to be most useful. It is wrong, however, to believe that ESL is synonymous to bilingual-bicultural instruction, or that it can replace a bilingual program. Experience has proven that two-language instruction is best. The old ESL practice of never using the child's native language in the classroom, usually because the teacher could not speak it, is definitely not what I propose. The teacher who greets the child and bids good-bye, and perhaps gives a compliment in Spanish immediately creates rapport and respect for the child's native language and culture. Those few short phrases go a long way to establish self-confidence and an atmosphere of friendliness and relaxation. I oppose the ESL programs in which instructors have a superior attitude about the English language and the people who speak it and try to inculcate this attitude in Chicano youth. This type of program subscribes to the philosophy that Spanish is inferior and has to be substituted rather than supplemented with a mastery of the English language. Whenever I meet ESL teachers teaching English to Spanish-speaking children I ask them the question, "Do you speak Spanish?" Some answer, "No, I do not think it's necessary." I do not recommend this kind of teacher for Chicano children learning English any more than I would favor a Spanish teacher who cannot speak English.

The Chicano's desire is to experience a revitalization of intellectual and social philosophy on a level that will be inspiring to all Mexican Americans. It has been suggested that the founding of a national university would be a first step toward stimulating specialized studies, the organization and administration of a special library, publications, and above all intellectual leadership to abstract and conceptualize Chicano problems and potential. The precedent for such a university would presumably be Yeshiva or Brandeis universities of the Jewish community or Howard University or Tuskegee Institute, which were founded for Black Americans or other more recently developed institutions of higher learning. To the criticism that this constitutes segregational practices the Chicano might answer that social reform must rest on the ability of the reformer to document his own condition and articulate his own persuasions. As of 1977 the Chicano community had no polarization, only an awakened political conscience that could not distinguish foe from friend, or free itself of *caciquismo* or political bossism. César Chávez, however, serves as an example of the growing moral unity based upon integrity, legal action, and nonviolence, which is the sign of our maturity, as well as progress and commitment.

On the lower levels of education Chicanos feel an urgency for child counseling, textbooks and texts for Spanish-speaking children, and a corps of teachers and librarians trained in the language and the culture of the Chicano child in order to more successfully meet his needs.

Whether or not in the course of time Chicano universities become a reality, state universities in the Southwest should be regarded as having an obligation to develop programs for teachers, counselors, librarians, and administrators, in preparation for the task of ministering to the Chicano community.

The forward-looking Chicano is eager to point out that once many of the educational problems which have been discussed here are resolved, bilingualism and biculturalism imply talents, assets, and virtues, both personal and social. The concept of liberal arts education, predicated on the humanistic tradition and the rich American heritage that is basically pluralistic in origin, endeavors to achieve what many Mexican American bilinguals will have already attained.

Bibliography

Córdova, Ignacio R. 1970. "The Relationship of Acculturation, Achievement, and Alienation Among Spanish American Sixth Grade Students." *Educating the Mexican American.* Edited by Henry S. Johnson and William J. Hernández-M. Valley Forge, Pa.: Judson Press: 160–82.

*Enciclopedie de bilinguisme.* 1971. Quebec, Canada: Loval University.

Espinosa, Aurelio M. 1930 and 1946. *Estudios sobre el Español de Nuevo Méjico: Parte I. Fonética.* Buenos Aires: Instituto de Filología, Facultad de Filosofía y Letras de la Universidad de Buenos Aires. *Parte II. Morfología.* Buenos Aires.

Guerra, Manuel H. 1968. "Analysis of Mexican American Psycholinguistic and Sociolinguistic Problems and Talents," in Edward R. Roybal's "Linguistic and Cultural Pluralism in America's Southwestern States." *Congressional Record,* 90th Cong. 2d sess., 1968, vol. 114, pt. 2:2574.

————1965. "Why Juanito Doesn't Read." *Journal of the California Teachers Association* 71 (October issue): 17–19.

*The Invisible Minority.* 1966. National Education Association. Department of Rural Education, Washington, D.C.

John, Vera P., and Horner, Vivian M. 1971. *Early Childhood Education.* New York, N.Y.: Modern Language Association.

Lado, Robert. 1957. *Linguistics Across Cultures: Applied Linguistics for Language Teachers.* Ann Arbor, Mich.: University of Michigan Press.

Lambert, Wallace E., and Peal, Elizabeth. 1962. *The Relation of Bilingualism to Intelligence.* Washington, D.C.: American Psychological Association.

Levenson, Stanley, and Kendrick, William. 1967. *Readings in Foreign Language for Elementary School.* Waltham, Mass.: Blaisdell.

Madsen, William. 1964. *The Mexican Americans of South Texas.* New York, N.Y.: Holt, Rinehart, and Winston.

Morin, Raúl. 1962. *Among the Valiant: Mexican Americans in WW II and Korea.* Los Angeles: Borden Publishing Co.

Rivera, Feliciano. 1970. *A Mexican American Source Book.* Menlo Park, Calif.: Educational Consulting Associates.

Rivers, Wilga M. 1964. *The Psychologist and the Foreign Language Teacher.* Chicago: The University of Chicago Press.

Sánchez, George I. 1940. *Forgotten People, A Study of New Mexicans.* Albuquerque: University of New Mexico Press.

Texas State Advisory Committee to the United States Commission on Civil Rights. 1967. *The Civil Rights Status of Spanish-Speaking Americans in Kleberg, Nueces, and San Patricio Counties, Texas.* Washington, D.C.: Government Printing Office.

U.S. Commission on Civil Rights. 1970. *Mexican Americans and the Administration of Justice in the Southwest: A Report, March, 1970.* Washington, D.C.: Government Printing Office, pp. 66–67.

Ureña, P. Henríquez. 1921. "Observaciones sobre el Español en América." *Revista de filología Española* 8 (julio-septiembre): 374–75.

Wonder, John P. 1965. "The Bilingual Mexican-American As a Potential Teacher of Spanish." *Hispania* 48 (March issue): 97–99.

# THE SPANISH LANGUAGE IN THE SOUTHWEST: PAST, PRESENT, AND FUTURE

*Fausto Avendaño*

IN THE YEARS THAT FOLLOWED the Mexican War (1846–1848), English-speaking Americans began immigrating en masse to the Southwest, bringing with them their language, religion, and customs. As they arrived and settled within the Spanish-speaking community, they learned Spanish and their children spoke it like the natives. Spanish continued to be the language of commerce, entertainment and the arts. For the newly arrived it was the language used outside the home. Assimilation at that time meant incorporation into the Spanish-speaking realm, except in purely Anglo-American settlements. Inter-marriage, therefore, became a way of assimilation and incorporation into Mexican society. In San Antonio, for instance, many prominent members of the Anglo community are the descendants of those first intermarriages with Mexican families. Spanish also played an important role in political and legislative processes, especially in New Mexico and California. The constitutions of these two states were written in both Spanish and English.

This linguistic dominance lasted approximately forty years, or until 1880 when English began to prevail in commerce and in the street. Spanish survived, however, remaining sufficiently strong in the home, entertainment, and in the arts. The prestige and stability of the language were evident in that newspapers, magazines, and literary periodicals were published in Spanish and read throughout the Southwest. *El Eco Mexicano, El Clamor Público, La Prensa Mexicana,* and *El Correo Mexicano* were but a few of the literally hundreds of Spanish language newspapers and periodicals published in the Southwest during the second half of the nineteenth century. With new immigrations from the Republic of Mexico in 1910 Spanish was assured the distinction of being the second language in the Southwest. Today Spanish is commonly spoken in California, Colorado,

[133]

New Mexico, Arizona and Texas. And until 1942 in New Mexico, it was recognized as an official language (see footnote in Guerra, p. 121).

Notwithstanding the prestige that it enjoyed and continues to enjoy in some sectors of our society (quite often among the upper classes), cultural and economic prejudices relegated Spanish to an inferior category. Even in New Mexico the well-established families, who spoke Spanish proudly, found themselves in such a disadvantageous economic situation in contrast to the recent settler, that they abandoned their tongue for English in the hopes of material and status gains in exchange. Many were the pressures on Mexican Americans to forsake their tongue. English was not learned for the joy and pleasure of acquiring a second language. It was felt that knowledge of English was necessary *para defenderse* (in order to defend oneself).

Unequal application of the law and abuse by law-enforcement authorities were commonplace. Businesses with Spanish names were boycotted. In many communities, especially in Texas, Spanish-named citizens simply did not serve on criminal juries. Mexican Americans who understood no English were punished in state institutions for disobeying orders, all of which were given in English. In school, Mexican American children were punished for speaking Spanish. In New Mexico, statehood did not come before 1912 principally because the Anglo population had not fully taken control. The widespread use of the Spanish language in courts, schools, and businesses was the reason given for not granting statehood. In 1971 Robert W. Larson, a New Mexico scholar, wrote: "Some remarks concerning the widespread use of Spanish in the schools, courts and businesses of the territory had merit" (Ellis 1971, p. 206). The prejudice toward the language and the people of New Mexico is also evident in the remarks of a congressman at the turn of the century; he characterized New Mexicans as a "race speaking an alien language" and not representing the "best blood on the American Continent" (Ellis 1971, p. 206).

The results of the pressures to abandon the Spanish language appear to be corroborated by Aurelio M. Espinosa, a noted Mexican American linguist, who asserted that when he left New Mexico in 1909 everyone spoke Spanish, but since then it has waned considerably. Nonetheless, in the Interpacific Congress of San Francisco (1915) New Mexican delegates asserted that 75 per cent of New Mexico's school teachers spoke and taught in Spanish. Although we should exercise caution with statistics, since many times they are manipulated by political forces, undoubtedly the report represents the widespread use of Spanish in many sectors of that state's society. At any rate, the importance of Spanish in New Mexico is undeniable when one takes into account that the House of Representatives with a Spanish-speaking majority used both languages until 1953 when Spanish was deemed unnecessary because all Spanish-speaking members of the House were fully bilingual.

Our historical past and the realities that confront us today point unequivocally to these conclusions: Spanish is not only the second American tongue, but initially was the principal language in the Southwest. Even through the years of transition it has survived in the home, in entertainment, and in the arts. Loss of prestige has come about primarily through cultural and linguistic prejudices as the Anglo population surpassed the Mexican American in numbers. Finally, the influx of thousands of Mexicans since 1910 and the Southwest's proximity to the Republic of Mexico continues to give new vigor and stability to the Spanish language.

Loss of prestige, however, remains one of the factors affecting our linguistic-cultural identity. In the past, Anglo-American institutions have discouraged the use of Spanish, even underrating the language's intrinsic value by suggesting, in one way or another, that it was manifestly deficient. That is to say, Mexican Americans, unlike other Spanish-speaking people across the world, spoke a bastard version of Spanish. Ironically, American scholars and educators have not been the only ones to disparage our language, but have been backed up by men of letters from the Spanish-speaking world. These men have censured the corruption of the Spanish language by the penetration of English in the Southwest.

Commentaries, articles, and books have been written and are still being printed today wherein this preoccupation is expressed. For the purpose of this study we will examine one of the earliest of these. In 1936 Francisco Castillo Nájera, a Mexican scholar, lectured at the Instituto de las Españas about the Spanish spoken in Mexico. His views were later published in New York (Castillo Nájera 1936). In his talk he touched upon the linguistic problems of the American Southwest. Emphasizing the surprising unity of the Spanish language, he recognized its value in the brotherhood of all Spanish-speaking people, but warned that the unity was being threatened by the English language at the linguistic borders of the Hispanic world, the Southwest.

Castillo Nájera had the prestige of the Spanish language in mind when he called for American and Mexican institutions to alleviate what he saw as a deplorable state of affairs. More specifically, he wanted the United States and Mexico to set up a joint program of education in Spanish and English so as to improve the cultural and linguistic levels of the Mexican community in the United States.

He considered the influence of English in the Spanish language to be a universal problem, attributable primarily to the lack of Spanish technical terms. He concluded that the great majority of these hybrid words were being propagated at the U.S.-Mexican border. His long list of vocables is so impressive that most readers would find themselves convinced that the Spanish in the Southwest has become a generalized patois, almost unintelligible to all other Spanish-speaking people. Since the generalization of vocabulary has far-reaching significance in the evolution of a language, it is important to determine if Castillo Nájera's list of terms has truly become generalized and incorporated into our vocabulary, and if the essential structure of the Spanish language of this geographical area differs to any significant degree from other regions of the Hispanic world.

The following examination of selected words from Castillo Nájera's list constitutes a preliminary study in an effort to determine the true picture of the Spanish language in the Southwest. I do not purport to say that the study is free of error, but I believe it to be sufficiently valid because the list was examined over a time perspective of more than thirty years. The study represents my own life-long experience with the language and the experiences of others from the four major regions of the Southwest, California, New Mexico/Colorado, Arizona and Texas; it includes conversations, observation, and interviews.

Vocables are listed here that have been generalized to a great extent in the Southwest, although in most cases alternate with the world standard word.

> 1. *Mechas (cerillas, fósforos* or *cerillos)*. Very generalized. Believed to have derived from "match." Most people consider it an Anglicism; a good number believe it to be generalized, while others point out that *fósforo* is just as common. Actually, there is serious doubt that this vocable is an Anglicism, since *mecha* means "wick" in Spanish. In

the "old days," cigarettes, cannons, lamps, etc., were lit with flint and a *mecha,* that is, a wick. Therefore, it is more than probable that the phrase *dame una mecha* has been handed down from that time on and is not necessarily a translation of "match."

2. *Dipo (estación, terminal).* From the English "depot." This word is highly generalized. However, *terminal* and *estación de autobuses,* and *de tren* are used with growing frequency. To my surprise many of the younger people that I interviewed who speak Spanish fluently said they had never heard the word. Based on my own experience I can say that during my childhood *dipo* was very frequent, but today I seldom hear it. Perhaps *dipo* is being replaced by the standard term as communication grows with Mexico and other parts of the Hispanic world.

3. *Traque (vía, carril).* From the English "track." Undoubtedly, one of the most generalized Anglicisms. In contrast to the others, many times the Spanish speaker is not even aware of its foreignness. Very few persons claim to have ever heard it. It is noteworthy, however, that railroad terminology is an old problem in the Hispanic world. There simply was none. Therefore, most terms in Spanish derive from the English. We may also note that although there has been resistance to the English terms with Spanish equivalents, *rail* or *riel* (both Anglicisms) continue to alternate with *carril* and *vía.*

4. *Troque* or *troca (camión* or *camión de carga).* From "truck." These two vocables are so widespread that they are heard not only in the Southwest and in Northern Mexico, but as far south as Guadalajara. In Mexico, however, they are considered affectations, or words taken from another tongue and used pedantically or pretentiously, such as the excessive use of French words or phrases in English. In the Southwest they have become part of the standard lexicon; however, Spanish radio and television opt for the standard vocable and the majority of the Mexican Americans here are familiar with it, though they may not use it.

5. *Parquear (estacionar).* From "to park." The verb is sufficiently common. Virtually no one negates its general use. *Estacionar* is heard occasionally and in the border

towns it alternates with *parquear*. It is worth noting, however, that this Anglicism appears in other parts of Spanish
America and is, therefore, not a linguistic phenomenon
exclusive to the Southwest or to Northern Mexico. In Spain
*aparcar* is of frequent use (to put away, to place munitions
and other war materiel in stores), but the Spanish Royal
Academy prefers *estacionar* (despite its French origin),
since *aparcar* is truly a military term.

6. *Pompa (bomba).* From the English "pump." *Pompa*
means "pomp" in Spanish, but in Northern Mexico and in
the Southwest it acquires the English meaning. Most people
believe that its entrenchment in the Spanish lexicon is due
primarily to the general influence of English technical terminology in the Spanish language. However, in Spanish
maritime terminology a *pompa* is a ship's water pump and
may be a legitimate Spanish term.

7. *Brecas (frenos).* From the English "brakes." It is very
common in the Southwest, but alternates with the standard
modern term and with the old *maneas*, or handbrakes, used
in carts or buggies. Once again the power of English technical terminology has bearing. Ricardo Alfaro, the re-
nowned lexicographer, lists this vocable and its variant *bre-
que* in his dictionary of Anglicisms, pointing out its use in
various parts of Spanish America. Again, we can see that
this phenomenon is not limited to the U.S.-Mexican border.

8. *Sanhuish.* From "sandwich." This word is clearly in
general use in the Southwest as well as in the rest of the
Hispanic world. At times, especially in Spain, sandwiches
are called *emparedados*. In Mexico they are called *tortas de
carne*, but in both countries when we have bread and meat *a
la inglesa* the term used is *sanhuish* or *sangüich*. Most
people consider it logical and acceptable to utilize the native
nomenclature for foreign foods and thus temper their linguistic stuffiness. After all, they would consider it ridiculous for English-speaking people to invent terms for paella,
tacos, enchiladas, etc.

There are many more words which could be studied and placed in
this category. But I think that for the purpose of this essay those cited

clearly indicate that generalized Anglicisms in the Southwest, in many cases, also appear in other parts of the Hispanic world. Some are of doubtful English origin, and notwithstanding their generalization, most alternate with the standard world term. All this leads to one conclusion: linguistic studies of the Southwest must be undertaken with great care. It is not enough to make lists upon lists of hybrid Anglo-Spanish words—with the sole criterion of having heard them one or two times—and then generalize about the language. To do that would be distortion of reality.

The following terms appear in Castillo Nájera's list as Anglicisms common to the Southwest. However, I would differ with that contention. In my estimation, they may have been used with some frequency during the 1930s, but were never accepted universally. By the late 1970s they were seldom used. In many cases they appear to be spontaneous errors or Anglicisms more common to other parts of the Hispanic world.

> 1. *Chorcha* (for *iglesia*). From "church." Of those interviewed not one said they had ever heard the word. The term seems to be more common to other areas of Spanish America. Ricardo Alfaro includes it in his dictionary, indicating its use in some Spanish-American countries to designate the Protestant church. He also points out its general use in northeastern Mexico and in the Southwest. This Anglicism appears to have originated in Spanish America to designate not the Catholic *iglesia*, but the foreign Protestant church; therefore, if used in the Southwest it was probably introduced from Spanish America. One thing is clear, however; today *iglesia* is the term used in the Southwest. I have come across *chorcha* only among natives of the northern state of Sonora, Mexico, and in a dictionary of Sonoran regionalisms. *Chorcha*'s introduction into Spanish America is probably attributable to American Protestant missionaries.
> 2. *Cola* (for *cuello de camisa*). Believed to derive from shirt "collar." No one that I interviewed has heard it, nor have I. Most likely it is a spontaneous error (English interference), or perhaps a deliberate argot, but not a generalized vocable, since everyone knows the true meaning of *cola* (tail, rear, posterior, the buttocks). Semantic conflict of this

type would generally prohibit the acceptance of the English meaning.

3. *Tabla* (for mesa). Probably from "table." *Tabla* is not an Anglicism; it is an old Spanish word for table. It is seldom used today. No one whom I have talked to has heard the term. (Both the Spanish *tabla* and the English "table" ultimately derive from the Latin *tabulam.*)

4. *Esencia (gasolina)*. Included in Castillo Nájera's list of Anglicisms of the Southwest, though the word is an obvious Gallicism (derived from the French *essence*). Perhaps it exists or existed in other parts of the Hispanic world, but not here. No one whom I have interviewed knows the word. (*Esencia* in Spanish means "essence" and in chemistry it is used to designate a volatile substance. This latter meaning is the probable reason why in some Hispanic areas it has been used, as in French, to designate gasoline.)

5. *Grosería (expendio de abarrotes, tienda* or *provisión)*. From the English "grocery." According to those interviewed *grosería* is heard only in New Mexico with any frequency, but resists generalization because most everyone knows the true meaning of *grosería;* that is, grossness, coarseness, rudeness, or ill-breeding.

6. *Boila* or *boiles* (for *caldera* or *calentón*). From "boiler." I have never heard the word in the Southwest, but it apparently has been heard by others in some areas. By all estimates, it has no claim to generalization here. The Spanish usage invariably is *calentón* [(water) heater]. Surprisingly, I came across this vocable in Mexico City among fairly well-educated people, an indication that perhaps the term is more common to other parts of the Hispanic world, and if known here, it is due to influence from without.

7. *Gloves* (for the Spanish *guantes*). I have never come across this term. It is not part of the Spanish lexicon. Spontaneous, individual error or memory lapse are probably instigators of this particular vocable. Bilinguals and polyglots quite often borrow words from another language when, at a particular moment, they forget the term in the language they are speaking. *Gloves* plays no significant role in the standard speech of the Southwest.

8. *Drinques* (*bebidas* or *tragos*). From the English "drinks." It may be used jokingly because of its foreignness. I know that in Brazil it constitutes an affectation. The term may be popular in other areas of Latin America. In the Southwest *drinque* (mixed drink) would not have the ring of elegance or sophistication that it apparently enjoys outside the United States. In the Southwest the standard terms are *bebida* and *trago*. In my inquiry I have found that very few persons recognize the term *drinque* and a very small number consider it of general or standard use.

9. *Jol* (*pasillo, zaguán, salón*, etc.). From "hall." This term is more common to other parts of the Spanish-speaking world. We should note that the Spaniard Ramón Franquelo y Romero in 1911 includes it in his vocabulary of foreignisms in Spain. *Zaguán, corredor, pasillo, salón* are the most common terms in the Southwest. In my estimation *jol* is a linguistic influence from south of the border, as revealed by its inclusion in Latin American literature. (*Jol* and *living* are affectations common among higher levels of Hispanic society.)

Although I do not contend that this preliminary study is error free, my experience and that of others have led me to the conclusion that the Spanish-speaking person in the Southwest is conscious of a level of standard expression and, as in any language group, strives to express himself within the linguistic norms of his area. Although he may use accepted Anglicisms when speaking Spanish, he perceives those speech patterns which are still considered foreign or unacceptable to the standard. That is why he may use words like *troque* and *traque* in a natural manner, but shun Anglicisms such as *huayfa* (wife), *drinques* or *grosería* (grocery). Any given English word may be Hispanicized for comic effect. In fact, it is a universal practice among linguists and polyglots to play with the languages they speak, thus creating ridiculous-sounding vocables. The Mexican American's bilingualism grants him that same privilege, but such combinations are not generally seen as legitimate forms of expression.

Contrary to popular belief the Spanish-speaking person in the Southwest does not truly mix English and Spanish, though there are exceptions. That is to say, a person will rely on one language, Spanish or English, but will choose certain words or phrases from the other language for emphasis, comic effect or shade of meaning. This is the *piquete* (spicy ingredient) which gives *sal y pimienta* (salt and pepper) to the conversation and is not a true mixture of the languages. For example, someone speaking English may say: "Then he stood up on the chair, *tamaño viejo,* and broke it all to pieces," and "Who was that *vieja fea* you were with last night?" This is not unlike the practice of using French words or phrases in English for emphasis or elegance. Now, a true mixture of the languages of the above sentences would be: *Entonces* he *se subió en* the *silla, tamaño viejo,* and *quebró* it *todo* to *pedazos,"* and "Who *era* that *vieja fea* you *estabas* with last *noche?"* \* If this were done we would have a truly embryonic language on our hands for it would merge two essentially different linguistic structures and imply a loss of essential Spanish vocabulary such as *él* (he), *yo* (I), and *quién* (who).

The mixture of the English and Spanish languages in this manner is highly unlikely because, as I said, there is a natural desire to conform to the speech norms of the Spanish language. Spanish language radio, television, various publications in Spanish and the proximity to Mexico are all factors that work and will continue to work against the mixing of the languages. Moreover, the speech of the well-educated persons differs little from that of their counterparts in the rest of the Hispanic world. When educated persons use Anglicisms these are usually the very same ones prevalent in Spanish America or Spain.

Surprisingly, the folk people in many instances use fewer Anglicisms and are more fluent in Spanish, even though their speech may be laden with archaic forms no longer in use in the educated levels of our society. Finally, there is enough evidence to suggest that many Anglicisms used here originated in other Spanish-speaking countries and later were introduced in the Southwest through the media and the influx of Spanish-speaking people.

Castillo Nájera also includes some terms in his list of hybrid words that are definitely not Anglicisms. The following are a few with my comments.

1. *Carro (automóvil).* Popularly believed to have derived from "car." Without question *carro* is a Spanish word. Its use is generic, since it does not always refer to the

---

\*Complete translations of these two sentences are: "Then he climbed on the chair, such a big kid, and he broke it into pieces" and "Who was that old bag you were with last night?"

automobile. Juan Corominas' *Diccionario crítico etimológico de la lengua castellana* includes *carro* as the Spanish
derivative of the Latin *carrus* (Gallic origin) and one
finds it in literature as far back as the works of Gonzalo
de Berceo (thirteenth century). Surprisingly, however, most
people believe it to be a patent Anglicism. Ironically, if we
really want to find a true Anglicism, we should point out
that *automóvil*, though based on two Latin words, was
coined in the English-speaking world from which Spanish
borrowed it.

2. *Máquina* (literally "machine" for *automóvil*). A legitimate Spanish vocable. I have never heard it in the Southwest in place of *carro* or *automóvil*. The few people who
recognized *máquina* used in this way deny its generalization
and its English origin. I have heard the word only among
natives of other countries, especially from the Caribbean
area. I believe *máquina,* as *carro,* is used generically since
an automobile is one of many machines.

3. *Rueda* (literally "wheel" for *bicicleta*). Castillo Nájera
argues that *rueda* is a translation of the English "wheel." It
is neither an Anglicism nor common in the Southwest. As
far as I have been able to ascertain, only in New Mexico
does it appear among the youth. Doubtless, it belongs to the
youthful argot, but does not derive necessarily from
English. Drawing on my own experience, I know that as
teenagers we would employ words in a different manner
deliberately among ourselves. It is a universal practice and
corresponds to the fact that each teenage generation has a
language of its own.

There are many more words taken for Anglicisms without justifica-
tion. Many times this is due to similarities in the languages, since both
Spanish and English have their share of Latin derivatives (Spanish
many times more than English). Therefore, the question of Hispanicized English words in the Southwest and elsewhere must be
examined very carefully and with a good knowledge of the history of
the Spanish language. Only in this manner can one bring forth the true
picture of the linguistic intricacies of our area.

Despite the apparent aversion to foreign words in Spanish, Anglicisms per se are not necessarily negative factors. As with other

languages, Spanish has been enriched by the introduction of numerous foreign words. Many Anglicisms are useful and necessary, as long as their penetration in Spanish is general and measured, so as not to break up the linguistic unity of the Spanish-speaking world. Although Ricardo Alfaro condemns the great majority of the hybrid words in Spanish as corrupt and divisive, he confesses that many are useful and necessary. The Royal Academy of the Spanish Language agrees with that position and has officially accepted many Anglicisms (though not always with everyone's approval) like *filmar* (to film), *flirtear* (to flirt; Alfaro does not agree with the Academy here because he deems the term unessential; curiously, it is not known in the Southwest), *planificar* (to plan), *reporte, reportero, reportaje* and *test* (many do not agree with this last word because it is seldom heard in Spanish America and there are perfectly good Spanish equivalents). Surprisingly, however, the Academy was slow to recognize the acceptability and universality of *aeropuerto* (from ''airport''), insisting on *aeródromo* until 1947.

Alfaro points out the existence of important precedents concerning the utility of foreignisms in the Spanish language when no native equivalent is found. In this spirit he suggests the assimilation into the Spanish lexicon of the following Anglicisms: *overoles* (overalls; appears in Castillo Nájera's list, but Alfaro does not condemn it because he sees no suitable equivalent in Spanish). He justifies *panqueque* (pancakes) because it is an Anglo-American food without an equivalent term in cuisine. Curiously, he opts for *emparedado* (sandwich) but admits that *sanhuish's* consistent and universal use demands its acceptance.

Alfaro has accomplished an immeasurable task in the field of language studies, and his explanations and judgments reflect a high degree of professionalism. However, some of his statements about the language of the Southwest are dubious, most likely due to his use of secondary sources. For example, I do not believe words such as *youk* (joke), *feca* (?), *quidnapear* (to kidnap), *jolopear* (?), *muvis* (movies), *corna* (corner), *yob* (job), *chopear* (to shop), *norsa* (nurse) and many others are or have been part of the standard speech of the Southwest. These words are no doubt spontaneous errors or deliberate efforts among the youth of the 1930s and 1940s to create a slang only they could understand. This was the celebrated *caló pachuco*, extreme and colorful at times, but spoken by a small sector of the population, namely, the youth. As we know, every generation in whatever language creates its own argot whether or not social ills exist to spur extremes. It is a universal phenomenon, but in our case bilingualism contributes to a more complicated and colorful creation.

In my conversations with various members of the generation of the 1930s and 1940s, I have asked if today they would use the *caló* of their youth. They replied with astonishing uniformity that those expressions were almost forgotten, and that they would feel ridiculous using them today. It is apparent that slang is a short-lived linguistic phenomenon (with some exceptions) that depends almost exclusively on the teen-age generation of the times. In English we find the same tendency to abandon youthful slang as a particular generation comes into adulthood.

Whenever we confront the problem of the unity and standardization of a language, we must keep in mind that some foreignisms are inevitable. When certain sports, foods or inventions appear on the scene, the world community, generally, is obliged to accept the term used in the country of origin. This is why Spanish has accepted and assimilated *béisbol, fútbol, tenis, golf, aeropuerto, filmar, automóvil* and many other technical neologisms taken directly from English. In like manner, the English language also borrows from Spanish when it has no adequate terms of its own. For instance, the following Spanish words form part of the English vocabulary: Don Juan, toreador, picador, patio, guerrilla, armada, aficionado, armadillo, junta, rodeo, arroyo, lariat, chocolate, cacao, maize, lasso, ranch, rancher, bronco, desperado, siesta, fiesta, plaza and many, many more.

As we have seen, lexical influences of one language on another are a common and universal phenomenon. In Spanish, as with other languages, the process of assimilation of useful foreign terms will continue, as long as the need arises. However, affectations and individual linguistic idiosyncrasies which come and go will have generally no significant effect on the universal standard. Doubtless, many more hybrid Anglo-Spanish vocables will appear in the Southwest, primarily due to the inclinations of the individual as will be true in the rest of the Spanish-speaking world. But from what we know of the past, the great majority of these affectations will remain passing fancy.

It is important to note, for example, that the Spaniard Franquelo y

Romero in 1911 testified to such affectations in the Spain of his day, which save for a few, have been completely forgotten. Surprisingly, many of these Anglicisms are the same ones attributed to the speech of the Southwest. For the following examples Franquelo y Romero's spelling was retained as it was originally: *lench* (lunch), *pícnic, spich* (speech), *bil* (bill for a "proposed statute"), *bisquit, interviu, intervienar* (both from the English "to interview"; *entrevistar* has been sanctioned as the correct term, though it, too, stems from the combination of inter/*entre* and view/*vista*), *mitin* (meeting), *brindis* (toast), *boicotear* (to boycott), *fáchenabel* (to be in style), *chokin* instead of *espantoso* (shocking), *jai laif* (high life), *suit* instead of *salón, recámara* (suite), *nerse* instead of *enfermera* (nurse), *mach* instead of *apuesta* (match), *ful* (fool; *tonto* would be one of the Spanish equivalents), *yoqui* instead of *jinete* (jockey), *claun* instead of *payaso* (clown), *flirt* instead of *coqueta* (flirt); *ditective* for *policía secreta*; presently *detective* is universally accepted and alternates with *policía secreta*.

Again we can see that the majority of these terms was a passing fancy, quickly forgotten except for those words which represented true deficiencies in the language. Most lists of neologisms and hybrid words correspond to spontaneous foreign interference or are due to deliberate affectations, and as such only a reduced number reach the stage of general acceptance and inclusion in dictionaries. Francis M. Kercheville's list of Anglicisms which he attributes to the standard speech in New Mexico serves as a good example of this linguistic phenomenon. Upon researching his findings, I have discovered, as with Franquelo y Romero's list, that the great majority of the Anglicisms recorded by Kercheville are not truly generalized and have not, therefore, sustained the test of time. The following words which appear in Kercheville's list have no claim to acceptability for generalization in the standard speech of New Mexico: *estopear* for *parar* (stop), *juipe* for *látigo* (whip), *laya* for *mentiroso* (liar), *loque* for *suerte* (luck), *taya* for *llanta* (tire), *fuliar* for *engañar* (to fool), *jamochi* for *cuánto* (how much), *tumoro* for *mañana* (tomorrow), *charchar* for *sacar fiado* or *agregar, cargar a la cuenta* (to charge), *restar* for *descansar* (to rest). Although there is room for error, the words cited here are no longer used with any significant frequency. Those interviewed were outraged that anyone would characterize their speech in that way. The problem stems from the fact that Kercheville relied on information supplied by a group of listeners who went out into the field to record any and all phenomena. On the other hand, the people that I interviewed agreed on the frequent use of the following words, although they alternate with the universal term: *chitear* for *engañar, hacer trampa* (to cheat), *breca* (brakes), *esmart* (smart), *tritear* for *agasajar, convidar* (to treat), and *baquear* or *bequear* for *retroceder* or *recular* (to back up).

Notwithstanding these Anglicisms and the fact that some English interference exists, the language eludes any easy generalization. To be sure, there is no standardized Mexican American Spanish spoken; some speak little Spanish, others are Spanish dominant, and still others enjoy a command of both Spanish and English. The main problem is that Spanish-speaking persons have learned the language without the aid of formal education. Consequently, individuals who barely read and write in Spanish manifest a vocabulary deficiency common to all people across the world who have had little or no schooling. Educators in the Southwest have begun to recognize this problem and to reorient their Spanish language programs to include the specific problems and potentials of Mexican Americans.

Difficulties that existed in the past are now being remedied to some degree by special university seminars, conferences, and publications for language instructors, with the primary objectives being to stimulate in students an interest and pride in our Spanish language and further to avoid pedantism. We can take heart in what the Cubans are doing in Florida to encourage bilingualism in Spanish and English. Along these lines, progress is also being made in institutes of higher learning in states such as California, Arizona, Texas, and New Mexico.

In many instances, the problems between teachers and students have stemmed from the misinterpretation of the terms Castilian (*castellano*) and Spanish (*español*). There are still instructors who refer to Castilian and Spanish as two different tongues. The truth is that the terms are synonymous. Castilian became the official language in Spain, and, therefore, by the seventeenth century it was universally known as Spanish. This very same language was exported to the New World by Imperial Spain. For this reason we do not speak Galician, Catalan, or Portuguese, the other Romance languages in the Iberian Peninsula. Moreover, Spain shares linguistic hegemony with Spanish America, especially with Mexico, Colombia, and Argentina. The fact that Mexico today is the most populous Spanish-speaking country, and one of the most active in the literary arts, inevitably widens its share of influence in the Spanish-speaking world.

A lot is being done to further the study and preservation of Spanish in the Southwest, but these efforts must continue and expand. The future looks promising provided Chicanos take definite steps to preserve the Spanish language. This will involve rejecting the premise that its abandonment is the price that must be paid for economic and social status gains. The Spanish language is a unifying force that strengthens our cultural identity. Chicanos in the Southwest have much to gain by preserving this single cultural element in our heritage.

Past and present *movimientos*, such as the Chicano movement, with their goals of cultural and political reaffirmation, have pressed American society to give Mexican Americans the recognition due them. Now, we must take care not just to give lip service to bilingualism and biculturalism but to diligently pass on to our children the significance of maintaining our Spanish language. As the depository of collective experiences and ideas, and a reflection of the wisdom of ages, the Spanish languages must be preserved as an integral part of our heritage.

Bibliography

Alfaro, Ricardo. 1964. *Diccionario de anglicismos*. Madrid: Editorial Gredos, S.A.

Castillo Nájera, Francisco. 1936. *Breves consideraciones sobre el español que se habla en México*. New York: Instituto de Las Españas en los Estados Unidos.

Corominas, Juan. 1954-57. *Diccionario crítico etimológico de la lengua castellana*, 4 vols., Madrid: Gredos.

Coseriu, Eugenio. 1967. *Teoría del lenguaje y lingüística general*. Madrid: Editorial Gredos, S.A.

Ellis, Richard N., comp. 1971. *New Mexico, Past and Present*. Albuquerque: University of New Mexico Press.

Espinosa, Aurelio M. 1930. *Estudios sobre el español de Nuevo Méjico: Parte I. Fonética*. (Biblioteca de dialectología hispano-americana, tomo I). Buenos Aires: Instituto de Filología, Facultad de Filosofía y Letras de la Universidad de Buenos Aires.

———. 1946. *Estudios sobre el español de Nuevo Méjico: Parte II. Morfología*. (Biblioteca de dialectología hispano-americana, tomo II). Buenos Aires: Instituto de Filología, Facultad de Filosofía y Letras de la Universidad de Buenos Aires.

Franquelo y Romero, Ramón. 1910. *Frases impropias, barbarismos, solecismos, y extranjerismos de uso mas frecuente en la prensa y en la conversación*. Málaga: Tipografía de El Progreso.

Henríquez Ureña, Pedro. 1938. *El español en México, los Estados Unidos y la América Central*. Buenos Aires: Imprenta de la Universidad de Buenos Aires.

Kercheville, Francis M., comp. 1934. *A Preliminary Glossary of New Mexican Spanish Together with Some Semantic and Philological Facts of the Spanish Spoken in Chilili, New Mexico by George E. McSpadden*. Albuquerque: University of New Mexico.

Menéndez Pidal, Ramón. 1968. *Manual de gramatica histórica española*. 13th ed. Madrid: Esposa-Calpe, S.A.

Ramírez, Karen G. 1973. Lexical Usage of and Attitude Toward Southwest Spanish in the Ysleta, Texas Area. *Hispania* 56 (April issue): 308–15.

Teschner, Richard V.; Bills, Garland D.; and Craddock, Jerry R., eds. 1975. *Spanish and English of United States Hispanos: A Critical, Annotated, Linguistic Bibliography*. Arlington, Virginia: Center for Applied Linguistics.

Trejo, Arnulfo D. 1968. *Diccionario etimológico latinoamericano del léxico de la delincuencia*. México, D.F.: Union Tipográfica Editorial Hispano Americana.

# BILINGUAL-BICULTURAL EDUCATION: A MUST FOR CHICANOS

*David Ballesteros*

MANY CULTURES HAVE PLAYED a part in the development of the United States, including those of the American Indian, African, Asian, European, and the Mexican American. Instruction in languages other than English is not an alien concept in the United States. During the 1700s instruction in schools was given in German and French. In the 1800s the Cherokees had an instructional system which produced a population 90 percent literate in its native language. In 1884 a school law was passed in the state of New Mexico allowing for bilingual instruction (González 1975, p.6). The migration of a large Cuban population to Florida in the 1960s had a great impact on bilingual-bicultural education in the United States. Coral Way Elementary School in Miami became the model where Spanish and English are taught to both Anglo and Cuban students.

These instances, however, seem to have been the exception rather than the norm. Unlike European schools where children grow up with the notion of cultural diversity and frequently learn two or three foreign languages in the course of their formal schooling, schools in the United States commonly isolate the students from cultural exchange (Howe 1969, p. 15). Some might claim that European countries need foreign languages for economic existence; others contend that the United States could profit from this type of interaction for the sake of social existence. In a speech at Austin, Texas, Harold Howe II, former United States Commissioner of Education, said:

> This argument, that wider cultural exposure will help our international relations, stresses both national purposes and international amity. Perhaps the most important reason for bicultural programs, however, is not international but

[151]

domestic—our relations with each other here at home. The entire history of discrimination is based on the prejudice that because someone else is different, he is somehow worse. If we could teach all children—black, white, brown, yellow, and all the American shades in between—that diversity is not to be feared or suspected, but enjoyed and valued, we would be well on the way toward achieving the equality we have always proclaimed as a national characteristic. And we would be further along the way toward ridding ourselves of the baggage of distrust and hatred which has recently turned American against American in our cities (Howe 1969, p. 16).

Bilingual education is the concurrent use of two languages in learning; bicultural education is the concurrent use of two ways of life, two cultural points of view outside the school as well as in the school. Language is an integral part of culture. Thus, to be truly bicultural implies being bilingual; however, a person may be bilingual without being bicultural. Knowing the language of the people does not guarantee that one understands their way of life, but knowing about a culture is not enough either. To be bicultural one must feel, experience, and be part of it. Biculturalism is a state that indicates knowing and being able to operate successfully or comfortably in two cultures (Ulibarri 1972, p. 3).

In addition to speaking and understanding two languages, having exposure to two cultures, and reading and writing two languages, bilingual-bicultural education means teaching the student educational concepts in his mother tongue while at the same time teaching him English (or Spanish) and problem-solving using two different perspectives. This latter approach prevents his educational retardation while reinforcing his language and culture. The important thing is that the thought processes are enhanced and not limited by degrees of Spanish-English bilingualism.

As early as the 1930s George I. Sánchez, a Mexican American educator, scholar, and spokesman for bilingual-bicultural studies, was promoting and analyzing the dual experiences of language and culture among the Spanish-speaking people of the Southwest and attacking the use of IQ tests to determine the intellectual ability of Chicanitos. He viewed bilingual-bicultural education not only as a way to preserve Hispanic culture but also as a means of intellectual development for all Americans.

In spite of these early beginnings, progress has been relatively slow. According to a 1971 report of the U.S. Commission on Civil Rights, out of every one hundred Mexican Americans who enter first grade, only sixty graduate from high school, compared to eighty-six for Anglos (U.S. Commission on Civil Rights 1971, p. 6). This is attributable in large measure to the language barrier. The number of Mexican Americans and other Spanish-speaking students who begin school in the American educational system without speaking English is significant. The trend has been to force these students to repeat grade levels and to postpone all serious academic work until they learn English. This approach commonly leaves the Spanish-speaking student three to five years behind his Anglo counterpart by the time he is a teenager. According to the U.S. Civil Rights Commission there is a strong relationship between grade level repetition and low student achievement. The state of Texas, which has had the largest proportion of grade repetition for Chicanos in the first and fourth grades, also had 74 percent—the largest proportion—of Mexican American eighth graders reading below grade level (U.S. Commission on Civil Rights 1971, p. 31).

The enactment of the Bilingual Education Act of 1968, commonly known as Title VII of the Elementary and Secondary Education Act, gives impetus to the education of the Spanish-speaking student. It provides a national commitment for important changes in the educational policy of most school districts. It gives recognition to the assets of people whose mother tongue is not English. First priority under the Bilingual Education Act is to strengthen the education of the non-English and limited-English speaking children; and second, it is the intent of the Act to promote bilingualism among all students. Even so, as of the mid-1970s, a large number of Chicano students were still isolated in schools predominantly Mexican American, situations caused by de facto segregation or gerrymandered school boundaries. While the segregated Anglo American students are equally deprived of a heterogeneous environment which could lead to increased educational development, they are rarely confronted with a school environment which directly rejects the culture of their home environment. I had this feeling of isolation when I started school in Orange County, California. It was a Mexican American school, yet all the teachers were Anglo and none spoke Spanish.

Soon after entering the primary grades, the Chicanito begins to realize that he is different and the differences are taken by society at large as a sign of inferiority. Further, it is not only his schoolmates who teach him this; frequently the teachers themselves betray an ill-disguised contempt for the schools and neighborhoods in which they work. Seldom do teachers and administrators blame themselves. It is usually the fault of the student or the fault of the parents. Remarks which I have heard in teachers' meetings and coffee rooms when referring to Chicano students include: they can't read; they never bring their homework; they are scheming and lazy; they talk back; the children do not want to learn and do not try; the children do not use standard English; they speak Mexican, not Castilian, that is why I cannot understand them; the parents do not care about the children; the children are always filthy; they blow with the wind, here today, gone tomorrow; what can you teach them?; I have got to get him tested for Special Education. The opinions and attitudes of these teachers are also reinforced by history books, in which the youngsters read of the Spaniards' greed for gold, of Mexican bandits, of the massacre at the Alamo (Ríos 1969, pp. 25–26). The result of this kind of teaching by both school and society is that the Chicanito is kept ignorant of the significant contributions that his forbears made to the development of this land, *nuestra tierra* (our land). At a time when he should be developing pride in his history and his own unique kind of Americanism, he is made to feel that he is an outsider, an intruder in his own country.

In my opinion the most important function of the total educational experience is the interaction between teacher and student. It is through this exchange that the school system makes its major impact upon the student. The manner of interaction between teacher and student to a large degree determines the quality of education the child obtains. A stereotype by the majority culture can become a tremendously damaging element for the Chicano student, since the perpetuated stereotype often becomes a self-fulfilling prophecy. It is easy to see how a teacher or counselor who believes a Chicanito to be a poor student will soon have this person behaving accordingly (Rosenthal 1968, p. 240).

Report V of the U.S. Civil Rights Commission on the Mexican American states that many teachers in the Southwest display poorer teaching behavior toward Chicano students than they do toward Anglo students. The average teacher, according to the report, praises and encourages Anglo pupils 35 percent more often than Chicano students, accepts or uses Anglo students' ideas 40 percent more often, and questions Anglos 20 percent more often than Chicanos (U.S. Commission on Civil Rights 1973, p.17). This consistent disparity suggests that our teacher training institutions are failing to prepare teachers to provide equal educational opportunity for Chicano students.

Disproportionate numbers of Spanish-speaking students are placed in classes for the mentally retarded because they cannot cope with the placement and IQ tests that are given in English. Many are also placed in remedial classes and non-academic subjects. A very important question to raise is whether IQ tests measure intelligence or language proficiency. In practice, Chicano students frequently are placed in Educable Mentally Retarded (EMR) classes because many teachers equate linguistic ability with intellectual ability. In many schools in the Southwest, Chicano students are overrepresented in low ability groups and underrepresented in high ability groups. In California, Mexican American students account for more than 40 percent of the so-called mentally retarded.

We often err in viewing bilingualism as a handicap, or at least as some sort of special problem in education. A low socio-economic status is usually accompanied by a lack of knowledge of the English language, but this is nearly always interpreted as a language handicap, not a socio-economic one. Educators should take into consideration, too, that great differences exist between individual children with regard to language facility in general, quite apart from any influence of bilingualism. The great majority of the studies on bilingualism have not compared bilinguals with monolinguals of the same socio-economic status, but have matched monolingual English speakers with bilinguals of lower socio-economic status. In studies which compare the performances of monolinguals of different socio-economic status, the groups with lower socio-economic status have scored lower (Sánchez 1966, p. 15). Therefore, bilingualism itself cannot be considered as the only possible reason in poor test performance. A 1970 memorandum from J. Stanley Pottinger, director, Office of Civil Rights, Department of Health, Education, and Welfare to school districts with more than 5 percent minority children directed them not to assign minority students to classes for the mentally retarded on the basis of tests which essentially measure English language skills. Also, school districts were directed not to deny these students access to college preparatory courses on a basis directly related to the failure of the school system to inculcate English language skills (U.S. Commission on Civil Rights 1975, p. 205).

The Chicano student's language and culture need not be obstacles to his success in school, but rather effective tools for learning. To destroy his language and culture is to destroy his identity, self-image and self-esteem. To enable him to survive in our Anglo-dominated society he must be able to put into that society an extra ingredient that marks him as a person with a valuable asset to be used for the enrichment of the total society. That extra ingredient is his linguistic, cultural and ethnic pride. Pride, dignity, concern, and feelings for his own self-worth are especially strong in the Chicano youth who is struggling to find his self-identity and a positive self-image.

> Who am I? asks a young Mexican American high school student. I am a product of myself. I am a product of yours and my ancestors. We came to California long before the Pilgrims landed at Plymouth Rock. We settled California, the Southwestern part of the United States, including the states of Arizona, New Mexico, Colorado, and Texas. We built the missions; we cultivated the ranches. We were at the Alamo in Texas, both inside and outside. You know we owned California—that is, until gold was found there. Who am I? I am a human being. I have the same hopes that you do, the same fears, the same drives, same desires, same concerns, same abilities; and I want the same chance that you have to be an individual. Who am I? In reality, I am who you want me to be (Johnson and Hernández-M. 1970, pp. 17–19).

This same concern for dignity and respect is found in the words of the Chicano poet, Alurista:

*Mis ojos hinchados,*
    *flooded with lágrimas*
*de bronce*
*melting on the cheek bones*
*of my concern*
        *rasgos indígenas*
*the scars of history on my face*
        *and the veins of my body*
*that aches*
        *vomito sangre*
*y lloro libertad*
        *I do not ask for freedom*
*I am freedom.*

(Alurista 1968, p. 6)

Why is it that the Mexican American is not prepared to attend and remain in institutions of higher learning? The reasons are primarily that the American educational system is not geared to meet the educational needs of Spanish-speaking students, thus developing an atmosphere of discouragement. The Chicano college population is relatively small; smaller yet are the number of college graduates, which the Chicano community desperately needs. The importance of an education cannot be taken lightly. One of the most important routes by which the Mexican American may reach some measure of equal opportunity with other Americans is schooling. For every successful Chicano or Chicana there will be innumerable others who will be inspired and motivated by them.

In meeting the instructional needs of Chicanos, both in public schools and in institutions of higher learning, standards should be reassessed regarding achievement and IQ tests, admission and academic requirements, and teaching competencies for both prospective and experienced teachers. The need is to look at standards in terms of the future, not the past, in terms of the changing times, in terms of diverse ethnic groups. We do not need fewer standards but better standards. To require that teachers—both Anglo and Chicano—working with Chicano students have a bilingual-bicultural background, certainly is not a requirement which lowers standards.

A humanistic approach to education means equality of opportunity for all students—it is respect and concern for students regardless of the language and culture they bring to school. It is the positive climate established for students to develop their full potential by taking advantage of their cultural and linguistic assets. It is the belief in the dignity of all students regardless of race, color, creed, or sex. Bilingual-bicultural education recognizes cultural diversity as a fact of life, and it affirms that this cultural diversity is a valuable source that should be preserved and extended in order to meet the curricular needs of Chicano students. The content of the curriculum and the teaching strategies used in our schools should be tailored to the unique learning and incentive-motivational styles of Chicano children. In his attempt to study biculturalism and establish bicultural programs, Manuel Ramírez has isolated unique learning and incentive-motivational styles in Mexican American children. His research shows that Chicano students need a more personalized teaching style and culture-matching curricula (Ramírez 1970, pp. 45–46). Equal educational opportunity is denied when educational policy and practice favor one teaching and cognitive style over another.

School programs for Chicanitos will fail in the long run if they define educability in terms of a student's ability to perform within an alien culture. Thus, the amount of time spent in school matters little if the experience concentrates on compensation instead of enrichment. Innovation must take place in developing policies, procedures, and teaching materials used in schools.

Educational litigation has challenged discrimination by school officials in cases of the suspension and/or expulsion of Mexican American students, prohibitions on speaking Spanish in school, failure to hire Chicano teachers and administrators, and the lack of material on Mexican American history and culture in school curricula. The courts are also looking into school districts which offer segregated bilingual education programs, or those districts which offer integration without bilingual-bicultural education (Cárdenas 1975, p. 20).

In 1973 the Mexican American Legal Defense and Educational Fund (MALDEF) participated in a U.S. Supreme Court case *Lau* v. *Nichols*, which dealt with non-English-speaking Chinese American students. This case has important implications for Spanish-speaking people because the court ruled that a school system's failure to provide an educational program for Chinese American students violated the 1964 Civil Rights Act proscribing discrimination on the basis of national origin. Under *Lau* v. *Nichols*, the Supreme Court held that school districts receiving federal funds cannot discriminate against children who have limited ability in English by denying them the language training they need for meaningful participation in the educational process (U.S. Commission on Civil Rights, 1975, p. 137). In another case, *Serna* v. *Portales*, the MALDEF counsel argued that the absence or inadequacy of bilingual-bicultural programs in a New Mexico school system which has many Chicano students violates the Fourteenth Amendment's equal protection clause. The decisions of *Lau* v. *Nichols* and *Serna* v. *Portales* have illustrated the viability of using the courts to legally establish bilingual programs.

It is most important that professional as well as paraprofessional personnel understand and recognize the unique cultural and linguistic differences of Chicano students. We need, in our schools' components, proficient teachers. Frequently, we equate certification with qualification. There are thousands of qualified Spanish-speaking persons who could be working in bilingual-bicultural programs, but who do not have the necessary teaching credentials because of antiquated requirements. Credentials, unfortunately, are still granted on the basis of unit requirements and not necessarily on teaching competencies. As I have already mentioned, the teacher is the key person in the school who helps the student develop to his full potential. In addition to the basic educational core curriculum, teachers' training should include courses in language and ethnic studies to expose the individual to cultural differences which can affect classroom practices and teacher-student interaction. I feel that the following components are essential in the development of a bilingual-bicultural teacher:

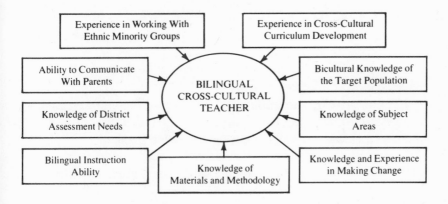

An example of a sound bilingual-bicultural, teacher-training program is the Teacher Corps at the University of Texas, Austin. Instructional staff, participants and community members work together to develop objectives and criteria designed to better prepare the teacher to do an effective job. The teacher's objectives are: (1) to understand his own attitudes, insecurities, and prejudices through a program of sensitivity development; (2) to understand the nature of the child's environment and culture (including language) through a program of teacher interaction in the school and community; and (3) to become knowledgeable of and competent in effective teaching techniques (Teacher Corps 1971, p. 13).

Another example of a teacher-training program is the model developed by the Mexican American Education Project at California State University, Sacramento (1968–73). This project had three components: (1) early childhood education, (2) prospective teacher fellowship, and (3) experienced teacher fellowship (Mexican American Education 1974). The Mexican American Education Project was one of the few nationwide efforts aimed at training teachers to develop skills and knowledge in order to stimulate alternatives to the existing patterns in our public schools. Additionally, a very important objective of this program was to develop community accountability among the Chicano population.

Contributions of the various ethnic groups to this country should be integrated in all aspects of the school experience: history, geography, art, music, literature. A cross-cultural experience means not only the integration of students and staff, but also the integration of the curriculum. The University of Texas, San Antonio, in recognition of this need has placed the Division of Teacher Education in the College of Multidisciplinary Studies. The emphasis for the teacher is to obtain a wide range of experiences outside the field of education, particularly as they relate to cross-cultural experiences. Teachers are prepared to work in a variety of settings and to obtain a linguistic and cultural understanding of minority students.

Cecilio Orozco, former director of Bilingual/Bicultural Studies at New Mexico Highlands University, has said that a teacher working with Chicano students should meet the following standards:

1. Everyone who teaches Chicano students needs to *know* and be keenly aware of the language differences between English and Spanish.

2. Teachers of Chicanos need to know the history of the Iberian peninsula (including its role in the Roman Empire), the history of the Virreinato and the history of the exploration and settlement of the Southwest. Without this, they cannot understand the greatness of the Chicano's culture.
3. Teachers need to understand the roles played in the family unit, the social unit and the political unit by both sexes in the Chicano culture (Orozco to Ballesteros).

The demand for a relevant educational experience is one of the most important features of the contemporary Chicano cultural renaissance. On high school and college campuses the demands for a relevant cultural experience have taken the form of proposals for Chicano Studies programs. Chicano Studies curricula should encompass the Chicano experience, past and present, in accordance with established cultural categories. Unity among Chicanos rests, in large part, on the knowledge of the Chicano heritage. Thus, in the teaching of Chicano Studies, formal study is designed to influence the student's self-realization either by showing him or eliciting from him diverse aspects of himself and of his community (*El plan* 1970, pp. 43–47).

Equality with other students must have priority in the education of Chicanos. In planning and implementing programs, the community, parents, students, faculty, and administrators must work together if the curriculum is to be relevant and viable. Setting criteria for measuring equal educational opportunity can no longer be the province of the established experts. The policymakers need to listen to those for whom they are working, which ultimately means that they should be willing to share the powers of decision making.

An effective bilingual-bicultural program is characterized by community and parent participation. Parents and other community members need to be involved in the planning and reviewing of any program. They can and should be involved in the training of staff and in classroom activities. Parent-advisory boards can serve as a liaison between schools and the community. There is no substitute for the personal communication between school, home, and community, which is vital if bilingual-bicultural programs are to succeed. We must continue to encourage parents to participate in all phases of programs which affect their children. The purpose of organizing Chicano parents to take a more active part in school affairs is to assure that they will be an influence in their children's education. Theodore Andersson, an advocate of bilingual-bicultural programs, particularly at the pre-school and primary grade levels, is a proponent of extending school learning into the home. Out-of-school learning has the advantage of involving grandparents, parents and older children as sources of information. The effectiveness of communicating ideas in this manner lies to a large extent in the use of their native language (Andersson 1975, p. 302). An example of this type of school-home communication is the Cuauhtemoc Home-Centered Bilingual preschool in Redwood City, California. This project involves forty-eight children ages three, four and five. Two-thirds of them are native Spanish-speakers and one-third are native English-speakers. Teaching is done in groups of six children by a bilingual teacher and a bilingual aide meeting in a different home each day of the week (Andersson 1975, p. 305). Test results showed high correlation between the degree of parent cooperation and the children's scholastic development (Hohn and Dunston 1974, p. 253).

The Spanish-speaking parent will support the goals and values of the school when the school begins to recognize the worth of his culture and realize that he or she can make a unique contribution to the educational process. Bilingual-bicultural education should help the child to make the transition from home to school more easily by reducing the differences between the language and culture of the home and that which prevails in the school. The Spanish-speaking population views the community not only as a physical setting but also as a spiritual experience—an extension of the immediate family. Whether we live in the barrio or not, we are concerned for the welfare and education of *Raza* students. As educators we depend on support from the community as the community depends on our support. The pursuit of academic excellence is fully compatible with service to the community. Some of the goals and objectives to strengthen school-community relations are:

1. to complement students' instructional and learning needs with community projects and activities
2. to involve parents in school decisions affecting their children
3. to increase the teachers' awareness of the children's life-styles

4. to interact in class sessions with community persons in both English and the target language
5. to work in a team effort along with parents, community, school personnel to better utilize school facilities and equipment
6. to facilitate educational opportunities for adults in the community
7. to learn techniques of family counseling and training parents in order to guide and counsel their children more effectively
8. to serve as public relations in the community, interpreting school programs in both English and Spanish (Ballesteros 1974, pp. 183–84).

The need for recognizing the bilingual-bicultural student as a positive force in our society is beyond question, but both schools and universities must change their teaching programs before any real benefit can reach our ultimate clients—our children. The commitment to alleviating curricula deficiencies in educational programs from the preschool through the university must continue and must be intensified in the years ahead. The Chicano student need not be considered deprived, disadvantaged or handicapped because of language and cultural differences. On the contrary, educators should capitalize on these differences and help the child appreciate his assets. Bilingual-bicultural programs must not be considered as compensatory programs but as integral parts of the linguistic-cultural-cognitive development of the student. Bilingual-bicultural education should be viewed as an enrichment program. With these goals in mind, not only will bilingual-bicultural education be an asset to Chicanos in relation to our fellow citizens and the rest of the world, but also of incalculable worth in the enhancement of the human spirit.

Bibliography

Andersson, Theodore. 1975. "Extending Bilingual Education into the Homes." *Foreign Language Annals* 8 (December issue): 302–5.

Andersson, Theodore, and Boyer, Mildred, eds. 1970. *Bilingual Schooling in the United States.* 2 vols. Austin, Texas: Southwest Educational Development Laboratory. (Sold by Government Printing Office.)

Ballesteros, David. 1974. "Community-Based Education: A Program to Improve Home-School Communication." *California Journal of Educational Research* 25 (November issue): 281–88.

Banks, James A. 1973. *Teaching Ethnic Studies: Concepts and Strategies, 43rd Yearbook.* National Council for the Social Studies.

Cárdenas, José. 1975. "Bilingual Education, Segregation, and a Third Alternative." *Inequality in Education* 19 (February issue): 19–22.

Castañeda, Alfredo; Ramírez, Manuel III; Cortez, Carlos E.; and Barrera, Mario, eds. 1974. *Mexican Americans and Educational Change.* New York: Arno Press.

*El plan de Santa Barbara: a Chicano Plan for Higher Education.* 1970. Analyses and Positions by the Chicano Coordinating Council on Higher Education. Santa Barbara, Calif.: La Causa Publications.

Gezi, Kal. 1974. "Bilingual-Bicultural Education: A Review of Relevant Research." *California Journal of Educational Research* 25 (November issue): 223–29.

González, Josue M. 1975. "Coming of Age in Bilingual/Bicultural Education: A Historical Perspective." *Inequality in Education* 19 (February issue): 5–17.

Hohn, Joyce, and Duston, Virginia. 1974. "Bilingualism and Individualized Parent Education: An Organic Approach to Early Childhood Education," *California Journal of Educational Research* 25 (November issue): 253–60.

Howe, Harold II. 1969. "Cowboys, Indians, and American Education." In *National Conference on Educational Opportunities for Mexican Americans. Proceedings.* Austin, Texas: Southwest Educational Development Laboratory. April 25–26, 1968: 9–18.

Johnson, Henry S., and Hernández-M., William J., eds. 1970. *Educating the Mexican American.* Valley Forge, Pa.: Judson Press.

Mazón, Manuel Reyes, ed. 1972. *Adelante: An Emerging Design for Mexican American Education.* Center for Communication Research, University of Texas, Austin.

Mexican American Education Project. Final Report. 1974. California State University, Sacramento.

Orozco, Cecilio. A letter to David Ballesteros. September 2, 1975.

Ramírez, Manuel III. 1970. "Cultural Democracy: A New Philosophy for Educating the Mexican American Child." *The National Elementary Principal* 50 (November issue): 45–46.

Ríos, Francisco A. 1969. "The Mexican in Fact, Fiction, and Folklore." *El Grito* 2 (Summer 1969): 14–28.

Rosenthal, Robert, and Jacobsen, Lenore. 1968. *Pygmalio in the Classroom: Teacher Expectation and Pupil's Intellectual Development*. New York: Holt, Rinehart, and Winston.

Sánchez, George I. 1966. "History, Culture, and Education." In *La Raza: Forgotten Americans (Papers in Memory of Charles de Young Elkus)*. South Bend, Ind.: University of Notre Dame Press.

*Teacher Corps Proposal, Cycle VII*. 1971. University of Texas, Austin. November 1971.

Ulibarri, Mari-Luci. 1972. "Toward a Philosophy of Education for the Chicanos: Bilingualism and Intellectual Development." *Adelante: An Emerging Design for Mexican American Education*. Teacher Corps Assistance Project, Center for Communication Research: University of Texas, Austin, pp. 1–33.

Urista, Alberto Baltazar [Alurista]. 1968. "The Poetry of Alurista." *El Grito* 2 (Fall issue): 5–12.

U.S. Commission on Civil Rights Clearinghouse Publication. 1975. *A Better Chance to Learn: Bilingual/Bicultural Education*, no. 51 (May 1975). Washington, D.C.: Government Printing Office.

U.S. Commission on Civil Rights. 1973. *Teachers and Students: Differences in Teacher Interaction with Mexican American and Anglo Students*. Mexican American Education Study Report, no. 5 (March 1973). Washington, D.C.: Government Printing Office.

U.S. Commission on Civil Rights. 1974. *Toward Quality Education for Mexican Americans*. Mexican American Education Study Report, no. 6. (February 1974). Washington, D.C.: Government Printing Office.

U.S. Commission on Civil Rights. 1971. *The Unfinished Education: Outcomes for Minorities in the Five Southwestern States*. Mexican American Educational Series Report, no. 2. (October 1971). Washington, D.C.: Government Printing Office.

# OF BOOKS AND LIBRARIES

*Arnulfo D. Trejo*

LIBRARIES HAVE PLAYED a major part in my life. Ever since my junior high school days, it seems that I have either been using libraries or teaching others how to use them. Unfortunately, books and libraries are of little importance to most of my people. I made this discovery early in my career. After I received my master's degree in Library Science, I visited my family in Tucson, where I grew up. Much of my two weeks was spent visiting relatives and friends. As I recall, they always wanted to know where I had been and what I had been doing. I would mention that I had been away studying; some of them showed slightly more interest than others, but invariably if I told them that I had been doing graduate work, the conversation changed to another topic. None of my friends knew that graduate studies were required to become a librarian, while some admitted they did not know that such a profession even existed. It easily follows, therefore, that books and libraries have not been part of the lives of most of my people. One experience I had points this out particularly well.

A couple of days before leaving Tucson, I had called on Don Ramón, a close friend of my family who lived in my barrio. We talked mostly about Mexico, since that had always been his favorite topic of conversation. I still remember how I enjoyed listening to my father and Don Ramón tell stories about their "good old days" in their homeland. In our talk we somehow drifted to the topic of education. I had discovered that the one criticism which he did not mind hearing against Mexico was its lack of adequate schooling for the poor. As an inquisitive, budding librarian I innocently started to ask about the books he read and if he used the nearby library. Before I could finish my question, he cut me short by saying: *"A mí no me hables de libros ni de bibliotecas, porque de eso no sé ni papa. Esas cosas son para la gente de bien."* (Don't talk to me about books and libraries, because I know nothing of that. Those things are for people who are well-to-do.) Then he went on to tell me that he could barely read and write. Ever since that time, I have been aware of the insignificant role which books and libraries have played in the lives of *La Raza*.

One of my early disappointments was to discover how poorly we were represented in library collections. The disappointment was heightened further when I found that almost everything available was written by authors who were not of my own cultural background. As a student I must have noticed how few books by and about Mexican Americans there were, but probably attributed this lack to my own inability to use the library satisfactorily. As the years went by, however, and I gained experience as a librarian and visited the more important libraries in this country and in Latin America, I finally had to acknowledge that there was very little written about my people, and what little was available had rarely been written by Mexican Americans. Increased reading, travel, observation, and years of experience convinced me that this lack of literature on *La Raza* had many facets and that its roots reached far into the past. Interestingly, what is true for Mexican Americans is also true for many of the people in Spanish America. Since education and books go hand-in-hand, my working experience in those countries revealed to me how frequently schooling, particularly beyond the elementary level, is a privilege reserved for the upper classes. In these countries, reading and writing are done by the educated, and since so few people are educated, it is understandable that books are few in number when compared with those of countries which have a written tradition and a high literacy rate such as France, Germany, Great Britain, Japan, and the United States.

Too frequently what is written about Mexican Americans has been authored by Anglos, whose works, well-intentioned though they may have been, contain distortions, inaccuracies and biases, at least in part, because they wrote as outsiders. With few notable exceptions, they failed to capture the real essence of the Mexican Americans. It is difficult to pinpoint the exact origin of the problem, but history tells us that the early American colonists who settled on the Atlantic seaboard brought with them memories, prejudices and pre-conceived ideas which to a degree had motivated their exodus. For instance, the sailing of the Spanish Armada to England was within the memory of the first colonists. Further, their philosophical and religious beliefs and opinions coupled with their hatred for their powerful rival—Catholic Spain—created among the first Anglo-Americans an insular nationalism. They had suffered persecution in their homeland and were determined to avoid it in the New World. Being far removed from Europe, America offered them freedoms and opportunities which they had not previously enjoyed. Jealously they guarded what they had gained. Thus the English colonists militated against all peoples who were not of their heritage. When these new Americans and their descendants later voiced the idea that all men are created equal and endowed with certain inalienable rights—life, liberty and the pursuit of happiness—they were thinking of people like themselves.

Much later when the Anglo frontiersmen invaded the Southwest, they were unable to accept on an equal basis the settlers of Hispanic American heritage, or anyone else who did not fit their mold. Historical records indicate that the vast majority of the Anglos who settled in Texas were from the South (Lowrie 1967, p. 32). The prejudices they held against blacks were transferred to the peoples of different cultures whom they met and later conquered. Thus Anglos did not bring with them to the Spanish-Mexican borderland social attitudes conducive to creating an integrated society where all men would have equal rights and opportunities to improve their social and economic status. There were, of course, exceptions when Anglo men married into the Spanish-Mexican families of the Southwest. But generally, Anglos nurtured their racial superiority as a means of self-preservation and justified their insatiable land-grabbing drive by proclaiming that Manifest Destiny gave them the right to extend the boundaries of the United States, legally or otherwise, as far as possible and furthermore to impose their way of life.

Power, acquired by annexation of vast areas of land—sometimes at the cost of shameful wars—made it possible for the Anglo frontiersmen to establish settlements with legal and social institutions based on their own traditions. As these settlements grew, separate and unequal worlds developed within them. The Protestant tradition ascended into dominance, as did the English language, customs and dress. The dominant values were now those of the competitive Anglo-American. Cecil Robinson has a chapter in his book, *Mexico and the Hispanic Southwest in American Literature*, entitled "Mexican Traits—An Early Portrait" which documents the fact that

nineteenth century Anglos who wrote about the Southwest generally
found little to admire in the people they called "Messicans," unless it
was their women or their horsemanship. Consequently, the Mexican
was, more often than not, unrealistically portrayed.

Beginning with Timothy Flint's 1826 novel, *Francis Berrian: Or
the Mexican Patriot*, Anglo writers found much to criticize in the
Mexican whom they portrayed in a manner which has contributed
much to the negative image which some people have of us today.
Evidence shows that early Anglo authors had a very superficial knowledge of the Mexican people who became the subject of their writings.
Easterners, however, were interested in reading about "Mexicans" in
the wild west, not realizing or admitting that after 1848 those "Mexicans" were Americans. Writers exploited this market. Since some
writers had never been to the Southwest or had never seen a Mexican
American they created caricatures to accommodate the imagination
and expectations of their prospective readers. Mexicans and Mexican
Americans were stereotyped in the dime novels of the last century as
dull, dirty, and liable to steal anything not nailed down. Men, in
particular, were labeled as lazy, cowardly, treacherous, and cruel to
animals. In his short story, "The Water-Witch," George Emery gives
an indication of the Anglo's racism and contempt for Mexicans. A
character in the story is described as "a ragged, dirty Mexican, whose
matted hair was a model of cactus-fence, whose tattered blanket served
to make more evident his nakedness, an unmistakable, unredeemed
'greaser' " (Emery 1971, p. 36).

Although women were usually seen with kinder eyes—probably
because the writers were mostly men—they did not escape reproach.
In *Wolf Song*, a novel by Harvey Fergusson, one of the characters
warns a friend of the danger in taking a "Mexican" girl too seriously.
He says, "Them women breeds like prairie dogs an' jest as careless.
They look good when they're young but after they've calved a time or
two they swell up like a cow in a truck patch an' you need a wagon to
move 'em" (Fergusson 1927, p. 102).

Those writers who did not degrade the Mexican American romanticized him. Bret Harte, for example, in his short story, "The Devotion of Enriquez," portrays the "Spanish" character as a happy-go-
lucky caballero who sings, dances, and is a master horseman, as well
as an expert in winning the love of the señoritas (Harte 1971, pp.
48–71).

More contemporary authors such as William Saroyan, Paul Horgan, and John Steinbeck continue the stereotyping. Steinbeck in *Tortilla Flat* characterizes the Mexican American as shiftless, dull-minded and dirty. Yet, more recently there is a noticeable trend away from degrading Mexican Americans. Ray Bradbury in his short story, "The Wonderful Ice Cream Suit," fails to give a realistic portrayal of the Mexican American people, but he does not denigrate them. His characters are comic figures who have Spanish surnames, but nothing else to portray them as Mexican Americans. The characters in this particular story could easily be substituted by individuals of any other ethnic group.

Non-fiction writers also stereotyped and romanticized the Mexican American. For example, Charles Lummis fell in love with the *Hispanos* of New Mexico, and praised them as different and fascinating. Another writer, J. Frank Dobie, the Texas folklorist, saw the "Mexican" with kind eyes and wrote about him with sensitivity and understanding. Yet, even the keen and sympathetic eyes of these writers did not distinguish the difference between the "Mexican" and the "Mexican American."

Were it not for Anglo writers, in some instances, there would be no written records to document various episodes in the life of the Mexican American. Within the Mexican American community of the Southwest there were very few writers and fewer who concentrated on the traditions, customs, songs, and legends of Mexican Americans. Carlos E. Castañeda, a noted historian of Texas; George I. Sánchez, a pioneer in bilingual education; and Aurelio M. Espinosa, a New Mexico philologist and folklorist, were among the few who gained recognition as scholars in this period. These writers, however, usually wrote for the academic world and not for the common people. Nonetheless, their ancestry served them well in identifying and researching topics which had a direct relationship to their own culture. Castañeda in his multi-volume work *Our Catholic Heritage in Texas* effectively interwove the history of Texas and the role played by the Hispanic Catholic Church in the state's development and growth. Sánchez's writing in the 1930s indicted the public schools for failing to be responsive to the cultural background of the Mexican American child. Espinosa's *Estudios sobre el español de Nuevo Mejico* provided specialists with the most comprehensive and in-depth study of the Spanish spoken in New Mexico. He proved that New Mexican Spanish is basically the same as the Castilian Spanish spoken in the sixteenth century. He also became one of the best folklorists, having compiled the largest and one of the most important collections of ballads gathered in New Mexico.

Two other prominent writers in the field of folklore, Arthur L. Campa and Juan B. Rael, also made significant contributions. Through their rich collections of tales, songs, legends, and religious folk plays, they have left a unique legacy which provides useful insights into the Mexican American's heritage. Since their works were primarily scholarly in nature they did not filter down to the general public and thus had little impact on changing the attitudes of either Anglos or Mexican Americans.

Regrettably, books are not a major part of either Spanish or Indian heritage. For the Mexican American, the spoken language has been the primary means of transmitting from one generation to another information which is considered significant and/or unusual. This tradition continues today. Corridos—a musical narrative dating from the romance of medieval Spain—capture and perpetuate singular events in the life of the people. Although traditionally a form used by folk people, today some are written by well-educated individuals. Along with proverbs, and folktales, they have served to transmit religious doctrines, morals, superstitions, beliefs, and legends. The spoken language, however, has definite limitations. One of its major drawbacks is that with each transfer of information, facts may be left out and/or details added, deleted or changed to suit the occasion.

To explain why the spoken word has been given preference over books, let us recall that when the conquistadores arrived in the New World, they came armed with the cross and the sword and only rarely with books. In sixteenth-century Spain from whence they came, reading materials were reserved for the privileged classes. The books that did find their way to New Spain usually fell into the hands of the clergy and the few learned men of the upper social classes. Many of the religious orders brought from Europe books on theology, history, philology, and law as well as some of the classics. Many of these books became the nuclei of libraries which were established in seminaries and churches. What is today the Biblioteca Palafoxiana in Puebla, Mexico, for example, started with 6,000 volumes donated by the Mexican prelate, Juan de Palafox y Mendoza, to a seminary, the Colegio de San Pedro y San Pablo which he founded in 1646 (Thompson 1970, p. 8).

The new consciousness of man's power and dignity which emerged during the Renaissance and Reformation in northern and western Europe had little effect on Spain or her colonies, where Catholicism thrived as a totalitarian and state religion. Furthermore, in the Spanish society of the sixteenth and seventeenth centuries, there was no concern for the common man except as a source of wealth for the Church and the privileged class. To assure that people in the colonized New World remained subservient to their European rulers, laws were passed and enforced to prevent the unauthorized publication and distribution of printed works. Only books approved by the King through the Council of the Indies were permitted and these were mostly of a religious nature (Toribio Medina 1958, vol. 1, p. 6). But regardless of these restrictions, some prohibited reading materials did manage to find their way to New Spain. A case in point is the library of Pedro de Mendoza which contained the works of Erasmus (Thompson 1970, p. 12). In spite of restrictive measures, by the 1800s the liberal ideas of Diderot, Montesquieu, Rousseau, Voltaire, and other writers were known in Mexico and other Latin American countries. As liberal ideas began to take hold, and a trend toward democratic government began to develop, the privilege of formal education in Mexico nevertheless still continued to be reserved for the wealthy classes with the masses remaining largely illiterate.

Our Indian heritage also encompassed a caste system in which education for the most part was the right of a privileged class. Glyphs were used by the learned men to record, preserve, and impart knowledge. The Olmecs' form of writing has been traced to at least 600 B.C. (León-Portilla 1969, p. 9). Later picture writing was greatly advanced during the Mesoamerican Classic and Post Classic periods by the Mayan, Mixtec, Zapotec and Aztec peoples. Picture writing culminated in some beautifully decorated Nahuatl codices or painted "books" like those belonging to the so-called "Borgia group" which are today in the custody of such European institutions as the Vatican Library and the University of Bologna.

Invaluable as picture writing has proven itself to be in recording and preserving information about the pre-Columbian peoples of Mexico, this form of writing had its limitations. With only the bare beginnings of phonetic writing, it was not possible to structure words with which to express abstract thoughts and ideas (León-Portilla 1969, pp.12–13). The picture books of the time, then, could not record detailed knowledge in depth and their use was limited to only a few of the privileged class. To gain information, the individual relied primarily on memory and the oral tradition to perpetuate knowledge accumulated over the years. Even in centers of higher learning, students were taught to learn by rote. The oral tradition became even more important after the conquest when the use of glyphs eventually died out. A few Indians became literate in Spanish and wrote books, but their writing did not reach the masses. Thus the people who came from Mexico into the Spanish borderlands brought with them the oral traditions of two cultures—the Hispanic and the Indian. It was natural that the oral tradition should continue to thrive in the semi-feudal agricultural economy which prevailed in the Spanish-Mexican borderlands. Reading and writing played an insignificant role among most of the people in this region, for the *patrón* needed working hands more than thinking minds. George I. Sánchez describes the frontier situation in this manner: "...There was little need for formal education. The priests and parents drilled children in church doctrine. Sometimes the local scribe or priest was employed by a family or two to give instruction in reading, writing, and counting to the children for a few weeks a year. Literacy was the exception rather than the rule. There was little to read, only an occasional agreement to sign, communications were by word of mouth and letters were rare" (Sánchez 1940, p. 8).

Later migrants to the United States were, for the most part, from the agricultural laboring class. As such, most of them had enjoyed limited social and economic advantages in Mexico. Functionally illiterate and equipped with few skills needed in a rapidly changing industrial society, they arrived to become members of the growing labor force who were psychologically pre-conditioned to assume subservient roles in this country (Gamio 1969, pp. 71–72). Further, many of the new immigrants left Mexico around the time of the 1910 revolution when Mexican nationalism was only beginning to develop. Lacking a sense of pride in his indigenous heritage, the emigré's self-image as a politically voiceless member of Mexico's Indian or mestizo working class was magnified many times in America. The immigrant was at a disadvantage when competing in the aggressive Anglo society whose institutions were geared for producing a monolingual, monocultural society. For the uneducated Mexican immigrant, these institutions were seen as cultural centers for the *Americanos*, but not for him. The children of the Mexican immigrant did go to school but found the curricula designed for the Anglo middle-class child and teachers insensitive to the Mexican way of life. The result is that even today at least forty percent of the Mexican American children who start elementary school fail to finish high school. By contrast, the Anglo dropout rate is only ten percent (U.S. Commission on Civil Rights, 1974, p.1).

The new immigrants made little use of libraries or museums either because they were unaware of their existence or because they had no meaning for them. The environment, organization, and personnel of these institutions exaggerated the foreignness of the immigrant user and made him feel uncomfortable. The Spanish language of the immigrant also inhibited his use of these cultural facilities. Indeed, the precedent for public libraries to serve primarily patrons of middle class background can be traced to the founding of the Boston Public Library in 1848, when it set forth its philosophy that libraries were for the educated (Lee 1966, p. 7). Present-day public libraries are still influenced by such concepts. If we consider the socio-economic background of Mexican Americans and couple this with the philosophies of Anglo educational institutions which have ignored our needs, it is understandable why the world of books as well as libraries and museums are irrelevant to our people.

It is no secret that children imitate their parents. If parents are readers and library users, the practice will be passed on to their children. Having books and magazines available in the home greatly reinforces the child's reading behavior. Educators have found that generally when a child does well in school he or she was introduced to books at a very early age. The introduction of books and writing into the child's way of life is usually informal. The mother or father or both will read to the child and encourage him to read and write. By the time the child is ready for school, books are no strangers to him. The importance of the printed word as a means of receiving and transmitting information is further strengthened in school. One of the first things that happens to the child as he starts his learning processes is to have paper and pencil placed before him. As he masters his reading and writing skills, he is also taught the use of the library. In other words, for a person to acquire the habit of using libraries, certain attitudes must have been developed at home during the pre-school years or at least in the early grades. Too often Chicano children, particularly those from poor families, enter school greatly handicapped by the strangeness of the new surroundings which have little or no resemblance to his past experiences. Not only is the child taught in a foreign language, but in some cases is made to feel that his native tongue is inferior.

School libraries have done little to improve the plight of the Chicano student. As with teachers, librarians too often do not speak Spanish and are not sensitive to the Chicano's way of life. I do not mean to imply that the situation is any better in academic or public libraries, for it is not; however, I feel that school libraries should bear the brunt of the criticism, for they have contact with the child during his formative years. School libraries—as part of the educational system—function under the social and philosophical values of the Anglo society. As a result, they have not met the needs of Chicanos. This is most evident when the organization, staff, collection, and services of the library in the barrio schools are identical to the libraries of predominantly Anglo schools.

What I would like to see is a conversion of the barrio school library into a community-oriented one. Libraries need to take advantage of the traditional custom of family unity among Mexican Americans. Yet school libraries are operating under Anglo practices which tend to separate children from their parents. Customarily, the Mexican American family participates together when events or activities are considered important.

For school libraries which operate in the barrios I would advocate a policy statement along these lines:

> The policy of this school library will be to complement and supplement the classroom instruction as well as to enrich and enhance the cultural heritage of students and their families. Since the ethnic composition of this school is largely Mexican American, the services, as well as the print and non-print materials, will be oriented to meet the needs of this group. However, this library will build concurrently a collection of print and non-print materials reflecting the pluralistic society of our country with special emphasis on the ethnic groups of the Southwest. As we acknowledge that the family plays an important role in the lifestyle of Chicanos, the school library will offer services to students

and their families. Whenever possible, the school library will make every effort to secure from its own sources or nearby sources, information requested by teachers, students, and families of students.

The school libraries that I envision, however, would not function in isolation, but rather would work as an integral part of a community information network, the central point of which would be the public library. And speaking of the public libraries, I am not thinking of the traditional ones which have geared the delivery of services and information to a relatively small number of middle-class patrons. In these libraries the patrons' needs are defined in accordance with the organization of the library, rather than in accordance with the needs, interests, and preferences of its patrons. Robert Haro, an experienced library administrator, conducted a survey of Mexican Americans in California to learn their views of libraries. He determined that "while most disadvantaged Mexican Americans generally perceive libraries indifferently and seldom frequent them, those who do, especially the young, harbor an uneasiness and a resentment toward them" (Haro 1970a, p. 738). He further explains that Mexican Americans do not use libraries because they lack an understanding of how these institutions function (Haro 1970b, p. 32). If Mexican Americans are unfamiliar with the organization and purposes of public libraries, it is understandable that their attitude will be one of indifference. If they do have an opportunity to use the library, it is doubtful that they will find it relevant to their needs, much less feel comfortable in the institutional-like formality of these libraries which are alien to their way of life. Further, since these libraries are usually staffed by librarians who neither speak Spanish nor are knowledgeable about the Mexican American historical and cultural background, it is not likely that Chicanos will be drawn to them.

These shortcomings have hindered communication between librarians and Mexican Americans. Haro confirms that the language factor is the greatest barrier to communication. He found "that eighty-nine per cent of those interviewed stated they would utilize their neighborhood libraries if Spanish were spoken and Hispanic themes were available" (Haro 1970b, pp. 31–32). Appreciation and recognition of the Spanish language is a means of showing respect and understanding for the individuals who speak it. Mexican Americans who are bilingual have an advantage over monolingual persons and should be made to feel that being bilingual is an asset.

It becomes obvious then that public libraries as we know them today will have to undergo drastic changes if they are to serve Mexican Americans effectively and responsively. Perhaps the initial starting point would be a commitment on the part of librarians to recognize libraries as existing to provide service and information to all members of the community. Libraries are intended to be service-oriented institutions, but unless they are responsive to the informational needs, interests and preferences of their many publics, they will not fulfill their goals.

Responsive librarians, since the mid-1970s in particular, have added a new dimension to public library service by incorporating neighborhood information centers or information referral services into their libraries or by establishing these information agencies as an extension of the library system. The I & R's, or whatever name is given to them, differ from the traditional libraries in that the collection and use of print and non-print materials is not their primary concern. Their major purpose is to acquire information from whatever sources are available, to analyze this information, and to give it to their clientele quickly and directly (Donohue p. 3284). As these information centers have already proven successful in fulfilling the informational needs of non-book oriented persons in public libraries in Atlanta, Cleveland, Detroit, Houston, and New York (Queens), it is appropriate to discuss these nonconventional information sources, as they could be adapted to meet the informational needs of the Chicanos ("Neighborhood" 1975, p. 699). Such centers have neglected the Mexican American population, not intentionally, perhaps, but because like so many libraries and other service agencies, they lack the trained staff and the techniques to market their services and programs in the Mexican American community. The function that these I & R's are performing is vital. They provide information on topics varying from health to family planning and from education and employment to welfare.

These centers could function as a bridge between the people of the barrio and the public library. The unifying bonds would be established and developed by a select staff of bilingual-bicultural information specialists who would also be advocates for their patrons. The primary purpose of the centers would be to deliver information in either

English or Spanish to those people, many of whom in the past have not received needed information because of ignorance, poverty, and prejudice. With the bridge established by information centers, eventually their users would be guided to the public library.

For these new patrons, however, to continue making use of the public library, its librarians ideally should be knowledgeable about the cultural background of the Mexican Americans and be able to speak Spanish, but even if librarians lack these special qualifications, their willingness to help is the most powerful asset that the staff can possess.

Isidro Ramón Macias writes: "As an educational vehicle, libraries are almost non-functional in our Chicano communities. At best, the barrio is served by a branch library which is almost always poorly stocked in books, magazines, and reference materials...." (Macias 1970, p. 735). In this particular case, what appears to a Chicano to be a poorly stocked library could well be judged as a perfectly sound collection by a middle-class Anglo. After all, the collection, in all probability, was selected according to criteria that met the established standards of the dominant society. These standards, in turn, were set up to follow traditional library policies. To me, therein lies the problem. The guiding policies of American public libraries which were established more than a century ago direct libraries to become institutions "to which the young people of both sexes, when they leave schools, can resort for those works which are needful for research into any branch of useful knowledge" (Lee 1966, p. 8). This explains why public library collections are generally made up of scholarly books.

Ann Allen Shockley remembers that in 1959 "most libraries were still placid places to borrow books, read, study, meet people, and do research on usually pedantic subjects while being guided by bland librarians" (Josey 1970, p. 226). Only as recently as the late 1960s did a few libraries in the Southwest venture to purchase the paperback Spanish novelettes. By this time more librarians had come to realize that the public library could also be a source of entertainment for Spanish-speaking people. The book collections they started to build were supplemented with various kinds of print and non-print materials which were selected not solely on the merit of erudition, but on their expression of insights and the enjoyment they could offer the patron as well. If in the past public libraries have been relevant mainly to Anglo, middle-class people, there now are indications that efforts are being made to serve a greater representation of groups in the community.

Yet school and public libraries have not been the only ones to neglect the needs of Mexican Americans. Academic libraries have also fallen short in this respect. In the 1960s when militant students rioted in universities, a Black wrote: "The reason the students didn't burn libraries is that they didn't know the libraries were there" (Cloud 1969, p. 787). A Chicano could have said the same. Some undergraduate students have boasted to me about how they were getting through college by never having to use the library except for the reserve book room. The most striking evidence of the insignificance of libraries to Mexican Americans came when the first Chicano Studies programs and curricula were established and the role of the library was ignored or relegated to an afterthought. Even if this had not been the case, few librarians would have been ready to meet the challenge of a Chicano Studies program. Too often when ethnic studies became a part of college and university curricula, librarians were caught rehashing the cataloging code and planning libraries for the year 2001, but doing little or nothing to meet the demands of today. If there were monies to employ professionals with a foreign language background, those most frequently hired knew French and German. Spanish-speaking librarians were given low priority. In an unpublished survey which I conducted in May 1973, among eleven universities in the Southwest, including California, it was found that two of these libraries had a Spanish-speaking professional librarian in acquisitions; and another had two Spanish-speaking professional librarians in reference. It should be noted, however, that four other libraries had Spanish-speaking professional librarians who worked part-time in either reference or acquisitions. From observation, I know that most of those universities which listed Spanish-speaking librarians first employed them during the 1960s.

At the height of the Chicano Movement no university located in the Southwest had a Spanish-speaking professional on the library staff who could establish a dialogue with students who were asking for Chicano Studies programs. There were at least two reasons for this. First, there had been no concerted effort to recruit Chicanos into the library profession, and second, librarianship as a career has had little appeal for Mexican Americans. Chicano students have a negative image of librarianship and many male students think it feminine. Those Chicanos who enter college with a good scholastic record already have plans to study medicine, law, engineering, business, or education. Librarianship is not even considered because Chicanos generally do not know of existing opportunities in this field. Some students have admitted to me that they did not realize that it took a graduate degree to become a librarian. Librarianship for both men and women just does not have the attraction or the status which they associate with other professions. This further illustrates how alienated Mexican Americans are from libraries.

But, if Mexican American students find themselves disaffected by their college or university libraries, the sources of the problem lie in the reasons which previously have been identified. Deficiencies of earlier school years take their toll during college. These students were not book-oriented at home, and school libraries, in turn, did little to encourage or help them sharpen their library skills. Librarians, like so many teachers, have continued to operate on the premise that their patrons, regardless of their background, are equipped with the knowledge needed to take advantage of the educational and cultural facilities available. The fact is that Mexican American students have lived in a world closed off from books and libraries. These students see libraries as institutions of the dominant society to which they do not relate.

Academic libraries in the last few years have been challenged by Chicano students who are now becoming aware of the importance that libraries can play in their lives. As a result, they have approached the university and college administrations to ask for and, in some cases, to demand change. A few universities and colleges have anticipated these demands and responded to them. There are, of course, exceptions. Some librarians always do their homework quietly and well. For example, the student problems of the 1960s were skillfully anticipated at the library of California State University at San Francisco. Barbara Anderson, a librarian there, said: "Months in advance (i.e., as much as six months to a year before any of the demonstrations) we were taking note of the movements toward Black Studies and Ethnic Studies. As responsive librarians, we naturally set about ordering the important books and periodicals in these fields" (Anderson 1970, p. 1276). In other cases, student and faculty pressures have been successful in changing the traditional roles of libraries.

Academic libraries can become the right arm of ethnic studies, but only if librarians commit themselves to these programs. To alleviate at least a portion of the problem at university and college libraries, it will be necessary to permit the establishment of a separate library, apart from the main library, to support Chicano Studies programs. Where lack of funds does not permit the organization of a separate library, at least a section in the established library could be designated as the Chicano Studies area. If students learn how to use a smaller library and feel comfortable in its setting, it is very likely that they will make their way to the more complex libraries as they advance in their academic studies.

In the survey already mentioned, one library estimated its book holdings as high as 3,900. Not all libraries provided such a high estimate; nonetheless, every library gave evidence of having a substantial number of books as well as non-published materials such as theses, dissertations, manuscripts, and microfilms. The problem then is not a lack of material, but being able to locate them and knowing how to use them. With few exceptions, the reporting libraries indicated that their Mexican American collections were dispersed. This suggests the need not only to have Chicano materials brought together to facilitate their use, but the employment of a specialist who will identify with Chicano students.

In reviewing the multi-faceted problems Mexican Americans have had with libraries, it becomes evident that solutions will not be simple. Pressed for an answer, however, I would point to library schools as a starting point to attack the problem. After all, libraries are the products of librarians, and librarians, in turn, are the products of library schools. The library school curricula that have developed over the years continue to prepare librarians for the conventional library; it fails to acknowledge that our society is in a constant state of change. If previously librarians were content to be guardians of books and serve only those of the privileged classes, librarians today are faced with different types of needs and demands from new library users whose numbers are progressively increasing as they become aware of the importance of libraries as a source of information. If those needs and demands are going to be met effectively, we must have librarians trained to see members of ethnic minorities as members of the public to be served in addition to the Anglo, middle-class library user. Certainly, librarians who will serve the Chicano population should make a special effort to learn about the history, customs, values, and traditions which are a part of Chicano heritage. Ideally, these librarians should be bilingual and bicultural. Equally important, they should be equipped with the skills and attitudes to enable them to function without the restraints which are the product of racial prejudice and ignorance. Moreover, they should be imbued with a new philosophy which teaches that librarians are dispensers of information and as such they have a responsibility to all people regardless of economic status or heritage. Library service should extend beyond the walls of the library building, utilizing whatever print or non-print materials meet the needs of the patrons. This will involve identifying with the people of the barrios.

Library schools will also need to develop and implement well-organized recruitment programs to attract top-calibre Mexican American students. The few Chicanos already in the profession have charged, in the last few years, that librarianship is one of the most racist professions in the country. A recently published American Library Association survey of library graduates in 1973–74 (*Survey 1973-1974*, p. 5), lends credence to this view. Given all the minorities in the United States, the Spanish-speaking and the American Indian are proportionately the fewest among those being recruited into librarianship. The study of ethnic groups further shows that of the 7,221 persons who received master's degrees in library science in 1973–74, only 99 were Spanish-surnamed (*Survey* 1973–1974, p. 9). The critical shortage of Spanish-speaking librarians is even more evident when one considers their number in the Southwest in relation to the Spanish-speaking population. In compiling a who's who of Spanish-heritage librarians in the United States, my findings show that California, with a Spanish-origin population of 2,639,000, has 50 Spanish-heritage librarians; Texas, whose Spanish-origin population is 1,841,000, has only 23 Spanish-heritage librarians; New Mexico, with a Spanish-origin population of 308,000, has only 4; Arizona has 10 Spanish-heritage librarians for a population of 265,000 Spanish-origin people; and Colorado has 6 Spanish-heritage librarians for a Spanish-origin population of 226,000 (Trejo 1976, p. vi). Considering that there are at least 115,000 librarians listed in the 1975 American Library Association directory (Miele and Prakken 1975, p. 285), the Spanish-speaking population is greatly underrepresented. With so few Spanish-heritage librarians, it is easy to understand why libraries have not been able to serve the Mexican American community satisfactorily.

The task confronted by librarians is big in all dimensions. There is need for understanding and interaction among the Mexican American community, students, teachers, librarians, and administrators as well as between minorities and majorities. No individual group can resolve the complex human problems involved. Library service for Mexican Americans is in the embryonic stage. A unique potential exists. The alert, willing, and foresighted librarian should and will accept the challenge. Knowledge is power. Power in the hands of the informed with a commitment to improve conditions in our society points to a brighter future. Information is the right of everyone and we as librarians need to be committed to respond to the social, economic, and intellectual needs of all people.

## Bibliography

Anderson, Barbara Elaine. 1970. "Ordeal at San Francisco State College; a librarian who went through the violent days of the student uprisings of 1968 weighs the questions it posed librarians." *Library Journal* (April 1 issue): 1275–80.

Bradbury, Ray. 1971. "The Wonderful Ice Cream Suit." In *The Chicano: From Caricature to Self-Portrait*. Edited by Edward Simmen. New York: New American Library.

Cabello-Argandoña, Roberto. 1976. "Recruiting Spanish-speaking Library Students," *Library Journal* 101 (May 15 issue): 1177–79.

Castañeda, Carlos E. 1936–1958. *Our Catholic Heritage in Texas, 1519–1936*. Supplement 1936–1950. 7 vols. Prepared under the auspices of the Knights of Columbus of Texas. Austin: Von Boechmann-Jones Co.

Cloud, John M. 1969. "Why Didn't They Burn the Libraries?" *Wilson Library Bulletin* 49 (April issue): 787–812.

Donohue, Joseph C. 1972. "Planning for the Community Information Center." *Library Journal* 97 (October 15 issue): 3284–88.

Emery, George. 1971. "The Water Witch." In *The Chicano: From Caricature to Self-Portrait*. Edited by Edward Simmen. New York: New American Library.

Espinosa, Aurelio M. 1930 and 1946. *Estudios sobre el español de Nuevo Méjico: Parte I. Fonética.* (Biblioteca de dialectología hispanoamericana, tomo I.) Buenos Aires: Instituto de Filología, Facultad de Filosofía y Letras de la Universidad de Buenos Aires. *Parte II. Morfología.*

Fergusson, Harvey. *Wolf Song.* 1927. New York: A. A. Knopf.

Gamio, Manuel. 1969. *The Mexican Immigrant.* New York: Arno Press and the New York Times.

Haro, Robert P. 1970a. "One-Man Survey: How Mexican Americans View Libraries." *Wilson Library Bulletin* 44 (March issue): 736–42.

————.1970b. "Library·Service to Mexican Americans." *El Grito* 3 (Spring issue): 30–37.

Harte, Bret. 1971. "The Devotion of Enríquez." In *The Chicano: From Caricature to Self-Portrait.* Edited by Edward Simmen. New York: New American Library.

Josey, E.J., ed. 1970. *The Black Librarian in America.* Metuchen, N.J.: The Scarecrow Press, Inc.

Lee, Robert Ellis. 1966. *Continuing Education for Adults Through the American Public Library, 1833–1964.* Chicago: American Library Association.

León-Portilla, Miguel. 1969. *Pre-Columbian Literatures of Mexico.* Trans. by Grace Lobanov. Norman: University of Oklahoma Press.

Lowrie, Samuel Harman. 1967. *Culture Conflict in Texas, 1821–1835.* New York: AMS Press.

Macias, Ysidro Ramón. 1970. "The Chicano Movement." *Wilson Library Bulletin* 44 (March issue): 731–35.

Miele, Madeline, and Prakken, Sarah, eds. 1975. *The Bowker Annual of Library and Book Trade Information.* 20th ed. New York: R.R. Bowker, Co.

"Neighborhood Information Centers: Update on an Experiment." 1975. *Wilson Library Bulletin* (June issue): 699–701.

Robinson, Cecil. 1977. *Mexico and the Hispanic Southwest in American Literature.* Tucson: University of Arizona Press.

Sánchez, George I. 1940. *Forgotten People: A Study of New Mexicans.* Albuquerque: University of New Mexico Press.

Simmen, Edward, ed. 1971. *The Chicano: From Caricature to Self-Portrait.* Introduction by editor. New York: New American Library.

Steinbeck, John. 1935. *Tortilla Flat.* New York: Covici, Friede.

*Survey of Graduates and Faculty of U.S. Library Education Programs Awarding Degrees and Certificates, 1973–1974.* Chicago: American Library Association, Office for Library Personnel Resources.

Thompson, Lawrence S. 1970. *Essays in Hispanic Bibliography.* Hamden, Conn.: The Shoe String Press, Inc.

Toribio Medina, José. 1958. *Historia de la imprenta en los antiguos dominios españoles de América y oceania.* 2 vols. Prólogo de Guillermo Feliu Cruz. Complemento bibliográfico José Toribio Medina. Santiago de Chile: Imprenta y Litografía Universo.

Trejo, Arnulfo D., ed. 1976. *Quién es quién: A Who's Who of Spanish-Heritage Librarians in the United States.* Tucson, University of Arizona, College of Education, Bureau of School Services.

———. 1977. "Modifying Library Education for Ethnic Imperatives." *American Libraries* 8 (March issue): 150–51.

U.S. Commission on Civil Rights. 1974. *Toward Quality Education for Mexican Americans. School.* Mexican American Education Study Report, no. 6. February 1974. Washington, D.C.: Government Printing Office.

# AS WE SEE OURSELVES
# IN CHICANO LITERATURE

*Arnulfo D. Trejo*

CHICANO IMAGINATIVE LITERATURE is experiencing a renaissance as a result of the *Movimiento*. In this essay I propose to give a bird's-eye view of the principal genres—poetry, short stories, drama and novels—which make up this body of literature and which illuminate the real world of Americans of Mexican ancestry. My intent is to show how imagined experiences have been used to present insights into the nature and conditions of our existence in the American Southwest. Historically, Mexican Americans have either been stereotyped, degraded, and ridiculed in literature, largely by Anglo writers who viewed them with contempt, or have been romanticized by other Anglo writers who admired them. (See "Of Books and Libraries.") The Chicano self-portrait is long overdue.

*Todos tenemos un poco de loco y de poetas* is a Spanish saying which loosely translated means we all have a bit of madness and the makings of a poet in us. Facetiously, of course, this could explain the reason why there are more Chicano poets than short story writers, playwrights, essayists, or novelists. A serious explanation might be that the Chicano has for many years lived with his thoughts bottled up inside himself but has not expressed them in literature. Now there is an opportunity to be heard. Poetry has often been selected as the vehicle for conveying these inner feelings and thoughts because words arranged in a rhythmic pattern have a special appeal and can reach deep into the hearts and minds of everyone. Then, too, a few simple verses can air long-suppressed emotions, manifest truths, and create allegorical references to the world in which we live. Other forms of literature also can, and do, penetrate the intellect and activate our emotions, our senses, and our imaginations, but they lack the economy of expression which can be found in poetry.

Poetry has played a unique role in capturing the thoughts and feelings which have propelled and nourished the *Movimiento*. The best single poem which illustrates this point is *I Am Joaquín* by Rodolfo Gonzales of Denver, Colorado. This narrative poem is undoubtedly one of the most significant pieces of creative literature that has yet been written by a Chicano. In the introduction to this poem, Gonzales refers to "a journey back through history, a painful self-evaluation, a wandering search for my peoples and, most of all, for my own identity." He adds, "The totality of all social inequities and injustices had to come to the surface...the truth about our flaws—the villains and the heroes had to ride together—in order to draw an honest, clear conclusion of who we were, who we are, and where we are going" (Rodolfo Gonzales 1972, p. 1).

No one writer can be said to typify the Chicano. Our ethnic group is much too large and heterogenous for any one individual to be our spokesman. Nonetheless, *I Am Joaquín* serves as the unifying catalyst as it reveals truths held by Chicano people from all walks of life. It is fitting, then, that this essay should begin with a commentary on this poem which the author has called "a mirror of our greatness and our weakness."

If one is to understand Chicano literature, it is important to be acquainted with Chicano writers. Needless to say, there are but a few, and they vary from self-taught individuals to authors with doctoral degrees who express themselves fluently in both English and Spanish. The multi-faceted life of Rodolfo Gonzales embodies the wide differences which are representative of Chicano writers.

Gonzales is the son of a Mexican emigrant who worked as a farm laborer and as a coal miner in southern Colorado. At the age of ten "Corky," as he is better known, worked beside his father in the sugar beet fields. Coming from a migrant family, who of necessity followed the harvest of the crops, he went to four grade schools, three junior high schools, and two high schools. Significantly, he does not attribute his education to his schooling but to living in the barrios and working in the fields. Bitterly he recalls, "The teachers taught me how to forget Spanish, to forget my heritage, to forget who I am" (Steiner 1969, p. 380). This may explain why, unlike other Chicano poets, he makes little use of Spanish. At the age of sixteen he graduated from high school. To help pay for his high school education he worked nights in a slaughterhouse, and to get away from the slaughterhouse he became a prize fighter. At the height of his boxing career, the National Box-

ing Association had him ranked as one of the top contenders for the
World Featherweight title. In his poem he reflects on those days with
these words:

*I bleed as the vicious gloves of hunger*
  *cut my face and eyes,*
*as I fight my way from stinking barrios*
*to the glamour of the ring*
*and lights of fame*
  *or mutilated sorrow.*
                    (Rodolfo Gonzales 1972, p. 60)

In the years that followed Gonzales had a variety of jobs including
soldier, lumberjack, poet, and playwright. He also attained considerable success in the insurance business and as a politician. In 1960 he
coordinated the "Viva Kennedy" campaign in Colorado and was rewarded by being named to important posts in the anti-poverty programs designed for implementation in the Southwest. He attended
conferences and more conferences. "What resulted was a lot of brave
words, promises, motions—and no action" (Steiner, p. 382). Finally,
he became disenchanted with party politics and went back to his
people. In 1965 he founded La Cruzada Para La Justicia (Crusade for
Justice) in the barrio of downtown Denver.

The opening lines of *I Am Joaquín* are presented here to illustrate
how Gonzales treats his subject, as well as to acquaint the reader with
his style of writing:

*I am Joaquín,*
*lost in a world of confusion,*
*caught up in a whirl of a*
        *gringo society,*
*Confused by the rules,*
*Scorned by attitudes,*
*Suppressed by manipulations,*
*And destroyed by modern society.*
*My fathers*
    *have lost the economic battle*
*and won*
    *the struggle of cultural survival.*

*And now!*
  *I must choose*
        *between*
  *the paradox of*
*victory of the spirit,*
*despite physical hunger*
        *or*
  *to exist in the grasp*
*of American social neurosis,*
*sterilization of the soul*
  *and a full stomach.*

*Yes,*
*I have come a long way to nowhere,*
*unwillingly dragged by that*
    *monstrous, technical*
    *industrial giant called*
        *Progress*
*and Anglo success...*
  *I look at myself.*
  *I watch my brothers.*
  *I shed tears of sorrow.*
  *I sow seeds of hate.*
*I withdraw to the safety within the*
*circle of life—*
            MY OWN PEOPLE.
        (Rodolfo Gonzales 1972, pp. 6–12)

The name Joaquín is used symbolically to represent the Chicano in the course of history and is borrowed from the legendary folk hero, Joaquín Murrieta, who robbed and killed in California in the middle of the last century to avenge the misfortunes which befell him and his wife at the hands of unscrupulous and rapacious Anglo frontiersmen. The pronoun ''I'' is employed in a generic way and with a cosmic connotation as a means of directly involving Chicanos with characters, scenes, and events which form nearly five centuries of their history.

The opening verses show the Chicano lost in what is identified as an Anglo-American mechanized world. The Chicano finds that he must choose between keeping his own identity and remaining poor, or, if he wants to eat well, assimilating American culture. Then the Chicano epic is traced to our indigenous ancestors and continues through Indo-Hispanic times. Whereas Cuauhtémoc is praised and viewed with pride, Cortés is dismissed with a single, demeaning term—gachupin, a derogatory name given to Spaniards. Yet the poet recognizes that the Mexican mestizo is a product of both the Indian and the Spaniard. In the conquest of Mexico, the Spaniard was victorious over the Indian, but three centuries later came the War of Independence and Spain was defeated. Did this solve Mexico's problem? No! "The crown was gone, but all its parasites remained," says Gonzales (Rodolfo Gonzales, p. 30).

Another revolt followed. Now it was a civil war. The heroes were Madero, Pancho Villa, and Zapata. This was the Revolution that drove many people from Mexico onto American soil. From this point on, Gonzales concentrates on the Chicano experience. He points out that the Chicano has worked hard in the United States and bravely fought the enemies of this country in a number of foreign lands, most recently in Viet Nam.

As the Chicano looks back he finds that despite his efforts, his situation has not improved. The poet describes this plight with the following verses:

> *I stand here looking back,*
> *and now I see*
> > *the present,*
> *and still*
> > *I am the campesino.*
> > > (Rodolfo Gonzales 1972, p. 51)

Worse yet the Chicano now carries an added burden:

> *in a country that has wiped out*
> *all my history,*
> > *stifled all my pride,*
> *in a country that has placed a*
> *different weight of indignity upon*
> > *my*
> > > *age-*
> > > > *old*
> > > > > *burdened back*
> *Inferiority*
> *is the new load . . . .*
> > (Rodolfo Gonzales 1972, p. 51)

But the Chicano does not see himself defeated:

> *Here I stand,*
> *poor in money,*
> *arrogant with pride,*
> *bold with machismo,*
> *rich in courage*
> *and*
> *wealthy in spirit and faith.*

(Rodolfo Gonzales 1972, p. 64)

As the poem draws to a close, the beginning of the *Movimiento* is signaled in this manner:

> *And now the trumpet sounds,*
> *the music of the people stirs the*
> *revolution.*
> *Like a sleeping giant it slowly*
> *rears its head.*
> (Rodolfo Gonzales 1972, p. 93)

The poem ends by affirming that the Chicano will endure, and whatever the American of Mexican ancestry calls himself, Raza, Mexicano, Español, Latino, Hispano, or Chicano, he refuses to be absorbed.

*I Am Joaquín* includes the five principal elements which are the essence of poetry: thought, tone, imagery, melody, and rhythm. Nevertheless, the one single element which overshadows all others is thought. From the beginning to the end the emphasis is on the narrative. The poet has a story to tell of the struggles of the past and present-day lives of Chicanos. He utilizes the techniques best suited to put the message across. The verses are short, but packed with power, like the jabs of a skillful prize fighter. The words are carefully chosen for their meaning and tone—one of fury. Once again we see the fighter, but this time he is fighting for a cause. The images are simple. Abstract metaphors have no place in this poem, for it is designed to be read and understood by the people of the barrio. And so Gonzales succeeds rather well in explaining the identity crisis of the Chicano and calling attention to the sufferings which finally culminated in:

*Tramping feet*
*clamouring voices*
*mariachi strains*
*fiery tequila explosions*
*the smell of chile verde and*
*soft brown eyes of expectation for a*
*better life.*
(Rodolfo Gonzales 1972, p. 93)

Again, in lyric poetry "thought" is the dominating element. The emphasis is on the themes that deal with la causa and social problems which among others are police brutality, oppression, poverty, self-determination, life in the barrio, the farmworker, and pride in Chicano culture. Seldom do we find themes of romantic love or the pastoral beauty of nature. Some of the poetry produced may be lacking in the literary quality that critics demand, but this does not bother the Chicano poet. His ultimate concern is to vent his feelings which are essential to the message he wishes to convey.

Unity and liberation are often the subject of Chicano lyric poetry. Both are dealt with in "Cambios," a poem written by Ricardo Pérez, an ex-convict.

*Yesterday, my carnal from that other barrio was my rival,*
*Today, the Brown Soul cries for eternal unity.*
*Yesterday, my ambitions toward my barrio were but a mere*
*    trivial,*

*Today, my carnal and I embrace our mentality. . . .*
*Yesterday Carnal, I saw a tear of anger in your eyes,*
*Today, I see a ray of total determination.*
*Yesterday, and the day before, they planted seeds of lies,*
*Today and tomorrow we must toil united for total liberation.*

Abelardo Delgado, a poet of the people, describes la causa in these verses:

*what moves you, chicano to stop being polite?*
*nice chicano could be patted on the head and wouldn't bite*
*and now, how dare you tell your boss, "go fly a kite?"*
*    es la causa, hermano, which has made me a new man.*
(Delgado 1972, p. 12)

Progressively more Americans of Mexican ancestry from all socio-economic levels are finding comfort and pride in identifying as Chicanos, acknowledging their Indian heritage, as well as their Spanish lineage, which earlier was the only source of pride. Sergio Elizondo, whose higher education includes a Ph.D. from the University of North Carolina, composed the following verses which express this feeling:

| | |
|---|---|
| *Yo, señor, pues soy Chicano* | *I, sir, am a Chicano,* |
| *porque así me puse* | *because that is the name* |
| *Nadie me ha dado ese nombre* | *I gave myself.* |
| *Y lo oí y lo tengo.* | *No one gave me that name* |
| | *I heard it and I have it.* * |

The poem concludes with:

| | |
|---|---|
| *Americano de ascendencia* | *American of Spanish* |
| *española* | *descent,* |
| *¿Qué es eso, mano?* | *What is that, my brother?* |
| *Qué largo y vacio suena . . .* | *How long and empty it* |
| | *sounds.* |

(Elizondo 1972, p. 24)

One unique characteristic of most Chicano poetry is its use of Spanish and English. Spanish adjectives describe English nouns; Spanish verbs keep company with English adverbs. It is natural that Chicano poets should follow this mode of expression, for the switching from one language to another is a common occurrence in our speech when conversing with other Spanish-speaking Americans. Most of us speak Spanish as our mother tongue. Even when we learned English in school, we continued to speak Spanish at home. Chicano poets generally write in English, but use Spanish to give their verse lyrical quality, rhythm, and mood. Spanish is also conveniently used to give lyrics authenticity—a feeling inherent in the Spanish, but lost in the English. In certain instances, there are no English words to convey the feelings and emotions which the mother tongue can express.

Does the bilingual aspect of Chicano poetry limit its number of readers? The answer to this question is obviously yes, particularly

---

*Translated by the editor.

when the writer uses *caló* or slang expressions. Poets are no doubt aware that this kind of writing carries with it definite limitations, but the *Movimiento* has instilled in Chicanos pride in their culture and language. The English language may not be completely ours, the writer tells himself, but when I add a part of my language to it, then it will tell who and what I am—a fusion of the Indo-Hispanic culture with that of the United States, and gifted in two languages. And so the use of bilingual poetry has a functional as well as a symbolic meaning.

The Chicano Movement has in the last few years brought to the forefront individuals who have the sensitivity as well as the talent of great poets. Among the best known is Alberto Baltazar Urista Heredia who writes under the pseudonym of Alurista. This Mexican-born Chicano who has lived in various parts of Mexico and the United States, and presently makes his home in California, has shown how Spanish and English can be effectively harmonized to create masterful lyrics. In the following verses, Alurista, in his characteristic style blends the two languages and cleverly uses the well-known Mexican legend of the wailing woman to show the sorrow felt by the Mexican nation for its "children" whom it has lost to a dehumanized society. Moreover, there is distress because the Chicano has forgotten the power that lies in his Indian ancestral and cultural background.

> *must be the season of the witch*
> > *la bruja*
> > *la llorona*
> *she lost her children*
> > *and she cries*
> *en las barrancas of industry*
> > *her children*
> *devoured by computers*
> *and the gears*
> *must be the season of the witch*
> > *i hear huesos crack*
> *in pain*
> > *y lloros*
> *la bruja pangs*
> > *sus hijos han olvidado*
> *la magia de durango*
> > *y la de moctezuma*
> > *—el huiclamina*

> *must be the season of the witch*
> *la bruja llora*
> *sus hijos sufren; sin ella.*
> > (Urista 1971, p. 26)

José Montoya is another poet who merits attention. A native New Mexican, he was as of 1978 an instructor at California State University, Sacramento. In composing "Resonant Valley" he drew upon his personal experiences as a migrant worker. The central symbol is the "green, iridescent worm" which represents the migrant worker. Montoya, as persona, sympathizes with the worm:

> *I was too quick to*
> *Sadden at the sight*
> *Of the green, iridescent worm*
> *Scorching itself in the*
> *Hot, planned-for-trays, sand.*
> > (Montoya 1972, p. 235)

He feels responsible for the death of the worm and refuses to "repeat the senseless carnage." The Montoya family shares the same work ethic as that of the industrious Japanese alluded to elsewhere in the poem. Their daily goal was to pick 500 trays of grapes. On this occasion, however, the poet was willing to have his actions miscounstructed and labeled as lazy.

> *But the worms, the wasps and the*
> *Black widow spiders—for a short*
> *Time, at least—frolicked*
> *Cooly in that green-leaf world*
> *Beneath the sun.*
> > (Montoya 1972, p. 236)

Metaphorically, the last stanza employs irony to describe the plight of the migrant worker who must find frolic "beneath the sun."

Still another poet who reveals much promise is Rafael Jesús González, the author of *El hacedor de juegos/The Maker of Games.* Born and raised in the bilingual, bicultural El Paso-Juarez metropolitan area and later educated in universities in Mexico and in the United States, this poet developed the skill to create "games" which widen and sharpen our contacts with existence. The extensive use of elusive imagery in his poems requires several readings before the seemingly random words produce identifiable symbols. Unlike other Chicano poets who mix both English and Spanish in their verses, González insists on the purity of a single language to express his ideas and emotions. This Chicano Walt Whitman sees no difference between the body and the soul, or the world around us and the realm of the spirit. The significance of González' poetry is that it transcends the Chicano plight. Consider the example in "Half-Truths":

> *The cat jumped on her lap,*
> *curled itself about her arm*
>    *like a storm cloud*
>    *flashing green lightning,*
> *scattering the sulfur-veined petals*
>    *of chrysanthemums.*
> *'I have written love letters*
>    *in my blood.*
> *& heard the hoarse voices*
>    *of old women begging*
> *& seen the glitter of crucifixes*
>    *on the bosoms of whores*
> *& lain on the laps of dowagers*
>    *like a dog.*
> *I have been upon the sea*
>    *heartless as the desert*
> *& been upon the desert*
>    *kind as the sea*
> *& –'*
>    *handing her the ghost of a flower,*
>    *'I have died in my sleep.'*
>                 (Rafael González 1972, p. 5)

Like the Spanish poet Federico García Lorca—whose influence becomes evident in *The Maker of Games*—González uses ordinary words to create elaborate metaphors and images. The lines above portray the picture of a woman holding a flower. The cat suggests wildness and yet serves as a symbol of femininity. With these few verses the poet has harnessed the restlessness of the mind.

In the verses that are preceded by a single quote, the reader is introduced to the lover reminiscing his experience with love in years past. First there is the tender love of youth, followed by the more sophisticated love of a grown man. In the course of his experiences, he prostitutes himself and fails in the end to realize a satisfying love. The poet's concern is not with beauty, or philosophical truth, but with experience, and yet he appeals to our senses and imagination.

In various ways the works of Chicano poets share similarities with the American "new poetry" which originated in the mid-1920s with Ezra Pound, William Butler Yeats, and T.S. Eliot. The language, symbolism and free association of imagery often make their poetry difficult to understand. Usually there is no standard metrical foot or rhyme scheme. The rhythm derives from the arrangement of the stanzas on the printed page and the presence, or more likely the absence, of punctuation. As such, this poetry is of interest to a limited audience.

It is not my intent, however, to evaluate Chicano poetry on the basis of literary standards, but rather to present a cross section of that poetry which portrays *La Raza* whether it be through the lyrics of the bard of the people or the sophisticated poet who develops his themes in abstract metaphors. Regardless of the poetic style, one can be sure that the verse reflects the core of human living. To date, few of our poets have transcended the Chicano plight in their poetry; however, in the years to come we can anticipate more themes of wider scope that will bring our poetry to a stage of universal appeal.

The short story is another genre which lends itself quite readily to expressing the Chicano experience. If our writers feel comfortable narrating *cuentos*, it is probably a carry-over from the past when the oral tradition was much more important in our way of life. Prior to the days of television and transistor radios, story-telling sessions were common in the family or whenever groups gathered for a *velorio* (wake) or a fiesta. The function of such narratives was to provide pleasure, to inform, and to preserve the cultural heritage of Mexican Americans. Some narratives had a moral twist and served as a way of teaching the young.

The real world of the Chicano did not come to light in literature until after World War II when a small number of Chicano authors began to write fiction. Chicanos most often write for the specific purpose of presenting the circumstances of life that affect them. These writers reflect a sense of outrage and a deep insight into our character. Their outrage against the oppressive majority invariably comes through. In Octavio I. Romano-V.'s short story "A Rosary for Doña Marina," one of the characters, Pedro, is employed to carry railroad ties soaked in creosote across his shoulder. As he looks at his inflamed shoulder he exclaims, "People around here can tell who is Mexican and who is not. It is not enough to be brown, but I must have this bloody brand in addition." Later the author states, "Pedro's foreman used to say that he was a very good Mexican worker, when he wasn't drinking" (Romano-V. 1969, p. 107). It takes little imagination to understand that he drank to tolerate his misery.

Nick Vaca, author of "The Week of the Life of Manuel Hernandez," a story told in diary form, shows a Chicano in the process of cultural transition from tomato picker to college professor. Through the various stages Hernandez experiences the emptiness of life in the impersonal Anglo world. At the end of the story he finds himself saying, "I am afraid there is no escape from this animal that plagues me. It has many masks. Nausea, boredom, depression" (Vaca 1972, p. 138).

The Chicano experience is also expressed in the longer prose form of the novel, but it is too soon to see the Chicano novel in its proper perspective. It was only in 1959 that the first Chicano novel appeared on the American literary scene with the publication of José Antonio Villarreal's *Pocho*. Also it is difficult to assess the Chicano novel when there are so few works that can be faithfully included in this category.

The elements which I attribute to novels of the Chicano school are: (1) an awareness of the need for political and social freedom among *La Raza;* (2) insights on the Chicano lifestyle through true-to-life experiences captured realistically; (3) contemporary themes, although there may be some historical background; (4) characters portrayed as real persons; (5) use of English or a combination of both English and Spanish in writing although there are exceptions; and (6) a message for the reader which is often the purpose of the work. It may not always be clearly defined, but the author in his prose is saying this is a real situation and real people are involved.

In my opinion as of 1977 there are only five works which can be designated as Chicano novels. In addition to *Pocho,* they are: (1) *Chicano* (1970); (2) ...*Y no se lo trago la tierra* ( ...*And the Earth Did Not Part*) (1971); (3) *Bless Me, Ultima* (1972); and (4) *Peregrinos de Aztlán* (1974). Not all of the characteristic elements I have listed may be present in each work. Certainly not all elements are represented to the same degree in each; however, it is not one factor alone that determines the school of a given literary work, but it is the overall content and the manner in which its structural components are developed which helps to place a novel, in this case, in a distinctive category. Of course, other novels have been written by, about, and for Americans of Mexican ancestry, but they do not belong to the Chicano school, as I perceive it. For example, there is Floyd Salas' *Tatto the Wicked Cross*, which does not concern itself with the Chicano experience, but rather with the plight of racial minorities in correctional institutions. *City of Night* by the Texas-born Chicano John Rechy, probably one of the most widely-read authors of the 1960s, depicts the harsh world of the homosexual in America's leading cities.

Of the five novels which I feel belong in the Chicano school, *Pocho* sets the precedent. It is a metamorphosis. It reaches back before the birth of the main character, Richard Rubio, and follows him through the different stages of his mental and physical development. Richard is born in California to newly arrived Mexican immigrants who eventually settle in Santa Clara. With each passing day, new problems are confronted by the Rubio family, as a unit and as individuals. Through Richard the author explains how the "pocho" evolves. The person who emerges is both an individual and a symbol—a symbol of the Mexican American who is portrayed as neither Mexican nor American and yet is both. The novel is intended for the Anglo reader who is privy to peep through a knothole in a board fence to watch a completely different world from his own. By providing insights into the social, economic and political conflicts that confront the Mexican American who is searching for self identity in a predominantly Anglo society, Villarreal wrote the first Chicano protest novel. In his desire to make a statement, he does not always accurately describe the world of a twelve-year-old boy but rather ascribes to him ideas perceived by the author in retrospect. Little Spanish is used in the narrative, even though the reader is told that neither the mother nor father knows English. But despite these challenges to its credibility Villarreal captures sufficient realism to make the Rubio family representative of persons of Mexican origin who have gone through the traumatic process of acculturation which in this case destroys the family.

After *Pocho*, eleven years passed before the next Chicano novel appeared, but this is not unusual since Mexican American novelists have been and continue to be few and far between. It is unusual, however, that both Chicanos and non-Chicanos illustrated a marked lack of awareness of our scanty literary production. The timing for *Chicano* by Richard Vásquez was right because it was published just as the *Movimiento* reached its peak in the late 1960s, creating a special market for Chicano writings.

It appears that the author of *Chicano*, a zealous Californian, took as his objective to chronicle the most comprehensive commentary of Mexican Americans in fiction. To achieve his ambitious objective he interwove the multi-varied life experiences of four generations of the Sandoval family. The novel begins in northern Mexico around the turn of the twentieth century, but the first part is mainly concerned with the efforts of the first and second generations of the family to assimilate into the American way of life in California. In an effort to expose the Anglo target reader to as wide a range of Chicano life experiences as possible, the author makes use of over fifty characters in the central plot and numerous sub-plots, some of which unfortunately have little or no connection to the main story. Few Spanish words are used throughout the text and when they are a translation follows which confirms that the novel was written for the non-Chicano. Transitions both in story development and in characterization are often awkward and inconsistent, all of which makes portions of the novel appear contrived.

In his attempt to engulf every Chicano life experience his characterization lacks depth and the overall story has tones of superficiality. To his credit the author does capture sufficient insights to educate the reader, particularly those who are unfamiliar with Chicanos. Even some Chicano readers may become acquainted with the socioeconomic problems of the less fortunate members of *La Raza*. Despite its shortcomings the novel does present aspects of the life of a Chicano of which not many people are aware. In some cases the presentation lacks authenticity and in others it is strained, but the fact is that the author has written another Chicano protest novel.

In 1970 Texas-born Tomás Rivera deservingly received the first Quinto Sol Chicano literary award for his novel *... Y no se lo tragó la tierra*. Some may question whether this work qualifies as a novel but if we accept the definition that a novel is a long work of prose fiction which deals with human experiences through a connected sequence of events and can vary in style and in structure, there is no question that Rivera's work can be classified unequivocally as a short novel. This work consists of twelve parts which symbolize the twelve months of the year, plus a brief prologue and a concluding episode in which it becomes evident that the characters, incidents, short stories, and vignettes are all a part of one year's experience of the nameless main character who is the fictional narrator. Unlike the previous novels discussed which had been written to make the non-Chicano reader aware of the plight of Mexican Americans, Rivera's work is anything but didactic or pedantic. Herminio Ríos C., who was editor of the literature division of Quinto Sol Publications, states in the introduction to the novel that Rivera has created an artistic world where "the literary characters move, speak, and feel as true and complex creations, not in the predetermined mold of a stock character or a sociological model" (Rivera 1971, p. xv).

The artistic and inventive mind of the author allows him to touch the intellect and stir the emotions of the reader. Using the Spanish of the ordinary people of whom he writes, Rivera deals with despair, oppression, love, fear, shame, and other anxieties which help give this work universal appeal. An English version, prepared by the author and Rios, accompanies the Spanish text. Although the novel is to be read for entertainment, it does provide insights into the nature of all men and the relationship of human beings to each other and to their environment. The author conveys the feeling of hope even under adverse conditions when the main character, caught in a helpless situation and despite a desperate search, fails to find an explanation for his dilemma in the blind religious faith which is a part of his life. Finally moved to curse God, he is surprised to find the earth did not swallow him up. The author's message is that if the Chicano builds on his strengths and accepts his weaknesses he will find his identity and determine his own destiny.

*Bless Me, Ultima*, winner of the Second Annual Quinto Sol award in 1971, was written by Rodolfo A. Anaya. The young writer grew up in Santa Rosa, New Mexico, and sets his novel in Guadalupe and Puerto de Luna, small towns in that state. The story covers about two years in the 1940s. Through the eyes of Antonio Marez y Luna, a six-year-old boy, Anaya weaves a sensitive story of his own New Mexican people, their traditions, customs, and legends. His style—

plain and direct—is consistent with the story he relates which concerns simple, unpretentious people. Written in English, the novel uses a few Spanish words to add color and authenticity to the story and the characters. The author's technique of focusing upon a young boy growing up is an excellent vehicle for presenting the basic conflicts churning inside of him: self identity, faith in God, catechism, truth in legends and magical powers, and questions concerning life and death.

Anaya's skill and eloquence as a writer lie in his ability to construct a regional story in the fashion of *costumbrismo* in which local color is combined with realistic elements and the characters are used to reflect a way of life. Under the surface story of the novel is a strong, symbolic, philosophical statement. The author is not content with the social conditions of his people, but he does not dwell on them. He prefers, instead, to outline symbolically his views regarding religion, the family, and good versus evil. He offers no black and white definition of good or evil, nor do his characters exhibit all good or all evil traits. The resolution of the novel is optimistic and based on a synthesis of many life experiences. In the end young Antonio is determined to gain strength from every maturing experience, no matter how terrible. After all, was he not taught by Ultima, the wise old *curandera* (folk healer) that "the tragic consequences of life can be overcome by the magical strength that resides in the human heart"?

Miguel Méndez-M., the author of *Peregrinos de Aztlán,* was born in Bisbee, Arizona, a small mining town near the Mexican border. His formative years, however, were spent in a village in Sonora, Mexico, where he received a rudimentary education. Returning to Arizona as a young man, he worked in the fields and later became a bricklayer, all the while furthering his education through self-study, reading the American classics as well as those of other countries. He says that his experiences are the principal source for what he writes. As for the purpose of *Peregrinos* he states: "Mi proposito ha side despertar resistencia para combatir la pasividad a la que ha estado subjecto el pueblo mexicano en ambos lados de la frontera."*

Unfortunately, the author's unorthodox style and use of symbolism plus the fact that he uses slang terms that will not be found in dictionaries make it difficult for the reader to fully comprehend this work;

---

*My purpose has been to awaken resistance to combat the passivity to which the Mexican working classes on both sides of the border have been subjected.

204 Ourselves in Chicano Literature

consequently, one may fail to understand its purpose. If there is a protagonist in this work, it is Loreto Maldonado, the poor, unkempt Yaqui who makes his living by washing cars in an unnamed Sonoran border city. There is no central plot, but this character serves as the spin-off for a series of short stories, character sketches, anecdotes, and incidents which together describe the way of life of the poor *Mexicano* on both sides of the border. These narratives are a social criticism, enhanced with mythical characters, folklore, and superstitions. In his faithful treatment of the poor, the writer depicts reality with all its crudeness and unadulterated truths. He gives credence to characters and their experiences through his versatile use of language. He writes in standard Spanish, but in dialogues especially he employs the speech of the Mexican peasant, and the Chicano, and the slang of the Pachuco. His insights to the conditions which have spawned and nurtured the poor leave the reader with a better psychological understanding of the wanderers who form a continual migration across the border in both directions. The dreams of gold in America lured many Mexicans, who thought their problems would be resolved by leaving Mexico, to cross the border. They only found that different problems awaited them in the United States. The Chicano of the novel is seen struggling, but the reader can surmise that he will not long tolerate the injustices and social conditions which victimized his forbears.

As Mexican Americans represent a very heterogeneous population, this marked diversity is reflected in these five works. Wide differences in the ethnic group make it difficult to identify a "typical" Chicano novel. Common to all, however, is deep emotional involvement in the plight of the Mexican American. The authors' discontent with the status quo, coupled with their proclivity to political and social reform, has, in some cases, overshadowed their creative literary qualities. Instead of revealing real life, contrived situations and stock characters are used by some writers.

Despite these shortcomings, I view the development of the Chicano novel with optimism. Already it has made a significant contribution in content to American literature. It has opened new vistas. Chicano authors have revived legends, traditions, and customs which are a part of our cultural heritage. Rivera and Mendez, with their use of the Spanish language, have realistically portrayed a world which has not yet been penetrated by writers using English. The Chicanos' conflicts—physical, mental, emotional and moral—have been captured as never before and in so doing these authors have created an awareness of the need to record accurately the life of our people.

Drama, the last genre to be discussed here, is the most successful literary expression that has surfaced as a tool of the *Movimiento* to create cultural awareness and to effect political and socio-economic reform. The main reason is that drama, like prose fiction, utilizes plot and characters to develop a theme, but the message is conveyed through action, making its impact direct, immediate and as effective as the actor's skills. Thus, performance of a play by skilled actors expertly directed gives drama a tremendous source of power, particularly among Chicano people who are not readers. I do not mean to suggest that drama per se will attract Chicanos. As a matter of fact, Chicanos for the most part are not devotees of the theater. This is understandable knowing that established theaters around the country have had little or nothing to offer the Chicano community in terms of relevant entertainment.

Drama, however, is not new to the people of Aztlán. On the part of our Indian ancestry, theatrical performances can be traced back to the Mayas. "Rabinal Achi," a ballet-drama, survives to the present as an example of the drama of that period (*Teatro* 1955, pp. x–xiii). In our Spanish heritage drama dates back to the morality plays of the Middle Ages. After the Conquest the Spanish used liturgical drama to teach Catholicism to their new subjects. Their use of plays for didactic purposes was made easier because the native people already had a theatrical-ritual heritage. Proselytizing by means of drama continued throughout the Spanish period in Mexico and was brought to what is now the American Southwest by the early Spanish colonizers.

The three most popular forms were the *auto sacramentales* (morality plays), the *pastorales,* and the *posadas*.* Sources of the *auto sacramentales* could be either secular or religious, but the story had to illustrate the basic fundamentals of Catholicism. The *pastorales* were usually representations of the story of Adam and Eve, and the *posadas* dealt with the birth of Christ. Secular plays were also performed in Aztlán although they were not as numerous as the religious ones and

---

*\**Posada* is Spanish for inn; hence *posadas* are Christmas plays in which Mary and Joseph seek lodging.

did not have the support of a strong institution such as the church. The first secular Spanish language play known to have been performed in the United States was given near El Paso on 30 April 1598, to celebrate Juan de Oñate's conquest of the territories of New Mexico (Bolton 1921, pp. 172–73). Since that first secular play many others have been performed in various parts of Aztlán. *Carpas* (theatrical troupes which perform in tents) and *Maromeros* (entertainers) from Mexico frequently performed folk drama in the border states (Castañeda Shular 1972, p. 44).

I have been unable to establish the origin of this form of entertainment, but my father recalled seeing traveling theatrical troupes giving performances in tents during his boyhood in Durango, Mexico, before the turn of the century. No doubt *carpas* existed long before then. Indeed, the term *carpas* means tents in Spanish. I recall that as recently as the 1950s groups of entertainers from Mexico came to share their talents with the people of the Southwest, but by then these events took place in neighborhood theaters. Important as the theater had been to the people of Aztlán, it faded with the coming of the radio, and the movies. Changing lifestyles in the post-World War II period, when Spanish-speaking peoples were dispersed from their previously isolated communities, served to hasten its demise.

Drama reemerged in Aztlán, however, in 1965 when Luis Valdez, a Chicano from California, started the Teatro Campesino. This theater was used to rally support for the *Huelga* in Delano, California, organized by the National Farm Workers' Association founded by César Chávez. Of this theater Valdez said, "We don't think in terms of art, but of our political purpose in putting across certain points. We think of our spiritual purpose in terms of turning on crowds" (Bagby 1967, p. 78). He went on to say, "The most characteristic thing about the Teatro as a theatre group is that we are dedicated to a very specific goal—the organization of farm workers" (Bagby 1967, p. 79).

The Teatro's repertoire is composed of *actos*, which are caustic, fast-moving, one-act plays dealing with the problems of the farmworkers. Singular characteristics, however, set them apart from other theatrical presentations. First, the *actos* are funny in a slapstick fashion. Valdez has said, "I think humor is our major asset and weapon, not only from a satirical point of view, but from the fact that humor can stand up on its own and is a much more healthy child of the theatre than let's say tragedy or realism" (Bagby 1967, p. 77). Since the audience for whom the *actos* are designed is functionally illiterate the performances make use of stock characters and are loosely put together but highly stylized. Signs hang from the actors to identify their roles for the audience. Gestures are used to the point of exaggeration. To characterize the grower as the boss, he always chomps on a cigar and "flicks [it] as if he had been taught by Groucho Marx" (Weisman 1973, p. 18). Unlike most plays the *actos* can be performed on the flatbed of a truck since elaborate sets are non-existent and props are usually improvised. To effectively communicate with the audience the *actos* are in English but include some Spanish words and phrases. To make a point or for special effect, coarse language is sometimes used as is *caló*—barrio slang.

*Las dos caras del patroncito* (*The Two Faces of the Boss*), a classic piece of farmworkers' theater, illustrates the content and some of the characteristics of an *acto*. The play opens with the boss contemptuously exhorting a farm laborer, who, shears in hand, is pruning grapevines. The boss demands he work harder because, after all, he is provided with housing, transportation, and a "good" wage. Besides while other growers hire Filipinos and Arabs, he prefers Mexicans. The boss also points out that the position of the farmworker is more desirable than his as a rich grower. The farmworker does not have to worry about maintaining an expensive house, a Lincoln Continental, and supporting a luxurious style of living. After this discussion, the grower and laborer agree to change roles. Although the farmworker begins somewhat timidly in carrying out his new duties, very shortly he manages to assume the aggressive, dominating characteristics of the boss. The grower who now must work under the physical and verbal abuse of his "new" boss quickly begins to see the wretchedness of the farmworker's life. The final irony comes when the grower throws down the shears and tells the audience: "You know that damn César Chávez is right? You can't do this work for less than two dollars an hour." The farmworker then agrees to give the boss back everything—except the cigar (Valdez 1972, p. 53).

From its early beginnings, the Teatro Campesino has gained in popularity and prestige and its repertoire has broadened manyfold. No longer is it restricted to the problems of the farmworkers; the urban Chicano and his concerns are also the subject of various *actos*.

Further, the Teatro Campesino has expanded to include puppet shows, full-length plays, films, and it also has a band. Nonetheless, the aim continues to be that of combating oppression and poverty.

One of the most significant contributions of the *Teatro* has been its influence on the development of drama in Aztlán. Under the leadership of Luis Valdez, an organization called TENAZ (El Teatro Nacional de Aztlán) was established. In its 1973 publication, *Chicano Theatre Two*, TENAZ listed thirty-three Chicano theater groups. Most are located in the Southwest but there are groups in Seattle and Chicago, as well as two in Spanish America. Urban theater groups aspire to educate the people of the barrios. Themes of their *actos* include, among others, police brutality, drug abuse, illegal deportations, housing, and unemployment. One of the urban groups which has taken the lead in developing the *teatro* for urban Chicanos is *El Teatro de la Esperanza*. This group is under the direction of Jorge A. Huerta, an instructor of dramatic art at the University of California, La Jolla. Like the Teatro Campesino, from whom they first borrowed *actos*, this group continues to capitalize on comedy to convey their message.

Though the audience may laugh at the *actos* they carry away ideas which will provoke thought and understanding of their status in life. *La Trampa Sin Salida* (A Trap With No Exit) describes the vicious cycle of poverty that traps poor Chicanos in the barrio which for many becomes a dead-end street. In this play the theme revolves around the brutal punishment Chicanos sometimes receive at the hands of sadistic policemen. In its original form the play contained numerous English and Spanish obscenities. At a Los Angeles high school the play was stopped by the principal after seven minutes because of the "vulgarities." The Chicanos in the audience applauded the principal's action (Verdugo 1973, p.13). This experience provided a lesson to the Esperanza group and no doubt has had an influence on other *teatros*. Important as a message may be it must be conveyed to the audience in a manner that does not offend them.

The objective of the Chicano theater, whether rural or urban, is to motivate, entertain, and educate the audience. If this objective is being successfully fulfilled it is because for the first time drama is dealing with the realities that are relevant to Chicano audiences. Moreover, through drama Chicanos are being educated and entertained, not by books which they may not or will not read, but through vivid dramatizations of experiences with which they can identify. Much about the *teatro* remains unknown for little of what is being done ever gets into print; however, the mission of the actors is to reach the people. This they are doing through their *actos*. The *teatro* and its horizons are eloquently captured by Huerta:

> The future of Los Teatros de Aztlán is very bright. The critical acclaim and the audience reactions seem to point to a true sense of pride in the Chicano as an artist, technician, actor and writer. Unlike Anglo American Broadway theater, the members of teatros are not concerned with "stardom." What matters to the Chicano in a teatro is that a message be understood. It seems that those sixteenth century missionaries have been replaced by a new religion and new apostles, equally, if not more fervent, in their purpose. Los Teatros de Aztlán are filling an essential role in the Chicano struggle for identity, justice and liberation (Huerta 1971, p.71).

In conclusion, the portraits drawn by Chicano authors depict resentment, oppression, struggle, and the tragedies of life. They bring to light those experiences which previously had never been accurately described until the *Movimiento* began. Making use of folklore, local color, and the Spanish language, including some of the crude speech of the working class, they unfold the drama of the Chicano. In some cases they reach into the past of our forbears. Our pre-Columbian Indian heritage is glorified, but as for Mexico, both in the past and the present, authors find conditions deplorable for the masses. The main concern of the writers, however, is to inform the reader of the Chicano experience and to present conditions as they exist in the United States. There is a vital interest in projecting the need for social reform. Noteworthy is the omission of Chicano women in Chicano literature. Their story is yet to be told.

Despite sorrow, toil and struggle the culture continues and the Chicano is viewed as " . . . poor in money, arrogant with pride, bold with machismo, rich in courage and wealthy in spirit and faith" (Rodolfo Gonzales 1972, p. 64). Gonzales recapitulates our historical journey by noting that we have endured bigotry, snobbery, dejection, exploitation, and racial hatred. Still " . . . the trumpet sounds and . . . we start to MOVE." (Rodolfo Gonzales 1972, pp. 93, 96).

Bibliography

Anaya, Rodolfo A. 1972. *Bless Me, Ultima.* Berkeley, Calif.: Quinto Sol Publications.

Bagby, Beth. 1967. "El Teatro Campesino: Interviews with Luis Valdez," *Tulane Drama Review* 11 (Summer issue): 71–80.

Bolton, Herbert E. 1921. *The Spanish Borderlands: A Chronicle of Old Florida and the Southwest.* New Haven: Yale University Press.

Brito, Aristeo. 1974. *Fomento literario: cuentos i poemas.* Washington, D.C.: Congreso Nacional de Asuntos Colegiales.

Castañeda Shular, Antonia; Garra-Fausto, Tomás; and Sommers, Joseph, eds. 1972. *Literatura chicana: texto y contexto.* Englewood Cliffs, N. J.: Prentice-Hall.

Delgado, Abelardo B. 1972. *Chicano: Twenty-Five Pieces of a Chicano Mind.* El Paso, Texas: Barrio Publications.

Elizondo, Sergio. 1972. *Perros y antiperros: una epica chicana.* Berkeley, Calif.: Quinto Sol Publications.

Gonzales, Rodolfo. 1972. *I Am Joaquín: Yo Soy Joaquín: An Epic Poem with a Chronology of People and Events in Mexican and Mexican American History.* Text in Spanish and English. New York: Bantam Books.

González, Rafael Jesús. 1972. *El hacedor the juegos/The Maker of Games.* San Francisco, Calif.: Casa Editorial Chapbook Number Five.

Huerta, Jorge A. 1971. "Chicano Teatro: A Background." *Aztlán: Chicano Journal of the Social Sciences and the Arts* 2 (Fall issue): 63–71.

Méndez-M., Miguel. 1974. *Peregrinos de Aztlán. Literatura chicana (novela).* Tucson, Ariz.: Editorial Peregrinos.

Montoya, José. 1972. "Resonant Valley." In *El espejo—The Mirror: Selected Chicano Literature.* 5th rev. ed. Edited by Octavio Ignacio Romano-V. and Herminio Rios C. Berkeley, Calif.: Quinto Sol Publications.

Pérez, Ricardo. 1969. "Cambios." *San Bernardino El Chicano,* December 5.

Rechy, John. 1963. *City of Night.* New York: Grove Press.

Rivera, Tomás. 1971. *...Y no se lo trago la tierra (...And the Earth Did Not Part").* Printed in Spanish and English. Berkeley, Calif.: Quinto Sol Publications.

Romano-V., Octavio I., ed. 1969. "A Rosary for Doña Marina." In *El espejo—The Mirror: Selected Mexican-American Literature.* Berkeley, Calif.: Quinto Sol Publications, 104–22.

Salas, Floyd. 1967. *Tatto the Wicked Cross.* New York: Grove Press.

Steiner, Stan. 1969. *La Raza: The Mexican Americans.* New York: Harper and Row Publishers.

*Teatro indigena prehispanico* (Rabinal Achi). 1955. Prólogo de Francisco Monterde. México: Ediciones de la Universidad Nacional Autónoma.

Urista, Alberto Baltazar (Alurista). 1971. *Floricanto en Aztlán*. Creative Series, no. 1. Los Angeles: Aztlán Publications, University of California.

Vaca, Nick. 1972. "The Week of the Life of Manuel Hernandez." In *El espejo—The Mirror: Selected Chicano Literature*. 5th rev. ed. Berkeley, Calif.: Quinto Sol Publications, 131–38.

Valdez, Luis. 1972. *Las dos caras del patroncito*. In *Literatura chicana: texto y contexto*. Edited by Antonia Castañeda Shular, et. al. Englewood Cliffs, N.J.: Prentice-Hall.

Vásquez, Richard. 1970. *Chicano*. Garden City, N.Y.: Doubleday and Co.

Verdugo, Jaime. 1973. *La trampa sin salida*. Jorge A. Huerta, ed. in *El teatro de la esperanza: An Anthology of Chicano Drama*. Goleta, Calif.: El Teatro de la Esperanza, Inc.

*Villarreal, José* Antonio. 1959. *Pocho*. Garden City, N.Y.: Doubleday and Co., Anchor Books.

Villaseñor, Edmund. 1973. *Macho*. New York: Bantam Books.

Weisman, John. 1973. *Guerrilla Theater: Scenarios for Revolution*. Garden City, N.Y.: Doubleday and Co., Anchor Books.

# Index

Abortion, 91, 97
Abuse of Spanish-speaking persons, 134, 135
Academic libraries: survey of Southwestern, 180, 182, *See also* Libraries
Acculturation, 5, 111, 112, 127
*Actos*, 206–7
*Adelita, La*, 83, 86
Adorador, María, 84, 88, 89
Aguilar, Linda Peralta, 98
Aimara, 121
*Alabados*, 27, 28
Alamo, 154, 156
Albuquerque, New Mexico, 32, 77
Alfaro, Ricardo, 138, 139, 144
Alianza Federal de los Pueblos Libres, 115
Alianza Hispano Americana, 112
Alurista. *See* Urista Heredia, Alberto Baltazar
Alvarado, Salvador, 82
American G.I. Forum, 113
American Library Association Directory, 183
American Revolution, 3
Anaya, Rodolfo A., 12, 202–3
Andalusian, 28, 31
Anderson, Barbara, 181
Andersson, Theodore, 162
Angagua, Mexico, 11
Anglicisms, 139–44, 146, 147. *See also* English language, influence on Spanish language
Anglo, defined, 102
Anglo control of politics, 103
Anglo family in the barrio, 41
Apaches, 3, 22
Apolitical attitudes of Mexican Americans, 111
Arabs: in Spain, 21; as farm-workers, 207
Argentina, 147

Arizona, 21, 108, 109, 115, 122, 134, 136, 147, 156, 183. *See also* individual cities
Art, 23–26, 83. *See also* Santos, Santeros
Artists, 24–26. *See also* names of individual artists
Asian Americans, 102
Assimilation, 1–3, 15, 133. *See also* Acculturation
Asturias, Spain, 28
Atlanta, Georgia, 178
At-large elections. *See* Elections, at-large
Austin, Texas, 151
Authors, Anglo, 187
*Auto sacramental*, 33, 205
Awards. *See* Quinto Sol Literary Award
Aztec beliefs and folklore. *See* Folklore and beliefs, Mexican Indians
Aztec foods. *See* Foods
Aztecs, 3, 6, 8, 13, 173; language, 9–10
Aztlan, 7, 8, 205, 206, 208, 209

Ballads. *See* corridos
Barraza, Maclovio, 118
Basques, 121
Becknell, William, 22
Beliefs. *See* Folklore and beliefs
Benitez, María, 32
Berceo, Gonzalo de, 143
Bernalillo, New Mexico, 20, 21, 26
Biblioteca Palafoxiana, 172
Biculturalism, 152: bilingualism, 121, 122, 124, 127–28, 130, 141, 145, 147, 148, 153–56; education, 129, 151, 164; programs, 159, 162, 164; research, 128. *See also* Monolingualism
Bilingual Education Act (1968), 128, 153
Birth, 73
Birth control, 73

Bisbee, Arizona, 203
Blacks, 103, 113, 116, 130, 169
*Bless Me, Ultima* (Anaya), 12, 199, 202–3
Bogardus, Emory S., 122
Bolivians, 121
Bologna, University of, 173
Book-orientation, Chicano lack of, 172–75
Books and libraries, 167–84
Books: child's introduction to, 175. *See also*
　Reading, attitudes toward
Books in the New World, 172–73
Boston (Mass.) Public Library, 175
Boys, role in family. *See* Son, role in family
Bradbury, Ray, 171
Brandeis University, 129
Brazil, 27, 140
Brotherhoods. *See Hermandades*
Brown-white syndrome, 14–15
Bustos, Marilina, 32

California, 4, 21, 22, 77, 103, 108, 109, 110,
　111, 115, 133, 147, 155, 156, 162,
　190, 200, 206; constitution, 133; electoral
　districts, 108. *See also* individual cities
California State Advisory Committee.
　*See* U.S. Commission on Civil Rights.
　California State Advisory Committee
California State University, Sacramento,
　196. *See also* Mexican American
　Education Project
California State University,
　San Francisco, 181
California State University, San Jose, 95
*Calo. See* Slang
Calvin, Ross, 13
Campa, Arthur L., 7, 172
Cano, Eddie, 128
Cárdenas, Blandina, 92
Cárdenas, Lazaro 2, 9
Carlota, 30
Carr, Vikki, 128
Carranza, Venustiano, 82
Carrillo, Randy, 30
Castañeda, Carlos E., 171
Castilian. *See* Spanish language
Castillo, Elvia, 95
Castillo Najera, Francisco, 135, 136, 139,
　140, 142, 143, 144
*Castizo*, 4, 8
Castro, Raul, 106, 108
Catalan language, 147, Catalans, 121
Catholic Church. *See* Roman
　Catholic Church
Catholicism. *See* Roman Catholic Church
Causa, La, 193
Census, 1790, 8

Cervantes, Miguel, 21
*Changuitos Feos, Los,* 29–30
Chama, New Mexico, 77
Chastity, 11
Chávez, Alex, 32
Chávez, Cesar, 9, 115, 118, 119, 130,
　206, 207
Chávez, Geneva, 32
Cherokee, 151
Chicago, Illinois, 122, 208
Chicana, defined, 95: identity, 81, 95;
　literature, 83–84, 86; organizations,
　96–97; perspective, 91–92; research on,
　83, 84; role in the Movement, 90–91;
　role in U.S. society, 95. *See also*
　National Woman's Studies Association;
　International Women's Year Conference
Chicanismo, 6, 14, 34, 111, 114–15
Chicano, defined, 101–2: heritage, 9, 15,
　101–2; identity, 2–6, 44–48, 122, 156,
　190–92, 194, 202; leaders, 118; literature,
　15, 168, 187–211; Movement, 1, 2, 4,
　89–90, 91, 113–14, 148, 180, 195;
　population, 117, programs in universities,
　105–6; renaissance, 161; studies, 161–62,
　180, 181–82; theater, 33–35, 208–9; need
　for university, 129–30. *See also*
　*Movimiento;* Teatro Campesino
*Chicano* (Vásquez), 199, 201
Child-care, 84–85
Childhood experiences, 41–42
Children, role in family, 72–73. *See also*
　Daughter, role in family; son, role
　in family
Chimayo, New Mexico, 77
Chinese Americans, 158
Christ, 42, 205
Christmas, 27, 34
Church. *See* Roman Catholic Church
Citizens Organized for Public Services
　(COPS), 118
*City of Night* (Rechy), 200
Civilian Conservation Corps, 112
Cleveland, Ohio, 178
Cobos, Ruben, 33
Codices, 173
*Cofrade,* 28
*Cafradías. See Hermandades*
Colegio de San Pedro y San Pablo. *See* San
　Pedro y San Pablo, Colegio de
Colombia, 31, 147
Colonies, Spanish, 173
Colonists, English, 168
*Coloquios,* 33
Colorado, 54, 55, 78, 109, 115, 122, 123,
　133, 136, 156, 183, 188

Colorado College, 33
Columbus, Christopher, 3
Comanches, 3
Community Service Organization, 113
*Compadrazgo,* 13–14
*Conquistadora, La,* 21, 74, 75
Convent, 70. *See also* Roman
    Catholic Church
Cooley, C. H., 50
COPS. *See* Citizens Organized for
    Public Services
Coral Way Elementary School
    (Miami, Florida), 151
Corominas, Juan, 143
Coronado, Francisco Vásquez de, 21
*Correo Mexicano, El,* 133
*Corridos,* 30, 31, 172
Cortés, Hernán, 6, 11, 20, 191
Cortéz, Gregorio, 111
Cortina, Juan Nepomuceno, 111
Council of the Indies, 173
Cross-cultural education, 161
Crusade for Justice, 115, 189. *See also*
    Gonzales, Rodolfo
*Cruzada para la Justicia. See* Crusade for
    Justice
Crystal City, Texas, 115–16, 117
Cuauhtémoc, 191. *See also*
    *Hijas de Cuauhtémoc*
Cuauhtémoc Home-Centered Bilingual
    Pre-school, 162
Cubans, 147, 151
Culture, 38–40; Chicano, 19, 35, 41–48,
    56–57, 156; Hispanic, 13, 21; Indian,
    8–13; Mexican, 9–13, 26, 125; Mexican
    American, 9–13, 54, 55, 83. *See also* Oral
    tradition; Traditional culture
Cumbia, 31
*Curanderas,* 12, 70, 71, 95
Customs, 21; Mexican American, 127;
    Mexican compared to American, 42–43

Dance, 23, 26, 31, 32. *See also* Flamenco
*Danzantes,* 20
Daughter, role in Chicano family, 85, 90.
    *See also* Children, role in family
Death, 73–74. *See also* Mourning
Delgado, Abelardo, 193
Delinquency, juvenile, 126–27
Democracy, 4
Democratic Party, 114, 117
Denver, Colorado, 104, 117, 189
De Oñate, Juan. *See* Oñate, Juan de
Deportations, 112
Depression, 112
Desertation, 71, 72

Detroit, Michigan, 178
De Vargas, Diego. *See* Vargas, Diego de
*Día de los santos,* 24
*Día de Santa Ana,* 74
*Día de Santiago,* 74
Díaz, Porfirio, 112
*Diccionario Crítico Etimológico de la len-*
    *gua castellana* (Corominas), 143
Diderot, Donis, 173
Diet, Inadequacy of, 62
Discrimination, 58, 62, 96, 97, 106–7, 127,
    154, 158–59
Divorce, 70, 72
Divorce laws, Mexican, 82
Dobie, J. Frank, 171
*Dolores, Nuestra Señora de los,* 76
Dolores, Use of name, 76
Drama, Chicano, 33–35, 205–9; Chicano
    theater, 34. *See also Actos; auto*
    *sacramentales; Coloquios;* Comanches;
    *Maromeros;* morality plays; *Pastorales;*
    posadas; Religious plays; Specific names;
    Teatro Campesino; *Teatro de la*
    *Esperanza, El; Teatro Nacional de*
    *Aztlan,* El (TENAZ)
Drop-out statistics, 153, 175
Duran, Carla, 32
Durango, Mexico, 206

Easter, 27
*ECO Mexicano, EL,* 133
Economy, 69–70
Educable Mentally Retarded (EMR), 155
Education, 74, 157, 167, 168: attitudes
    toward, 56–57; U.S. Office of, 128.
    *See also Biculturalism,* education; Books
    and libraries; Grade Repetition; Reading,
    attitudes toward
Educational needs, 129–30, 163–64; reform,
    122–23
Elected officials, Mexican American,
    109–10. *See also* Appointed officials;
    specific names
Election statistics, 109
Elections, at-large, 108–9. *See also* Elected
    officials, Mexican American; Political
    process; Poll tax; Voter harassment; Voter
    registration; Voting; Voting
    requirements
Eliot, T. S., 198
Elizondo, Sergio, 194
El Paso, Texas, 32, 117, 196, 206
Emancipation of Mexican women, 81–82
Emery, George, 170
England, 168
English and Spanish, mixture of, 141–42

English as a Second Language (ESL), 129
English language, 125–26, 133, 154,
    194–95; instruction for Spanish
    speakers, 125–26; and influence on
    Spanish language, 136–47
Epiphany, feast of, 34
Erasmus, 173
Escudero, Mario, 32
Espinosa, Aurelio M., Sr., 134, 171
*Estudio sobre el español de Nuevo Méjico*
    (Espinosa), 171–72
Ethnic studies. *See* Chicano studies
Extended families, 44, 60–61

Farmworkers, 58, 206–7. *See also* Migrant
    laborers; United Farmworkers Union
Fatalism, 59
Father, role in Chicano family, 84–85,
    86, 88
Fender, Freddy, 33
Ferdinand, Maximilian Joseph, 30
Fergusson, Harvey, 170
Fernandez, Maya, 32
Fernando of Spain, 21
Festivity, 20–21, 74
Fiction. *See* specific types of literature
*Fiesta de San Lorenzo. See San Lorenzo,
    fiesta de*
*Fiesta de Santa Fe. See Santa Fe, fiesta* de
Fiestas, 20–21. *See also* Religious festivals
Filipinos, 207
Flamenco, 31–32
Flint, Timothy, 170
Florida, 147
Folklore, 10–12; 172
Folklore and beliefs: Mexican Indians,
    10–13; Mexican Americans, 11–13.
    *See also* Chicano culture
Folk medicine, 12. *See also* Curanderas
Food: Mexican, 9–10; New Mexican, 77
Foreignisms, 144, 145
France, 168
*Francis Berrian: Or the Mexican
    Patriot* (Flint), 170
Francis of Assisi, St., Third Order, 27
Franguelo y Romero, Ramón, 141, 145, 146
French language, 137, 140, 151
French Revolution, 9

Galicians, 121, 147
Galindo de Topete, Hermilia, 83
Gallicisms, 140
Gamio, Manuel, 11, 122
García Lorca, Federico, 197
Georgetown University, School of
    Linguistics, 122
German language, 151

Germany, 168
Gerrymandering, 108, 153
G.I. Forum. *See* American G.I. Forum
Girls, Chicanas compared to Anglo girls,
    44. *See also* Daughter, role in
    Chicano family
Glyphs, 173–74
God, 69, 70, 73
Gods, Indian, 6
González, Rafael Jesús, 196–98
Gonzalez, Rodolfo (Corky), 104, 115, 118,
    188–93. *See also* Crusade for Justice
González, Simón, 122
*Gorras Blancas, las,* 111, 115
Governors, Mexican American, 110
Grade repetition, 153
Granada, Spain, 21
Great Britain, 168
Gringos, attitudes toward, 44–45
Guadalajara, Jalisco, Mexico, 139
Guadalupe, Virgin of, 8, 9, 74
Guadalupe Hidalgo, Treaty of, 125
Guarani, 121
Gutíerrez, José Angel, 107, 115, 118

*Hacedor de juegos, el/The Maker of Games
    (Gonzalez), 196*
Haro, Robert, 177
Harte, Bret, 170
Heller, Celia S., 49
*Hermandades,* 26–28
Hernandez Trujillo, Manuel, 25–26
Heterogeneity of Mexican American
    population, 123, 204
Higher education, 157. *See also* Chicano,
    need for university;
*Hijas de Cuauhtémoc,* 81
Hispanization, 8, 9, 141, 143
Hispano, 8. *See also* Hispanoamericano
Horgan, Paul, 171
Houston, Texas, 96, 98, 178
Howard University, 129
Howe, Harold, II, 151–52
*Huapangos,* 31
*Huelga,* 8, 9, 39, 206
Huerta, Jorge A., 208–9
Huitzilopochtli, 6
Husband, role in Chicano family, 70, 88
Hybrid language, 127, 135, 139, 142, 143

*I am Joaquin* (Gonzales), 188–93
I & R's. *See* Neighborhood information
    centers
Illiteracy, 174. *See also* literacy
Immigrants, Mexican, 135, 174–75, 188.
    *See also* Migrations
Indian culture. *See* Culture, Indian

Indian heritage, 1–17, 68, 173, 194, 195, 209. *See also* Oral tradition
Indians, 1, 2, 3, 8, 9; American, 102. *See also* specific names of tribes
Indies, Council of the, 173
Information and Referral Services (I & R). *See* Neighborhood information centers
Intelligence Quotient Tests (IQ), 155, 157
International Women's Year Conference, 98
Isabel of Spain, 21

Jalisco, Mexico, 11
Japan, 168
Jilotlan, Mexico, 12
Job training, 58–59
José María, use of name, 76
Júarez, Benito, 9
Jude, Saint, 12

Kansas City, Missouri, 122
Kearney, Stephen Watts (Gen.), 6
Kercheville, Francis M., 146
Kino, Eusebio (Father), 22
Kluckhohn, Florence, 49
Korean War, 77
Ku Klux Klan, 103

*La Conquistadora. See Conquistadora, la*
*Ladinhas*, 27
Language and language learning, 124–25
Language categories of Chicano children, 123–24
Language skills, 63, 121–22, 155–56
*La Raza Unida. See Raza Unida, la*
Larson, Robert W., 134
*Las Gorras Blancas. See Gorras Blancas, las*
Latin America, 67
Lau vs. Nichols, 158–59
Law enforcement, 103, 134
League of United Latin American Citizens (LULAC), 2, 112, 113, 114
León, Marcos de, 122
León de la Barra, Francisco (President of Mexico), 82
Lewis, Oscar, 54, 122
Liberalism, 173
Librarians, bilingual/bicultural, 179, 182; Spanish-speaking, 180, 183; statistics on minority, 183; statistics on Spanish-speaking, 183
Librarianship, lack of appeal to Chicanos, 181
Libraries: academic, 180–82; philosophy, 175; public, 176–79; school, 176–77. *See also* Biblioteca Palafoxiana; Neighborhood Information Centers

Library materials for Chicanos, 179
Library schools, 182–83
Linguistic Research, 122–24
Linguistic Society of America, 122
Literacy, 174. *See also* Illiteracy
Literary awards. *See* Quinto Sol Literary Award
Literature. *See* Chicanas, literature; Chicano, literature; Drama, Chicano; Novels, Chicano; Poetry, Chicano; Short stories, Chicano
*Llorona, la*, 10–11, 24, 41
Local government, Mexican Americans in, 109
Longeaux y Vásquez, Enriqueta, 95, 96
López, Leo, 122
López, Trini, 33
López Tijerina, Reies, 114
Los Alamos, New Mexico, 77
Los Angeles, California, 32, 76, 103–4, 108, 115
Los Comanches. *See* Comanches, los
*Los reyes magos. See Reyes Magos, los*
LULAC. *See* League of United Latin American Citizens
Lummis, Charles F., 171

*Macarena, La Virgen de la*, 74
Machismo, 61, 75–76, 90–91, 92, 97, 98
Macho, 75, 90
Macias, Isidro Ramón, 179
McWilliams, Carey, 122
Madero, Francisco I., 191
Madsen, William, 49, 83–84, 122
Magdalena, Sonora, 41
Malinche, la, 2, 10–11
Mallorquinos, 121
Man, role in family, 75–76
Manifest Destiny, 169
Manuel, Herschel T., 122
MAPA. *See* Mexican American Political Association
María, use of name, 76
Mariachi, 28: Cobre, 30, Vargas de Tecalitlán, 29
*Maromeros*, 206
Marriage, 70–71, 77, 87–88, 89. *See also* Religious practices
Martínez, Gilbert, 122
Marx, Groucho, 207
Mary, Virgin, 21, 42, 74, 75
Massachusetts Institute of Technology, 122
Matachines, 20, 21
Maximilian. *See* Ferdinand Maximilian Joseph.
Maxwell Land Grant, 4
Mayas, 9, 173, 205

Mead, George H., 5
MECHA. *See* Movimiento Estudiantil
　Chicano de Aztlan
Médica, 70, 71
Medicine. *See* Folk medicine
Men, role of Chicano, 86
Méndez-M., Miguel, 203–4
Mestizaje. *See* Mestizos
Mestizos, 5–9, 29
Mexican American culture. *See* Culture,
　Mexican Americans
Mexican American, defined, 101–2
Mexican American Education Project,
　California State University,
　Sacramento, 160
Mexican American heritage. *See*
　Chicano, heritage
Mexican American Legal Defense and
　Education Fund (MALDEF), 158–59
Mexican American Political Association
　(MAPA), 113
Mexican American studies. *See* Chicano,
　programs in universities
*Mexican Americans of South Texas*
　(Madsen), 83–84
Mexican culture. *See* Culture, Mexican
Mexican food, 9–10
Mexican Revolution (1910), 81, 82, 86, 174
Mexico, 2, 8, 9, 21, 22, 27, 28, 31, 62, 104,
　111, 122, 123, 133, 136, 137, 138, 139,
　142, 147, 173, 174, 191, 195
Mexico, independence of, 9, 22, 191
*Mexico and the Hispanic Southwest in
　American Literature* (Robinson), 169
Mexico City, Mexico, 29, 140. *See
　also Tenochtitlan*
Miami, Florida, 151
Michoacan, Mexico, 11
Migrant laborers, 55–56. *See also*
　Farmworkers
Migrations, 123, 174
Miners, Mexican American, 106–7
Miscegenation, 4, 8, 22
Missionaries, 23, 42
Missouri, 22
Mixtecs, 173
Moctezuma, 6, 13
Modern Language Association of
　America, 122
Monolingualism, 155, 174. *See also*
　Biculturalism, bilingualism
Montesquieu, Charles de Secondat, 173
Montezuma. *See* Moctezuma
Montoya, José, 196
Moorish, 21, 28
Moors, 21

Morality plays, 205
Moreno, David, 32
Mother, role in Chicano family, 84–85,
　71–72, 75, 88, 89, 90
Mourning, 73–74. *See also* Death;
　Religious practices
*Movimiento,* 16, 187, 188, 192, 195
*Movimiento Estudiantil Chicano de Aztlan*
　(MECHA), 90
*Mujer Moderna,* 83
Murrieta, Joaquín, 190
Museums, 175
Music, 26, 28–33, 83, 127. *See also
　Corridos;* Flamenco; Mariachi

Nahuatl, 7, 173
Nájera, Francisco Castillo. *See* Castillo
　Najera, Francisco
Names, Use of Spanish, 8, 76. *See also*
　specific names
National Boxing Association, 189
National Chicana Conference, 96; survey of
　participants, 97
National Chicano Social Science
　Association, 105, 114
National Farm Workers' Association, 206.
　*See also* United Farmworkers' Union
National Woman's Studies Association, 98
Nationalism, 5, 8
Navajos, 3
Neighborhood Information Centers, 178–79
Neologisms, 145, 146. *See also* Hybrid
　language
Newman, Phillip (Judge), 128
New Mexico, 3, 6, 8, 10, 13, 20, 21, 23,
　24, 25, 27, 32, 67, 68, 74, 77, 109, 110,
　117, 122, 123, 128, 134, 135, 136, 140,
　143, 146, 147, 151, 156, 171, 183;
　constitution, 133. *See also* individual cities
New Mexico Highlands University, 161
New Mexico, University of, 33
New Spain, 173
New York, New York, 135, 178
Nisbet, Robert A., 53
North Carolina, University of, 194
Novels, Chicano, 199–205
Nuns. *See* Convent

Oakland, California, 116
Officials. *See* Appointed officials. *See also*
　Elected Officials
Olmecs, 9, 173
Oñate, Juan de, 21, 206
Oppression: of Chicanas, 84, 85, 86, 90, 91,
　92, 93, 96; of Chicanos, 119
Oral tradition, 10–12, 172, 174, 198

Orange County, California, 154
Orozco, Cecilio, 161
*Our Catholic Heritage in Texas*
(Castañeda), 171

Pachuco. *See* slang
Palafox y Mendoza, Juan de, 172
Paraguayans, 121
Paredes, Américo, 103
*Partera,* 70, 71
Partido Revolucionario Institucional
(PRI), 9
*Pastorales,* 205
Patriarchal society, 13
Pattie, James Ohio, 22–23
Penitentes, 13, 26, 27, 28, 70
Perdido, New Mexico, 22–23
*Peregrinos De Aztlan* (Méndez),
199, 203–204
Pérez, Bertha, 93
Pérez, Ricardo, 193
*Personal Narrative of James Ohio Pattie,
The,* 22–23
Peruvians, 121
Phoenix, Arizona, 98
Phonetics. *See* Pronunciation difficulties
Picture writing. *See* Glyphs
Place-names, 10
Plays. *See* Drama, Chicano
Pochismo, 127
*Pocho* (Villarreal), 14–15, 199, 200–201
Poetry, Chicano, 187–98; bilingual, 194–95;
elements of, 192–193. *See also* specific
names of poems
Poets, Chicano. *See* Poetry. *See also* specific
names of poets.
Po - he - ye - mu, 21
Police, 103–4
Political Association of Spanish Speaking
Organizations (PASSO), 118
Political consciousness, Chicano, 102
Political control, Anglo, 116, 134
Political experience, of Mexican Americans,
102–3
Political mobilization, 111
Political myths, 107
Political organizations, 113
Politcal process, 102–3
Politicians, 107, 117. *See also* specific
offices
Poll tax, 106
Pope, 21
Portuguese, 147
*Posadas* 205
Pottinger, J. Stanley, 156
Pound, Ezra, 198

Poverty, 54–55; 63–65; 69, 72
Pre-Columbian peoples of Mexico, 173
Pregnancy, 12, 72
Prejudice, 44–45; 77, 168–69; linguistic,
134–35
*Prensa Mexicana,* 133
Pronunciation difficulties, 125
Psychological problems among Chicanos,
57–62
Public libraries. *See* Libraries
Publishing, restrictions in New World, 173
Puebla, Mexico, 172
Pueblo Indian revolt, 21
Pueblo Indians, 21
Puerto de Luna, New Mexico, 202

Quechua, 121
Quetzalcoatl, 6
Quinto Sol Literary Award, 201, 202

Racial superiority, 169
Rael, Juan B., 172
Ramírez, Manuel, 158
*Rancheras* (songs), 31
Rangers. *See* Texas Rangers
*Raza, La,* 1, 2, 3, 5–6, 14, 15, 49, 51, 56,
96, 98, 192, 198, 201
*Raza, Unida, La,* 107, 114, 116, 117
Reading, attitudes toward, 174
Rechy, John, 200
*Reconquista,* (New Mexico), 21
Redfield, Robert, 122
Redwood City, California, 162
*Reforma* of Benito Juárez, 9
Religion, 26–28, 79
Religious festivals, 20–21, 74. *See also*
specific names
Religious plays, 205–6
Religious practices, 12, 13, 24–28, 70. *See
also* penitentes
*Remedios, Virgen de los,* 8
Renaissance, European, 173
Representatives, state, Mexican American,
109–10
Representatives, U.S. Congress, Mexican
Americans, 109. *See also* specific names
Republican party, 117
*Revista de Revistas,* 83
Rios C., Herminio, 202
Rivera, Feliciano, 125
Rivera, Tomas, 201–2, 204
Robinson, Cecil, 169
Rodríguez, Johnny, 33
Roman Catholic Church, 13, 19–21,
26–27, 70, 71, 72, 139, 171, 205.
*See also* Convent; Penitentes;

Roman Catholic Church *(continued)*
  Religious festivals; Religious
  practices; Vatican library
Romano-V., Octavio I., 198–99
Romero, Ramón Franquelo y. *See* Franquelo
  y Romero, Ramón
Romero, Vincente, 32
Roosevelt, Franklin D. (President), 112
Rousseau, Jean Jacques, 173
Royal Academy of the Spanish
  Language, 144
Roybal, Edward R., 118, 124, 128
Rubel, Arthur J., 49

Sabicas, 32
Sacramento, California, 160
Sahagún, Bernardino (Father), 28
Salamanca, Spain, 28
Salas, Floyd, 200
Salazar, Ruben, 104
Samora, Julian, 49
San Antonio, Texas, 19, 32, 118, 128
Sánchez, George I., 122, 152–53, 171, 174
Sánchez, Leopoldo, 128
San Diego, California, 32, 76
San Francisco, California, 76, 98
San Ildefonso, New Mexico, 8
San Jose, California, 95
San Juan, New Mexico, 8
San Juan Pueblo, 21
*San Lorenzo, Fiesta de,* 20
San Luis Valley, Colorado, 123
San Pedro y San Pablo, Colegio de, 172
*Santa Ana, Día de,* 74
Santa Clara, California, 200
Santa Clara, New Mexico, 8
Santa Cruz de la Cañada, New Mexico, 8
*Santa Fe, Fiesta de,* 21
Santa Fe, New Mexico, 19, 20, 21, 22, 26,
  32, 74
Santa Fe Ring, 4
Santa Fe trail, 22
Santa Julia, Mexico, 82
Santana, Carlos, 33
Santa Rosa, New Mexico, 202
*Santeros,* 24
Santiago, Día de, 74
*Santos,* 24
Saroyan, William, 171
Saunders, Lyle, 49
School-community relations, 163
School, discrimination in, 104–5
School, reasons for poor attendance, 56–58
School libraries. *See* Libraries
Schooling. *See* Education
Schools, 64, 104–5, 126, 127, 175

Seale, Bobby, 116
Seattle, Washington, 208
Segade, Gustavo, 46
Segregation, de facto, in schools, 153
Segundo, Pepe, 32
Senators, Mexican American, 109
Separation. *See* Divorce
Serna vs. Portales, 159
Serra, Junípero (Father), 21
Seville, Spain, 1
Sex, 88–89, 90
Sex roles, 88–90
Shockley, Ann Allen, 179
Short stories, Chicano, 198–99
Singers. *See* individual names
*Sisterhood Is Powerful* (Sutherland), 93
Slang, 10, 144–45, 195, 203
Socio-economic status, 106–7
Son, role in Chicano family, 84–85, 90. *See
  also* Children, role in family
Songs. *See* Music; *Alabados; Corridos*
Sonora, Mexico, 22, 139, 203
Spain, 3, 6, 21, 22, 27, 28, 31, 32, 67, 68,
  125, 138, 169, 173
Spanish America, 168
Spanish Armada, 168
Spanish borderlands, 169, 174
Spanish culture. *See* Culture, Hispanic
Spanish heritage, 29, 31–32, 68, 191, 194,
  205. *See also* Culture; Oral tradition
Spanish language, 7, 9–10, 68, 105,
  121, 122, 123, 124, 125, 127, 133–148,
  171–72, 188, 194–95, 203, 204, 207
Spanish language: instruction, 147; official
  use of, 121, 134; prohibition, 134;
  statistics on use, 134–35
Speech difficulties of Chicanos, 126
Steinbeck, John, 171
Stereotypes, 1–2, 64, 83–84, 154, 187
Storytelling, 198
Strategies of Mexican Americans, 116–18
Superstitions, 12, 59
Supreme Court, U.S., 107, 158
Sutherland, Elizabeth, 93
Symbols, Chicano, 9

Tarascos, 9
*Tatto the Wicked Cross* (Salas), 200
Teacher attitudes toward Chicanos, 105, 127,
  129, 154–55
Teacher Corps, University of Texas, 160
Teacher qualifications, 161
Teacher training programs, 129, 159–161.
  *See also* Teacher Corps
Teatro Campesino, 206–8
Teatro de la Esperanza, El, 208

Teatro Nacional de Aztlan, El
(TENAZ), 208
Teatros, 209. *See also* Drama, Chicano
TENAZ. *See* Teatro Nacional de Aztlan, El
Tenochtitlán, 6, 11
Texas, 21, 32, 33, 78, 107, 109, 111,
113, 115, 122, 134, 136, 147, 151, 153,
156, 171, 183. *See also* individual cities
Texas Rangers, 103
Texas, University of (Austin), 106. *See also*
Teacher Corps
Texas, University of (El Paso), 93, 106
Texas, University of, (San Antonio), 161
Theater. *See* Drama, Chicano; Teatros
Thomas, Jorge, 12
Three Rivers, Texas, 113
Tierra Amarilla, New Mexico, 77
Tijerina, Reis López. *See* López
Tijerina, Reis
Toltecs, 9
Tonantzin, 8
Torea, Lydia, 32
*Tortilla Flat* (Steinbeck), 171
Traditional culture, 40, 53, 62
Trujillo, Manuel Hernández. *See* Hernández
Trujillo, Manuel
Tucson, Arizona, 29, 32, 104, 106, 117
Tuskegee Institute, 129

Unions. *See* specific names
United Farmworkers' Union, 9. *See also*
National Farm Workers' Association
U.S. Commission on Civil Rights, 108,
153, 155; California State Advisory
Committee, 108
Universities, 105–6. *See also* Chicano, need
for university
Urbanization, 62
Urista Heredia, Alberto Baltazar, 156–57,
195–96
Utes, 3

Vaca, Nick, 199
Valdez, Luis, 34, 206, 208
Valencians, 121
Values: Anglo, 53–54; Mexican American,
49, 53–62
Varela, María, 93
Vargas, Diego de, 21, 74
Vasconcelos, José, 2
Vásquez, Enriqueta Longeaux y. *See*
Longeaux y Vásquez, Enriqueta
Vásquez, Richard, 201
Vásquez, Tiburcio, 115

Vásquez de Coronado, Francisco. *See*
Coronado, Francisco Vásquez de
Vatican library, 173
Vega, Benjamin, (Judge), 128
Vidal, Mirta, 90–91
Viet Nam, 191
Villa, Esteban, 24–25
Villa, Pancho, 191
Villarreal, José Antonio, 14–15, 199,
200–201
Violence, 81, 103, 111, 118
Virginia, 3
Virginity, 11–12
Voltaire, 173
Voter harassment, 107
Voter registration, 108
Voting, 107–8. *See also* Poll Tax;
Politics of Mexican Americans;
Voter registration; Voter harassment;
Voting requirements
Voting requirements, 107–8

Welfare, 55, 57, 58, 59–60, 63–64
Western Political Science Association
Chicano Caucus, 105
White image. *See* Brown-white syndrome
White Sands, New Mexico, 77
Wife, role in Chicano family, 70, 72, 75, 84,
85, 87, 88, 89
Witches, 12, 41, 71. *See also Llorona, la*
Wolf Song (Fergusson), 170
Women, New Mexican, 67–79
Women, role of, 75, 79, 81, 82, 86–87; in
family, 86–87; of unmarried, 70–71. *See*
also Wife, role in Chicano family; Mother,
role in Chicano family
Women's Liberation Movement, 96, 97
Women's rights. *See* Emancipation of
Mexican women; Women's suffrage
movement in Mexico
Women's suffrage movement in Mexico,
81–83
World War II, 76, 113, 123, 198, 206
Wyoming, 78

Yaquis, 71
Yeats, William Butler, 198
Yeshiva University, 129
*Y no se lo trago la tierra ( ...And the Earth
Did Not Part* (Rivera), 201–2
Yucatán, 82

Zapata, Emiliano, 9
Zapotecs, 9

78815

E
184
M5
C47

THE CHICANOS, AS WE SEE OURSELVES.